GEORGE LUCAS

INTERVIEWS

CONVERSATIONS WITH FILMMAKERS SERIES
PETER BRUNETTE, GENERAL EDITOR

Photofest

GEORGE LUCAS

INTERVIEWS

EDITED BY SALLY KLINE

UNIVERSITY PRESS OF MISSISSIPPI / JACKSON

www.upress.state.ms.us

Copyright © 1999 by University Press of Mississippi
All rights reserved
Manufactured in the United States of America

07   06   05   04   03   02   01   00   99   4   3   2   1

∞

Library of Congress Cataloging-in-Publication Data
Lucas, George.
     George Lucas : interviews / edited by Sally Kline.
        p.   cm. — (Conversations with filmmakers series)
     Filmography: p.
     Includes index.
     ISBN 1-57806-124-5 (cloth : alk. paper). — ISBN
1-57806-125-3 (paper : alk. paper)
     1. Lucas, George interviews.   2. Motion picture producers and
directors — United States Interviews.   I. Kline, Sally, 1962–   .
II. Title.   III. Series.
PN1998.3.L835A5   1999
791.43'0233'092—dc21   99-22658
                                                                     CIP

British Library Cataloging-in-Publication Data available

CONTENTS

INTRODUCTION

HE IS THE FORCE behind The Force.

As director, producer, writer, editor, technology innovator, and entrepreneur, the controversial George Lucas may well be the most identifiable and popular film maker in the history of the medium. He started out modestly in the early 1970's as the fringe visionary behind an esoteric cautionary tale, *THX 1138*, and a personal coming-of-age classic, *American Graffiti*. Before the end of the millennium, he could count the ticket receipts and merchandising profits from his *Star Wars* franchise in the billions. Along with his close friend and colleague Steven Spielberg, he established the modern blockbuster phenomenon.

For good or ill, Lucas has revolutionized an industry and created the most successful film series of all time. The dedication of his *Star Wars* fans is legend, a fact never more apparent than in 1999, the release year of the first "prequel" to the original trilogy. Yet a reading of his interviews over time implies that this uniquely autonomous powerhouse—this force behind The Force—submits himself to press questions mostly by force. Unlike his more publicly engaged contemporaries, such as Martin Scorsese and Francis Ford Coppola, the strikingly reticent George Lucas granted audiences only sporadically before an atypical public reemergence with the *Phantom Menace's* release.

The book title *George Lucas: Interviews* is almost an oxymoron. To archive the verbal output of a notoriously nonverbal impresario offers a rare opportunity and an ironic challenge. Consequently, it generates an unprecedented, especially useful final product: The man is all the more fascinating because he has been so little known.

A scan of Lucas's conversations begs the comparison of him to his most famous mystery characters. They show him to be as masked as Darth Vader, concise as Yoda, intrepid as Luke Skywalker, and defiantly independent as the appropriately named Han Solo. Unfortunately, at times, he can be almost as robotic in his answers as the linguistically challenged R2-D2. If the Modesto, California native doesn't use oratory as a light saber, it is rather through imagination, hard work, and entrepreneurial risk-taking that George Lucas has won the victory at the box office and in the hearts of millions of devoted fans worldwide.

Peter Bart, editor-in-chief of *Variety,* once made an astute analogy in a commentary about George Lucas: "Despite his extraordinary success, talking with Lucas is still like meeting with a small town banker to whom one owes money. He is impeccably polite and implacably distanced, as though fearing that you might ask an inappropriate question, or perhaps even request a loan."

Studying his films gives mere hints at the man. Only *American Graffiti* relates back directly to his specific personal experience. Thus, the infrequent in-depth interviews that he has allowed over the years provide the only explicit avenue into Lucas's motivations and dreams, making an anthology such as this important. There aren't many options in compiling such a collection, because of the limited amount of appropriate material available. Much has been written *about* Lucas, but little comes directly *from* him.

Lucas has given so few substantial and comprehensive interviews that a majority of the longer ones ever published can be included in this single volume. Lucas calls reports of his reclusiveness a media myth. In contrast to legions of more self-promoting or image-conscious show business types, however, George Lucas seems to have gone for whole years without talking to the media—particularly during select periods from the early 1980s to the middle 1990s. While over his career he has spoken somewhat consistently with *Time* magazine, the *New York Times* and the *Los Angeles Times,* these interviews tended to result in briefer pieces on limited topics.

In the last two decades, *Rolling Stone* magazine may be the only publication that has published involved, extensive interviews with Lucas on regular occasions. Lucas has also seemed more relaxed with the alternative music magazine than in other press venues. Two of his five *Rolling Stone* interviews were selected for *George Lucas: Interviews.*

Whether by his evasion or theirs, Lucas has sat down less frequently with the academic film journals. The question of whether Lucas is the artistic genius of *American Graffiti,* the commercial genius of *Star Wars,* or the resourceful genius of his technology companies (such as Industrial Light and Magic) arises perpetually in any consideration of him. Perhaps his high profile as a pop culture icon has played a part in the respect and interest he has garnered—or failed to garner—in scholarly quarters.

In the weeks leading up to the May 1999 premiere of the highly anticipated first *Star Wars* prequel, Lucas began raising his profile—appearing on Hollywood awards shows, opening up to several interviewers, and being uncharacteristically revealing in public. He had great incentive since Lucas's privately owned companies financed the reported $115 million budget of *The Phantom Menace,* a project with enormous implications on his assets and legacy.

With the "special edition" reissue of the original trilogy of *Star Wars* films in 1997, Lucas also came out of hibernation to a certain degree. He participated in several in-depth pieces that year. The best of these—interviews from *Playboy* and *The New Yorker* magazines—are included here. Perhaps more than any other, John Seabrook's extensive article subtitled "Why Is the Force Still with Us?" from the January 6, 1997 edition of *The New Yorker* is the definitive investigation of Lucas and his empire. It is a critical, impartial scrutiny of an individual who otherwise is inclined to get the hero-worship treatment from those who are hand-picked to interrogate him.

Interviewers rarely press Lucas to address tough issues in anything but a general way, it seems. As a producer, he has been responsible for some big flops. These include *Willow, Radioland Murders* and a film that became synonymous with cinematic debacle in its day, *Howard the Duck.* Yet in major interviews conducted after the releases of these films, he is seldom asked to explain his fiascoes.

Furthermore, only the aberrant reporter confronts Lucas about his part in causing to change (and, some would say, cheapen) the investment priorities of the Hollywood studios. In the post-*Star Wars* and Indiana Jones era, the most expensive Hollywood movies have taken a turn toward wide-release merchandising events with lowest common denominator appeal. A few writers mention Lucas's correlation to the trend. But only Jack Mathews, in this book's final piece from the *Los Angeles Times,* seems to have probed Lucas directly and thoroughly on such a crucial aspect of his long-term legacy.

Interviewers are inclined to pull their punches when it comes to his personal life as well. You will find very little in Lucas's own words about such matters in these interviews.

People can debate about how much an artist's private dealings influence his creative output. There is no doubt, however, that the events which affect one of the most influential figures in movie history could end up affecting his work and thereby his audience. But on-the-record conversations with Lucas mostly breeze over his inner life.

For example, his ex-wife Marcia Lucas was also his close professional collaborator. Yet with the exception of a 1999 *60 Minutes* interview, George Lucas either hasn't been asked or doesn't answer questions about his 1983 divorce, the impact of that loss on him as a filmmaker or as a human being. It isn't just a gossipy tidbit that the marriage allegedly broke up when she had an affair with an employee from one of his companies. Such a traumatic experience had to have had an effect on the viewpoint of someone who was described as conservative and reclusive even before his divorce. The fact that Lucas has been the primary caregiver of three children, two adopted as a single father, must also mean something in terms of his aesthetic. But his role as a family man arises during interviews almost exclusively in terms of his work schedule and time priorities.

Profound personal insights remain buried. Even in professional discussion, his usually guarded words seldom offer deep revelation. In a 1977 piece included in this volume, interviewer Stephen Zito said, "Lucas claims to be shy of the press but he is a good talker. He tells you nothing by accident, doesn't let you into his life."

Interviewers probably don't want to push their luck by pushing too hard on sensitive areas with Lucas, since it is such a scarce treat to get to talk with him at all. Naturally, more common questions would come up first if one only had a limited amount of time with the inaccessible filmmaker.

As much as on any other topic, interviewers repeatedly query director-producer-writer Lucas about the various roles he has taken on his projects, which of the behind-the camera jobs he favors, and—throughout a long hiatus—why he stopped directing. (Lucas became a director again, for the first time since the original installment of *Star Wars* in 1977, when production began on the prequel *Episode I: The Phantom Menace* in 1997.) Though these same questions persist over the years, it is interesting to notice how his answers have changed as you read the interviews chronologically. Consistent and resolute on most other subjects, Lucas comes around full circle about this dilemma of where to put his energies.

In 1974's *Filmmaker Newsletter,* for instance, mastering nuts-and-bolts filmmaking is his priority: "I'm working on being a director and writer... They are a challenge to me because I don't know them as well... I'm not a good writer, It's very, very hard for me. I don't feel I have a natural talent for it—as opposed to camera, which I could always just do. And the same thing for editing. I've always been able to just sit down and cut... Writing just doesn't flow in a creative surge the way other things do."

You can see the beginning inklings of auteur fatigue, even back then. He admits, "There's only so much that one human being can do, and as you get older you realize you have to make a choice."

By his 1977 interview in *American Film,* conducted during the production of *Star Wars,* he acutely feels the pressure of calling all the shots. He says, "I come from the filmmakers' school of doing movies, which means I do everything myself... If I left anything for a day, it would fall apart... Whenever there is a leak in the dam, I have to stick my finger in it. I should learn to say, 'Somebody else go plug it up.' "

Lucas had resigned himself to full-time producing by 1980, when he told *Rolling Stone* frankly: "I hate directing. It's like fighting a fifteen-round heavyweight bout with a new opponent everyday."

Not much had changed in 1983: "I dislike directing. I hate the constant dealing with volatile personalities. Directing is emotional frustration, anger, and tremendous hard work—seven days a week, twelve to sixteen hours a day. For years my wife would ask why we couldn't go out to dinner like other people. But I couldn't turn it off."

His attitude starts to rally back in 1987, after a decade without directing. He called producing "not as exciting as directing, but it is possible to do more this way." He also declared, "I will go back to directing one of these days."

By 1990, the desire to return to the intimate act of hands-on filmmaking is back in full flower. "It's not that I prefer producing, that's just where I find myself these days. It wasn't something I did by choice. I was just more effective in the producing area, which is where the opportunities have presented themselves over the last few years... Ultimately, I'm a director. I've done many other things, but that's where my heart is... I just want to get back to what I started doing."

It would take another seven years for Lucas to follow through on the sentiment.

Like being an eloquent interview subject, being an effective director requires good people skills. But interpersonal communication, especially towards actors, has never been the strong suit of a man so often described as "reserved," close-mouthed, a loner. Harrison Ford, who worked with Lucas as director on *Star Wars* and Lucas as producer on several films thereafter, bears witness in the 1997 *New Yorker,* "George isn't the best at dealing with those human situations—to say the least."

Lucas has a love-hate relationship to the specific occupation, directing, that made him so enormously successful. He exhibits little such ambivalence about the general mission of making movies. "I always see images flash into my head, and I just have to make those scenes," he said in 1974. His enthusiasm stays intact as the years progress. In 1987: "I derive pleasure from storytelling. It is fun to sit around a fireplace and tell a story and have everyone go 'Oooh' and 'Ahhh.' That's what I'm doing with *Star Wars* or *American Graffiti*. In my current position, I can tell stories through large, epic, entertaining movies."

"Some of my friends are more concerned about art and being considered a Fellini or an Orson Welles, but I've really never had that problem. I just like making movies," he once said, "I like to make things move, and I like to make them myself. Just give me the tools and I'll make the toys."

He sees the storytelling mission as a moral one, not an artistically pretentious one. In interpreting his films (with the exception of *THX 1138*), Lucas emphasizes their traditional appeal and hopefulness—a spirit often considered in opposition to what is hip, authentic, or avant-garde.

Back in 1974, after the peak of the counterculture, he took a rather reactionary stance for a young artist then, "Everybody looks at the fifties as complacent, but I look at the fifties as optimistic . . . I realized after *THX* that people don't care about how the country is being ruined . . . It's easy to make films about Watergate. It's hard to be optimistic when everything tells you to be pessimistic and cynical." He observed with some sarcasm about *American Graffiti* that "It's all that hokey stuff about being a good neighbor, and the American spirit and all that crap. There *is* something in it."

In 1977, Lucas's ambition to inspire persists. He described what motivated him about his defining work "Once I got into *Star Wars,* it struck me that we had lost [dreams and fantasies]—a whole generation was growing up without fairy tales."

In a *Playboy* interview two decades later, Lucas was articulating explicitly his vision to uplift: "*Star Wars* has always struck a chord with people. There are issues of loyalty, of friendship, of good and evil...I mean, there's a reason this film is so popular. It's not that I'm giving out propaganda nobody wants to hear." In a rare introspective moment, he continued, "I'm the son of a small-town businessman. He was conservative, and I'm very conservative, always have been...Knowing that the film was made for a young audience, I was trying to say, in a simple way, that there is a God and that there is both a good side and a bad side. You have a choice between them, but the world works better if you're on the good side."

Looking back on *Star Wars* in the *New Yorker*, Lucas crystallized a philosophy that one can see form gradually in these interviews: "I wanted it to be a traditional moral study...there is always a lesson to be learned."

Many Lucas films indicate a nostalgia for the innocence and purity of his Modesto roots. From his point-of-view, the simple ways and bedrock values of his childhood run in direct conflict with the industry he would eventually conquer. Nothing perseveres from his early career to the present more than George Lucas's antipathy toward the institution of Hollywood and its shallow Southern California lifestyle.

His animosity manifests itself in nearly every interview. Lucas rehashes over and over the anecdotes of how studio types violated him by slightly trimming parts of both *THX 1138* and *American Graffiti* against his wishes. He repeats again and again with smug satisfaction how so many studios turned down the unexpected hits *American Graffiti* and *Star Wars*; how studio dimwits had to be cajoled into releasing the brilliant *Graffiti* theatrically, even after they saw it; how he negotiated to keep the priceless sequel and merchandising rights to *Star Wars* because of Hollywood's shortsightedness and foolish lack of confidence in it.

He gets downright, uncharacteristically gabby when it comes to these stories. He is like a martyr on crusade, as he describes in *Film Quarterly*: "Everybody in Hollywood had turned down *American Graffiti*. Universal had already turned it down once. And they offered me $75,000 to do *Lady Ice*, which is more money than I'd made in my entire life. And I said no. I said, 'By God, I've got a movie here, and I'm going to get it made somehow.'"

Along with particular recollections, he continually bashes Hollywood out of general principle.

In 1971: "They tell people what to do without reason. The studios know that directors get emotionally involved, and then all hell breaks loose... Sooner or later, they decide they know more about making movies than directors. Studio heads. You can't fight them because they've got the money."

He's still mad about studio executives by 1979. "They're people who have never made a movie in their lives, agents and lawyers with no idea of dramatic flow. But they come in, see a movie twice, and in those few hours they can tell you to take this out or shorten that." And in 1980: "L.A. is where they make deals, do business in the classic corporate way, which is to screw everybody and do whatever they can to make the biggest profit... To them, the deal is the movie... I don't want to have anything to do with them."

Nothing had softened in Lucas by 1997: "Down there [in Hollywood] for every honest filmmaker trying to get his film off the ground, there are a hundred sleazy used-car dealers trying to con you out of your money."

Ironically, of course, the multiplex behemoths produced by George Lucas have helped boost the bottom-line mentality he so steadfastly scorns habitually in these interviews. Even at the height of his wealth and domination, Lucas's anti-establishment attitude belies his position as the ultimate symbol of that establishment. As you will read, Lucas's financial and logistic self-sufficiency, propelled by his diverse conglomerate of privately owned subsidiaries, allows him to maintain his paradoxical status as a maverick.

Control appears to be a major issue with Lucas—whether in terms of his films, his companies, or his person. Writer Stephen Zito observes in his piece in this volume that: "Lucas jealously guards his privacy—he was once recognized in a restaurant and has never returned... In a very public business, he is a very private person. He lives as far from Hollywood as he can... as if it were some kind of leper colony. He is, quite simply, a man who wants to have everything his way."

Lucas reserves his respect for the autocrats from Hollywood's golden age, the Louis B. Mayers and Jack Warners, masters of their fiefdoms. Lucas said in 1979: "The movie industry was built by independent entrepreneurs, dictators who had a strong feeling about movies. They knew what they wanted and they made it happen."

His desire for autonomy may explain why George Lucas has been such an elusive interview subject. He can't control the press. As *Phantom Menace* fever heated up in July of 1998, at a celebration of *American Graffiti*'s 25th anniversary, a TV reporter asked Lucas "Why are you being so secretive about the new *Star Wars*?" He answered, "Because the media always gets it wrong." In brief remarks with a photo preview of *Phantom Menace* in the February 1999 *Vanity Fair* magazine, Lucas said that the most difficult part of returning to *Star Wars* had nothing to do with the franchise itself. It was the idea of becoming a public figure again. "If there's any trepidation I have, it's issues with the media . . ."

George Lucas has impacted the culture as much as any filmmaker in the late 20th century. And yet he stays an enigma at least in part because he is not deeply reflective, at least not publicly. But *Variety*'s Peter Bart justifies the filmmaker's lack of self-analysis eloquently, recognizing, "He is too busy inventing the future to spend much time reinventing the past."

Lucas has said it himself: "I'm always sort of living for tomorrow, for better or worse."

George Lucas: Interviews conforms to the standards set by the University Press of Mississippi for its Conversations with Filmmakers series. This means that the book includes interviews as originally presented, in a mostly unexpurgated form. Such a quantity of material gathered in such a pure form in one volume offers a special opportunity for researchers and aficionados of a particular artist. Especially in the case of George Lucas, who bares so little about himself, surveying the man's thoughts and ideas in his own words provides exceptional insight.

By necessity, then, this kind of primary source collection includes some repetition of anecdotes and observations. But this is useful in itself. Attentive readers will gain understanding from noting the consistencies or changes in ideas and perspectives. There is much to be learned in examining George Lucas's spin on his history, how it distills over time, and which matters most spark this quiet man to speak.

Thanks to all the interviewers and publications included for their contributions to this anthology; to Peter Brunette, general editor of the University Press of Mississippi's Conversations with Filmmakers series; and, to the whole team at the University Press of Mississippi including Seetha Srinivasan, Anne Stascavage, and Elizabeth Young for their kindness and guidance.

Special thanks to my close friend and advocate Greg Economos, con-siglière Norma Kline, and colleagues Cindy Pearlman, Amy Longsdorf, Mary Ellen Webb, and Linda Shubert for their support during this project.

Most importantly: a dedication to the memory of my father Jimmie Kline for his confidence, inspiration, and unconditional love.

—Sally Kline, Washington D.C., February 1999

CHRONOLOGY

1944   Born George Walton Lucas, Jr. on May 14 in Modesto, California

1962   Near-fatal automobile accident has major effect, inspires new seri-
       ousness of purpose

       Graduates from Modesto's Thomas Downey High School

       Enrolls in Modesto Junior College

1964   Meets important influence, future collaborator, cinematographer
       Haskell Wexler

       Begins film school at University of Southern California

1966   Earns undergraduate degree from USC, continues graduate work

1967   Meets future best friend and colleague Steven Spielberg at a stu-
       dent film festival

1968   During six-month internship on Warner Bros. lot, meets and
       begins work with mentor/partner Francis Ford Coppola

1965–68 Directs eight student and short films, including *THX 1138:4EB*
       (*Electronic Labyrinth*), precursor to his future first feature

1969   Co-founds American Zoetrope with Coppola in San Francisco

       Marries film editor Marcia Griffin on February 22

1971   Directs first full-length feature, *THX 1138,* released March 11

       Lucasfilm Ltd. incorporates

1973   *American Graffiti* released August 2

1974   *American Graffiti* nominated by Academy of Motion Picture Arts and Sciences for best picture, director, screenplay, film editing, and supporting actress (Candy Clark)

Begins first drafts of *Star Wars*

1975   Industrial Light & Magic (ILM), subsidiary of Lucasfilm, established to create *Star Wars* special effects

1976   *Star Wars* principal photography commences in Tunisia and London

1977   *Star Wars,* also known as *Episode IV: A New Hope,* opens May 25, becomes most successful film of all time

1978   *Star Wars* wins Academy Awards for original score, film editing, art/set decoration, costume design, visual effects, sound, and special achievement award for sound effects; nominated for best picture, director, screenplay, and supporting actor (Alec Guinness)

1979   *More American Graffiti* released August 3

1980   *The Empire Strikes Back* opens May 21

Skywalker Ranch construction begins in Marin County

1981   *Raiders of the Lost Ark* released June 21, inaugurates hit *Indiana Jones* trilogy

Becomes father—daughter Amanda, first of three adopted children, born

1983   *Return of the Jedi* released May 25

Divorces Marcia Griffin Lucas

1984   *Indiana Jones and the Temple of Doom* opens May 23

1986   *Howard the Duck* opens August 1, promptly lays egg

1987   Attends first sci-fi convention ever, in honor of *Star Wars*'s tenth anniversary

1988   *Willow* released May 20, bombs shortly thereafter

Tucker: The Man and His Dream released August 12 to good reviews, poor box office

1989   *Indiana Jones and the Last Crusade* released May 24

ILM makes computer graphics breakthrough in work on non-Lucasfilm project *The Abyss*

Star Wars among the first 25 films to be included in Library of Congress's National Film Registry

"Razzie" Award nomination for Worst Screenplay, for co-writing *Willow*

1991   First spin-off *Star Wars* novel by Timothy Zahn released, tops *New York Times* bestseller list

1992   Honored by Academy of Motion Picture Arts and Sciences at March 30 ceremony with prestigious Irving G. Thalberg Memorial Award

1994   *Radioland Murders* released October 21 to scathing reviews

1995   Begins first drafts of three *Star Wars* "prequels"

American Graffiti added to Library of Congress's National Film Registry

1996   Lucasfilm establishes official *Star Wars* website

1997   Refurbished "Special Edition" reissues of original *Star Wars* trilogy run in theaters, set box office records

Star Wars—Episode IV: A New Hope becomes first movie in history to break $400 million in domestic grosses

Lucas directs again for first time in twenty years when production begins on *Star Wars—Episode I: The Phantom Menace*

1998   Release of first sneak preview trailer for *Star Wars—Episode I: The Phantom Menace* causes sensation in November.

1999   *Star Wars—Episode I: The Phantom Menace* released May 19

FILMOGRAPHY

Student and Short Films

Look at Life (1965)
Herbie (1966)
1:42:08 (1966)
The Emperor, (1967)
THX 1138:4EB also known as *Electronic Labyrinth* (1967)
Anyone Lived in a Pretty How Town (1967)
6-18-67 (1967)
Filmmaker (1968)

Feature Films

THX 1138 (American Zoetrope/Warner Brothers, 1970)
Producer: Lawrence Sturhahn (Francis Coppola, Executive Producer)
Director: (and editor) **George Lucas**
Screenplay: **George Lucas** and Walter Murch, from a story by **George Lucas**
Cast: Robert Duvall, Donald Pleasence, Maggie McOmie, Don Pedro Colley

American Graffiti (Lucasfilm Ltd./Coppola Company Production/Universal Pictures, 1973)
Producer: Francis Coppola
Director: **George Lucas**
Screenplay: **George Lucas**, Gloria Katz, Willard Huyck

Cast: Richard Dreyfuss, Ron Howard, Paul Le Mat, Charles Martin Smith, Cindy Williams, Candy Clark, Mackenzie Phillips, Wolfman Jack, Bo Hopkins, Harrison Ford, Suzanne Somers

Star Wars also known as *Star Wars—Episode IV: A New Hope* (Lucasfilm Ltd./20th Century Fox Film Corp., 1977)
Producer: Gary Kurtz
Director: **George Lucas**
Screenplay: **George Lucas**
Cast: Mark Hamill, Harrison Ford, Carrie Fisher, Peter Cushing, Alec Guinness, Anthony Daniels, Kenny Baker, Peter Mayhew, David Prowse

More American Graffiti (Lucasfilm Ltd./Universal Pictures, 1979)
Producer: Howard Kazanjian (**George Lucas,** Executive Producer)
Director: B. W. L. Norton
Screenplay: B. W. L. Norton, based on characters created by **George Lucas,** Gloria Katz, Willard Huyck
Cast: Candy Clark, Bo Hopkins, Ron Howard, Paul Le Mat, Mackenzie Phillips, Charles Martin Smith, Cindy Williams

The Empire Strikes Back (Lucasfilm Ltd./20th Century Fox Film Corp., 1980)
Producer: Gary Kurtz (**George Lucas,** Executive Producer)
Director: Irvin Kershner
Screenplay: Leigh Brackett and Lawrence Kasdan, from a story by **George Lucas**
Cast: Mark Hamill, Harrison Ford, Carrie Fisher, Billy Dee Williams, Anthony Daniels, David Prowse, Peter Mayhew, Kenny Baker, Frank Oz, Alec Guinness

Kagemusha also known as *The Shadow Warrior* (20th Century Fox Film Corp., 1980)
Producer: Akira Kurosawa (**George Lucas** and Francis Coppola, Executive Producers of international version)
Director: Akira Kurosawa
Screenplay: Masato Ide, Akira Kurosawa
Cast: Tatsuya Nakadai, Tsutomu Yamazaki, Kenichi Hagiwara, Kota Yui

Body Heat (Warner Brothers, 1981)
Producer: Fred T. Gallo (**George Lucas**, uncredited Executive Producer)
Director: Lawrence Kasdan
Screenplay: Lawrence Kasdan
Cast: William Hurt, Kathleen Turner, Richard Crenna, Ted Danson, Mickey
Rourke, Kim Zimmer

Raiders of the Lost Ark (Lucasfilm Ltd./Paramount Pictures, 1981)
Producer: Frank Marshall (**George Lucas** and Howard Kazanjian, Executive
Producers)
Director: Steven Spielberg
Screenplay: Lawrence Kasdan, from a story by **George Lucas** and Philip
Kaufman
Cast: Harrison Ford, Karen Allen, Paul Freeman, John Rhys-Davies, Alfred
Molina, Denholm Elliott

Twice Upon a Time (Ladd Company/Warner Brothers, 1982)
Producers: Bill Couturie, John Korty, Charles Swenson (**George Lucas**,
Executive Producer)
Director: John Korty and Charles Swenson
Screenplay: John Korty, Charles Swenson, Suella Kennedy, Bill Couturie
Voice Cast: Judith Kahan Kampmann, Marshall Efron, James Cranna, Julie
Payne

Return of the Jedi (Lucasfilm Ltd./20th Century Fox Film Corp., 1983)
Producer: Howard Kazanjian (**George Lucas**, Executive Producer)
Director: Richard Marquand
Screenplay: Lawrence Kasdan and **George Lucas**, from a story by **George
Lucas**
Cast: Mark Hamill, Harrison Ford, Carrie Fisher, Billy Dee Williams,
Anthony Daniels, Peter Mayhew, Sebastian Shaw, Ian McDiarmid, Frank
Oz, James Earl Jones, David Prowse, Alec Guinness

Indiana Jones and the Temple of Doom (Lucasfilm Ltd./Paramount Pictures,
1984)
Producer: Robert Watts (**George Lucas** and Frank Marshall, Executive
Producers)

Director: Steven Spielberg
Screenplay: Willard Huyck and Gloria Katz, from a story by **George Lucas**
Cast: Harrison Ford, Kate Capshaw, Ke Huy Quan, Amrish Puri, Philip Stone

Mishima (Zoetrope Studios/Filmlink Intl./Warner Brothers, 1985)
Producers: Mata Yamamoto, Tom Luddy (**George Lucas** and Francis Ford
Coppola, Executive Producers)
Director: Paul Schrader
Screenplay: Paula and Leonard Schrader
Cast: Ken Ogata, Ken Sawada, Yasosuke Bando, Masayuki Shionoya

Labyrinth (Henson Associates/Lucasfilm Ltd./Tri-Star, 1986)
Producer: Eric Rattray (**George Lucas**, Executive Producer)
Director: Jim Henson
Screenplay: Terry Jones, from a story by Dennis Less and Jim Henson
Cast: David Bowie, Jennifer Connelly, Toby Froud, Shelley Thompson,
Christopher Malcolm

Howard the Duck (Lucasfilm Ltd./Universal Pictures, 1986)
Producer: Gloria Katz (**George Lucas**, Executive Producer)
Director: Willard Huyck
Screenplay: Willard Huyck and Gloria Katz
Cast: Lea Thompson, Jeffrey Jones, Tim Robbins, Paul Guilfoyle, Holly
Robinson Peete

Captain Eo (Disneyland release, 1986)
Producer: Rusty Lemorande (**George Lucas**, Executive Producer)
Director: Francis Coppola
Screenplay: **George Lucas**
Cast: Michael Jackson, Anjelica Huston, Dick Shawn

Willow (Lucasfilm Ltd./MGM-UA, 1988)
Producer: Nigel Wooll (**George Lucas**, Executive Producer)
Director: Ron Howard
Screenplay: Bob Dolman, from a story by **George Lucas**
Cast: Val Kilmer, Joanne Whalley-Kilmer, Warwick Davis, Jean Marsh,
Patricia Hayes, Billy Barty, Pat Roach, Gavan O'Herlihy, Kevin Pollak

Tucker: The Man and His Dream (Lucasfilm Ltd./Zoetrope
Studios/Paramount Pictures, 1988)
Producers: Fred Roos, Fred Fuchs (**George Lucas,** Executive Producer)
Director: Francis Coppola
Screenplay: Arnold Schulman and David Seidler
Cast: Jeff Bridges, Joan Allen, Martin Landau, Frederic Forrest, Mako, Elias
Koteas, Christian Slater, Jay O. Sanders, Dean Stockwell

The Land Before Time (Universal Pictures, 1988)
Producer: Don Bluth, Gary Goldman, John Pomeroy (Steven Spielberg and
George Lucas, Executive Producers)
Director: Don Bluth
Screenplay: Stu Krieger
Voice Cast: Judith Barsi, Burke Byrnes, Gabriel Damon, Pat Hingle,
Candace Hutson, Helen Shaver

Indiana Jones and the Last Crusade (Lucasfilm Ltd./Paramount Pictures, 1989)
Producer: Robert Watts (**George Lucas** and Frank Marshall, Executive
Producers)
Director: Steven Spielberg
Screenplay: Jeffrey Boam, from a story by **George Lucas** and Menno
Meyjes
Cast: Harrison Ford, Sean Connery, Denholm Elliott, Alison Doody, John
Rhys-Davies, River Phoenix

Beverly Hills Cop III (Paramount Pictures, 1994)
Producers: Mace Neufeld, Robert Rehme
Director: John Landis
Screenplay: Steven E. De Souza
Cast: Eddie Murphy, Judge Reinhold, Hector Elizondo, Theresa Randle,
Bronson Pinchot, **George Lucas** (cameo as "Disappointed Man"), Joe
Dante, John Singleton

Radioland Murders (Lucasfilm Ltd./Universal Pictures, 1994)
Producer: Rick McCallum and Fred Roos (**George Lucas,** Executive
Producer)
Director: Mel Smith

Screenplay: Willard Huyck, Gloria Katz, Jeff Reno, Ron Osborn, from a story by **George Lucas**
Cast: Brian Benben, Mary Stuart Masterson, Ned Beatty, George Burns, Michael Lerner, Michael McKean, Jeffrey Tambor, Christopher Lloyd, Corbin Bernsen, Rosemary Clooney

Star Wars—Episode I: The Phantom Menace (Lucasfilm Ltd./20th Century Fox Film Corp., 1999)
Producer: Rick McCallum (**George Lucas**, Executive Producer)
Director: **George Lucas**
Screenplay: **George Lucas**
Cast: Ewan McGregor, Liam Neeson, Jake Lloyd, Natalie Portman, Samuel L. Jackson, Ahmed Best, Ray Park, Frank Oz, Pernilla August

GEORGE LUCAS

INTERVIEWS

George Lucas

JUDY STONE/1971

THOSE WHO KNOW GEORGE Lucas say that he has the tempera-
ment of an artist who works alone in an attic. Plus a keen business sense
aimed at the preservation of his work. A private sort of person with an
incredible visual sensibility. And, from an unusually sympathetic Warner
Bros. executive, "He's a real 'auteur' filmmaker, a guy who's going to come
up with a very personal film and as such, someone who is treated gingerly
by a large studio."

Not "gingerly," countered Lucas. "Arbitrarily." There was a running battle from start to finish over his first feature film, *THX 1138*, the hypnotic
panorama of a chillingly automated society from which one man breaks
free. At times, it seemed as if Lucas himself were that man. At the end,
Warners still thought it was a "turkey," Lucas claims, but its artistry evoked
hurrahs from *Life* and *Newsweek*.

Lucas, twenty-six, could still pass as a skinny teenager if it weren't for
the black beard, dark-rimmed glasses—and the manner of a man who
knows what he's about. As a director, he ran a taut ship, bringing the film
in under the $750,000 budget and under the ten-week shooting schedule.
The director of photography was David Meyers.

Lucas spent six months editing *THX 1138* in the attic of his small hilltop
home in suburban Mill Valley, working incessantly seven days a week with

From *Eye on the World: Conversations with International Filmmakers,* pp. 715–18, Silman-
James Press, Los Angeles, 1997. Originally published in *The San Francisco Chronicle,* May
23, 1971. © *The San Francisco Chronicle.* Reprinted with permission.

his wife, Marcia, and Walter Murch who collaborated with Lucas on the final script and developed the eerie, cacophonous soundtrack. Downstairs, for inspiration, there's a blowup of Eisenstein, brooding over a strip of film.

Lucas soon learned there's a vast difference between what a filmmaker sees in those frames and what businessmen want. Warners demanded a rough cut before the film was ready and then excluded Lucas from the screening. Dumbfounded by the abstract images and deliberately obscure soundtrack, they laid down the law to executive producer Francis Ford Coppola that the film had to be clarified.

Still dissatisfied with the finished print, Warners had a psychologist test audience reaction to find out just how much they understood. "It was insane," Lucas laughed. "I wish I had filmed it. It was like bringing an audience to the Mona Lisa and asking, 'Do you know why she's smiling?' 'Sorry, Leonardo, you'll have to make some changes.' At least the audience understood that *THX* was not a love story set in the 25th century, which was the way Warners had planned to advertise it. Instead, the company settled for 'Visit the future, where love is the ultimate crime.'"

As far as Lucas is concerned, it's not about love or the future. He had filmed a coldly sterile world in which everyone takes pills to stay calm and nobody makes waves, where the computers know everything about everyone. To Lucas, it was an "abstraction of 1970," an appalling vision of a future that is already here.

In essence, girl reduces pill intake for her roommate THX 1138, he finds self in unprecedented surge of passion, is arrested for illegal sexual activity, held in an infinite white prison limbo without bars and after a harrowing chase by police robots, incredibly manages to escape.

"The plot was a vehicle for the theme," Lucas explains, "and the theme is basically existential. The importance of self and being able to step out of whatever you're in and move forward rather than being stuck in your little rut. People would give anything to quit their jobs. All they have to do is do it. People would give anything for a divorce and there's nothing stopping them. They're people in cages with open doors."

Warners was less interested in the theme than the plot. "They thought the *1984* idea was great. I thought, 'Gee, gosh, that's pretty dumb,' but they loved it. The ideas we thought were in the background, they wanted in the foreground. All the actors' heads had been shaved to give a slight feeling of oppression and a kind of abstraction. If I had put everyone in crewcuts and gray suits like they really were where we were shooting, people wouldn't have been nearly so interested as they are because I shaved the heads and put white costumes on. But I never said the society was oppressive. Nobody was having any fun, but no one was unhappy. A lot of people live that way now. There is real doubletalk in the film like, 'We need dissent but creative dissent.' Nixon said that. The places are real and the people are more or less like that. We are the drugged society and in case anyone thinks we're not, go talk to Bristol-Myers."

When Lucas was a youngster, he lived in Modesto, and had a proper Protestant Republican upbringing against which he soon rebelled—if only "biologically" at first. His next film will be about that time and place, a rock 'n' roll musical comedy of the 50s. "It was a time when the music was inane and everything was like Eisenhower. The most important thing was your car."

His father, a small retail-businessman, didn't think much of George's goal to become a professional car racer, nor was he overly enthusiastic when George switched to art after a nearly fatal smashup.

Following his graduation from the University of Southern California's film school, Lucas would probably have become a cameraman, but he couldn't get into the union. While working on a United States Information Agency film about President Johnson's trip to Asia, he became fascinated with editing—and with his assistant, Marcia, a winsome long-haired brunette with a wispy voice and shy manner, whom he later married.

Lucas soon discovered he didn't like editing films about people he didn't care for "saying things I didn't really believe in just because I had to make a living. The Johnson film wasn't terrible. I just didn't agree with the politics. I'm not a fan of big government and propaganda films are distasteful."

The present nature of things is natural, Lucas said philosophically. "If you hire a photographer to take your picture, you want to look good. If you make a picture for government, it wants to look good. It's Hollywood invading everything. There were a lot of stupid directives on the Johnson film. You couldn't show Lady Bird's profile. It always had to be a ½ view. You couldn't use any angle of the president where his bald spot showed. I had put in a shot of a bunch of horses in Korea running down the street to help control the huge crowds. Someone thought it looked a little too fascist—which it wasn't—and made us take it out. I just liked the shot."

When Lucas returned to graduate school in 1966 for one semester, he completed work on his film short *THX-1138-XEB.* ("It doesn't mean anything.") It had been filmed as an exercise in shooting without light when Lucas was helping to teach a class of Navy combat photographers.

He won a national Student Film prize for the short and a six-months scholarship to observe at Warner Bros.

At Warners, he met Coppola, then directing *Finian's Rainbow.* When Coppola formed his own company to make *The Rain People,* he asked Lucas to help.

Deciding to "get out of Hollywood and all that craziness," Coppola opened American Zoetrope in December 1969 in an old San Francisco warehouse decorated with photos of early movie heroes and filled with the latest equipment. It was financed by Coppola's profits from *Finian* and Zoetrope's exclusive deal with Warners to make seven films. Since then, Lucas said, "Primarily because of arguments about *THX,* Warners has cancelled the other six and Zoetrope has been reorganized. If you're going to use your own resources and not rob a bank, you have to figure out a way to make money. Francis can earn a great deal writing scripts and directing if he does it a certain way. He doesn't like it, but he couldn't have made *The Rain People* if he hadn't made *Finian.* Now he has to do *The Godfather* to make *The Conversation,* his next film."

Does that mean that Coppola is not likely to be upset by elimination of the "Mafia" and "Cosa Nostra" names from *The Godfather?*

"Well, he does because you end up getting involved emotionally and when they say, 'You've got to do this,' you go crazy. They tell people what to do without reason. The studios know that directors get emotionally involved, and then all hell breaks loose. It happened to me, to Elaine May, to anyone who makes movies now. Sooner or later, they decide they know more about making movies than directors. Studio heads. You can't fight them because they've got the money. The terrible thing about this country is that the dollar is valued above the individual. You can buy another person no matter how talented he is and then tell him he's wrong. They do not like to trust people."

American Zoetrope functions in the opposite way, Lucas said. "We say, 'We think you are a talented, functioning person and we are hiring you because of your abilities, and whatever you come up with, we're going to take.' If we make a mistake, it will be in picking the wrong person. What we're striving for is total freedom, where we can finance our pictures, make them our way, release them where we want them released and be completely free to express ourselves. That's very hard to do in the world of business. In this country, the only thing that speaks is money and you have to have the money in order to have the power to be free. So the danger is—in being as oppressive as the next guy to the people below you. We're going to do everything possible to avoid that pitfall. But if we fail, it's another saga in the history of man..."

THX 1138—Made in San Francisco

AMERICAN CINEMATOGRAPHER/1971

WARNER BROS.' *THX 1138* is a mind-bending look into a future century and into a civilization that exists totally underground, its hairless citizens computer-controlled, euphoric with compulsory drugs and having arrived at the ultimate in human conformity under a robot police force.

The American Zoetrope production for Warner Bros. release was directed by 25-year-old George Lucas, produced by Lawrence Sturhahn and written by George Lucas and Walter Murch. Francis Ford Coppola, head of American Zoetrope was the executive producer. The film editor was George Lucas, the art director Michael Haller and the cameramen were Albert Kihn and David Meyers.

The story is concerned with the efforts of Robert Duvall, who plays THX 1138 in a society where a prefix and a number suffice for a name, to escape his drug-induced state, which leads to love, an unknown and even forbidden emotion in his dehumanized surroundings, and finally his attempt to escape completely from the subterranean world itself.

The *THX 1138* company traveled to no less than 22 locations in the San Francisco Bay area, filming in such places as the Oakland Coliseum, the San Francisco Pacific Gas and Electric Building, the Marin County Civic Center in San Rafael and the various tunnels and tubes of the a-building Bay Area Rapid Transit system, scheduled to go into operation in 1972.

From *American Cinematographer*, October 1971, pp. 992–93, 1018, 1031. Reprinted by permission.

One of the chilling scenes shows Robert Duvall undergoing a medical examination of the future. To simulate this, director Lucas moved the company to a tumor research center in San Jose, where a four-million-volt linear accelerator and a laser treatment machine provided the necessary appearance of the medical machines of centuries hence.

The *THX 1138* company left the San Francisco area for one week to film a sequence involving a stark prison of the future without walls. The set, best described as absolute whiteness in all directions, served as a futuristic confinement facility without borders or boundaries.

Director George Lucas grew up in Modesto, Calif., and became interested in films while attending the University of Southern California. *THX 1138* is his first feature picture, either as a writer or director, but it is based on a short he made while at USC which took the grand prize at the National Student Film Festival. Lucas has several other films planned for American Zoetrope production.

Francis Ford Coppola, the executive producer and creator of American Zoetrope, is only 30 but has had a decade of experience in motion pictures, much of it as a writer. He attended Hofstra University in New York before going to UCLA for his master's degree in filmmaking, where he won first prize in the 1962 Samuel Goldwyn writing competition. He made his professional debut in 1967 as writer and director on the highly acclaimed *You're a Big Boy Now,* then directed Warners *Finian's Rainbow* and wrote and directed *The Rain People* for the same studio. It was while he was in the post-production phases on that film that he realized his "ultimate dream" with the founding of American Zoetrope and its ultra-modern film facility in San Francisco. Coppola won an Academy "Oscar" last year for his screenplay of *Patton.* He has recently completed co-scripting and direction chores on Paramount's *The Godfather* and is currently in the process of editing the picture at Zoetrope.

The production of *THX 1138* was unique in several significant respects, among which were the following:

(1) Though financed and released by Warner Bros., the film, in its creative concept and execution, was in no way a "major studio production;" on the contrary, it was totally the product of American Zoetrope, the San Francisco-based film-making "commune," founded and funded by Francis Ford Coppola for the purpose of attracting, encouraging and utilizing talented young film technicians new to the industry.

(2) Except for a couple of short sequences requiring set elements that did not exist locally, the picture was produced, photographed and completed entirely in San Francisco, with post-production utilizing the highly sophisticated technical facilities of American Zoetrope.

(3) Only one small "set" (an austere apartment of the future) was actually built for the production. Enormous production value and an atmosphere of great scope were achieved by utilizing carefully selected structures and locations existing in the San Francisco area.

(4) *THX 1138* was made by a relatively small crew of primarily young technicians, most of whom had never before worked on a feature film.

(5) The picture, filmed in Techniscope, is highly stylized in its photographic treatment. A distinctive visual aura, perfectly adapted to the subject matter, was achieved by breaking established photographic rules—not haphazardly, but with a high degree of skill and control.

The Concept of *THX 1138* By George Lucas

My primary concept in approaching the production of *THX 1138* was to make a kind of *cinema verité* film of the future—something that would look like a documentary crew had made a film about some character in a time yet to come.

However, I wanted it to look like a very slick, studied documentary in terms of technique. I come from a background of graphics, photography, art and painting—and I'm very graphics-conscious. So, I don't believe that a documentary has to look bad because it follows a *cinema verité* style. It can look good and still look real. Simply stated, that was my approach to every element of the production—the sets, the actors, the wardrobe, everything.

At the same time that I wanted the picture to look slick and professional, in terms of cinematic technique, I felt that the realism of the film's content would be enhanced by having the actors and their surroundings look slightly scruffy, even a little bit dirty, as they might well look in the society depicted. They wore no makeup, which helped to keep them from appearing too slick and clean.

I had in mind a certain "honest" look for the film, which I felt could best be achieved by using documentary cameramen. However, the main approach would be in the lighting. The idea was to not light anything unless it was absolutely necessary. Only if we walked into an area where there was no light at all would we put up a few low-wattage lights here and there. Otherwise, we would just let everything go the way it really was.

Another graphics concept in the film would be very flat lighting, with everything quite two-dimensional. Aside from its stylistic value, I knew that the no-lighting approach would enable us to move very fast in shooting. Obviously, we would have to do something to compensate for the lack of light, and that led to our decision to force-develop practically the entire film. We decided to "push" everything, except for the shots to be used for making opticals. By not pushing those shots, we hoped to achieve a consistency of graininess throughout the film.

I was well aware that there would be those in the audience who would be shocked by the graininess at first, but I was sure that after the first minute or two they would get used to the grain and simply accept it as part of the stylistic concept, the documentary approach.

As I said, I felt that *THX* should be photographed by someone with a very thorough documentary background, someone who was used to thinking fast and making quick technical decisions — also someone who had a feel for riding focus on unrehearsed action, without having to measure things off.

When production-planning first began on *THX*, I was living in Los Angeles. Haskell Wexler, ASC, is an old friend of mine from the time when I was going to school at USC. He's a great guy and a real friend of the student. While I was writing the script in L.A. I asked him if he would be interested in photographing the picture and he said that he would be. But by the time we were ready to go into production, I had moved up to San Francisco with American Zoetrope and, because we were a San Francisco company, the decision was made to use only San Francisco technicians.

Later, when we came down to Hollywood on location, Haskell was our standby cameraman. He did some of the shooting (three Directors of Photography, no less!) and helped us out of some of the tight situations that can break you on a low-budget feature. He was always there when we needed advice.

As for our two full-time Directors of Photography, both of whom live in San Francisco — Al Kihn had worked as a TV newsreel cameraman for four or five years and had shot a few documentaries for the USIA. Dave Meyers, who is older than Al, has had a great deal of experience and is highly respected in San Francisco as a documentary cameraman. He shot many of those fine documentary sequences in *Woodstock*.

We talked to every cameraman in San Francisco and looked at their film. We selected these two primarily because I liked the way they "thought" on the screen and the way they followed the action. They were both obviously good technicians who knew how to make the best of a situation. These things are important because it's tough doing a documentary. It's a real exercise.

As an example of what I mean, when we got into the actual shooting, I would set up a scene and rehearse it maybe once. A lot of the time I didn't rehearse at all. There were no marks and no measurements. The cameramen just had to guess where the actors were, while riding focus blind in a lot of cases. We were shooting at such low light levels and with such a shallow depth of field that it was very hard to keep things in focus, but they did an excellent job. Very often we'd get it in one take, and I almost never shot more than three takes on a scene. This was due mostly to the fact that I had a very professional cast of excellent actors.

If a take was acceptable, but not perfect, I would move the cameras before doing it over, instead of making take after take from the same positions. This gave me a vast number of different angles for each scene. Since I planned to edit the picture myself, I wanted to be able to "make" the film in the editing. The shooting was designed for me to end up with a lot of documentary coverage so that, hopefully, I would be able to cut together a perfect performance in every case.

I got so that I knew which actors gave their best on the first take and which ones needed a couple of takes to warm up. We would zero in on their closeups accordingly, using long lenses, so that the actors literally never knew when they were being filmed in closeup. This resulted in more natural performances, because they were playing to each other all the time (instead of to the camera) and they didn't get uptight, as actors often do when they know they're in a closeup.

While we shot with available light almost exclusively, this wasn't always as difficult as it sounds. We were shooting mostly modern interiors, which usually have ten times more light than they really need. It's just an architectural phenomenon of the sixties and seventies to way over-light interiors.

However, sometimes we'd walk into places where it was so dark that we'd have to turn on a flashlight just to read the needle on the exposure meter. Very often the meter didn't indicate any reading at all, but we didn't let that stop us. Our pet phrase during the entire shooting was: "Just put on your fastest lens, open it up all the way and shoot."

Despite all that, we kept getting back dailies that looked good. Everyone kept saying: "Gee, I never thought we'd get that one." But as long as it kept coming out all right, we kept doing it. We always ordered one-light dailies—never a timed print—and, incredibly enough, almost the entire picture printed on light 12.

I wanted to shoot *THX* in a wide-screen format because it is, basically, an environmental film and I felt it was essential to get it as big as possible. I chose Techniscope over the available 35mm anamorphic processes because we could use faster lenses and our Eclair cameras could easily be switched over to the Techniscope format. Also, while the Eclairs normally carry 400-foot magazines (which are awkward for the shooting of a feature), the Techniscope format gave us the equivalent of an 800-foot load of straight 35mm. I wasn't afraid of the blow-up involved, because I had shot a lot of 16mm that had been blown up to 35mm. To me, Techniscope is just another form of Super-16. Or maybe "Super-duper-16" is more like it.

There was one sequence in the picture that we went all out to light completely. That was the "cathedral" sequence near the end of the picture that was actually shot in a TV studio. They had all of these lights electronically controlled by push buttons so that we could do whatever we wanted in the way of lighting. We sort of ran amuck with back-lighting and everything else we could think of. It was a lot of fun, and it relieved the frustrations of the gaffer. It gave him a chance to actually light something.

No film ever ends up exactly as you would like it to, but, with minor exceptions, *THX* came out pretty much as I had visualized it, thanks to some excellent assistance—and a whole lot of luck.

The Filming of *American Graffiti*

LARRY STURHAHN/1974

"Graffiti" are defined as ancient drawings or writings scratched on a wall or other surface; as words or phrases written on public sidewalks, on the walls of buildings, public rest rooms, or the like; as the images of a past culture.

It is said that half the people at Universal hated the title, American Graffiti. *They didn't know what it meant, thought it sounded like an Italian film or a film about feet.*

When I told George Lucas that "graffiti" are now looked at as the statements of people establishing their being, their existence; that on the sides of New York subway trains they are folk art, Lucas said the title was "controversial" at Universal Studios, but that was "essentially what the movie is."

In 1969 I was producer of THX 1138, *George Lucas' first feature film. That picture, innovatively made for very little money, was finally very controversial too. I wrote something about it which appeared in* Kansas Quarterly *(spring issue, 1972) which derived from an interview I did with George prior to the shooting in September, 1969. Here and there in the following material are references, either to that interview or the production of that film, which I hope have been made clear. The roots of a tree are as important to its growth as the flexibility of its branches are to its ability to bend in the wind.*

From *Filmmakers Newsletter*, March 1974, pp. 19–27.

L S : *Back in the days before* THX *started shooting we talked, and at that time you described yourself as a "filmmaker," putting this order to it: first editor, second cameraman, third director, and fourth writer. Would you change that order now?*

G L : On *Graffiti* I would flip the cameraman and director. But who knows, I might flip back on the next one. As a film student I was all technical. Now I'm working on being a director and a writer, because those are the things I'm weakest at. They are a challenge, more interesting to me because I don't know them as well. But it all depends on how you define it. In film school, and on *THX*, I was all things. Now I'm less a cameraman because I'm starting to depend on people like Haskell Wexler. There's only so much that one human being can do, and as you get older you realize you have to make a choice.

L S : *An historical reason why film is compartmentalized is because it's physically impossible for one person to do everything.*

G L : I will always be concerned about the camera, but—as opposed to *THX*, which was designed in the camera—as I delve more and more into story and dramatics, they take more of my time. On *THX* some of the dramatic was sacrificed in favor of the camera.

L S : *If you didn't have the chance to work as closely with the cameraman as you have in the past, did you at least check every set-up?*

G L : I checked every set-up. Before, on *THX*, I knew exactly what the shot was, and I could watch the cameramen as much as I could watch the performance. I could see if they were hitting focus marks and following the right guy. I could see whether everything was going the way it should go, so when I saw the dailies they were more or less the way I thought they were going to look.

On *Graffiti* there were some depth-of-field and framing problems—people would shift, not know where to go—that kind of stuff; and I wouldn't see it when it happened. It's very hard; you really have to look through the camera all the time and then watch at rehearsals and keep aware of how the camera is moving so when someone moves you know how far he's moved and whether or not he's on the right spot.

L S : *I remember how meticulous you were about the camera on* THX, *so was this a problem for you?*

GL: Yes, it was. But once Haskell got there I was confident. He's really ter-rific, so I just let him do it and I didn't worry about it anymore. Everything came out beautifully, just the way we wanted it.

We had been shooting a week when Haskell came in. Originally we asked him to shoot the film, but he said he didn't want to shoot a wide-screen movie because he didn't like it. He didn't want to shoot Techniscope be-cause he felt it looked grainy and he didn't want to push it. And besides, he was writing his own script and shooting commercials, and he didn't really want to go back to being a cameraman.

But when we got in trouble and I asked him to do it, he did it—as a friend, to help me out. He shot a format he didn't like, using Techniscope which he didn't like. I had already locked in a look which he described as juke-box-like—very garish, bright blue and yellow and red.

LS: *Yes, I noticed that—the exteriors, the cars in particular.*
GL: Right, that's what I wanted for the film, and that was one of the prob-lems I was having early in the film. I wasn't getting the garish look I wanted. Haskell came in and made it look exactly the way I wanted.

LS: *Did he do it with lighting?*
GL: Yes, he did it with warm lights and cold lights. The existing lights were very blue (Mercury Vapor), so instead of compensating and overwhelming the blue light, he used it, played with it—used the blue and the red, the cold and the warm lights. Originally we had set it with red and yellow—very warm.

LS: *And shooting wide open must have been a serious limitation for the cam-eraman?*
GL: Oh, it was terrible. It was an impossible film to shoot. Very rarely did we have time for camera rehearsals; they just had to wing it. They were fol-lowing their own focus with 1.2 lenses, shooting at footcandles that ranged from 6 to 12—where normal is 250! And with the Arriflex which has lines inscribed on the viewing glass and a shutter bar that moves through, it's very hard to see what's going on. I couldn't follow focus—in fact, I could-n't even see focus half the time. At least the Eclair has a different viewing system; it's brighter and you can see. I'm used to working with the Eclair, and it's much easier.

LS: *The metaphors in* Graffiti *work on several different levels—like the cars that carry the characters through change. The cars are symbols too, and after all, in the United States the car is an enormously complex symbol. Isn't it true that our frustration with the energy crisis is partly due to this—our mobility is limited and we have no way to escape?*

In that first interview we talked of how you evolved into a filmmaker—because of a serious automobile accident. John has an accident in Graffiti—*like you did. To what degree are the characters in the film you?*

GL: On a realistic level, most kids start out like Terry the Toad. When they're 14 or 15 they hang out with the bigger guys and never quite make it. That's how I started: always the littlest guy, never quite able to make it. When I got to be 16 and got a car I started racing, hopping up cars, and ended up as a hot-rodder. That would be John. Then I had that very bad accident and spent time in the hospital. After that I started to apply myself to my studies and became sort of like Curt. I still went down to cruise, to hang out, but I was more detached. I wasn't John anymore; I wasn't the hot guy anymore. I was sort of over the hill, even though I still knew all the guys. But, I could reflect on it. I was still interested; it was still in my blood.

LS: *It seems to me that Steve (the fourth character) is less visible; I don't seem to remember him as I do the others.*

GL: Steve is the one we had the most problems with because, by definition, he's the most bland. Since that's what he really is, it was hard to make him interesting.

Also, because the other characters are based on myself I didn't really know Steve. He was more or less made up by the other writers, and I mean really made up. I had him in there, but he was terrible. They added as much life to him as there is now and made him acceptable. In my version, you would have just cut that whole story out because it didn't work. They got him up to where he worked, but they couldn't get him up to the level of the other characters who were infinitely stronger.

LS: *What about the other people who helped you write* Graffiti—*William Huyck and Gloria Katz? Since a great deal of the script is you, how much of it is them—in the mechanical sense of putting it on the page?*

GL: Originally I wasn't going to write it at all because I don't like writing and only do it if I have to. But Bill and I went to USC Film School together.

I had read all of his screenplays and loved them and thought he was a brilliant writer, so when I had the idea for the film about four guys who cruise
around and do all this stuff on the last night of summer, I sat down with
Bill and Gloria (they're husband and wife) and together we hacked out an
idea about four characters who do this, that, and the other thing.

Then it took me about a year to get the money because I wasn't the
hottest thing in Hollywood. By that time and with the miniscule amount
to write the screenplay, Bill had gotten the chance to direct a picture and
wasn't available, so I sat down and wrote the original screenplay.

Then I got the deal to make the film based on the screenplay, but I
wasn't happy with it because I don't have a lot of confidence in my
screen-writing ability. By that time—and due to begin shooting in two
months—Bill was available, so I suggested they come in and re-write it.
They didn't change the structure; what they did was improve the dialogue,
make it funnier, more human, truer. And they also wrote in the Steve and
Laurie relationship. They took those scenes and made them work. So
though they improved it a great deal, it was basically my story. The scenes
are mine; the dialogue is theirs. But it's hard to be cut and dry about something like that because, of course, they completely changed some scenes,
and others were left intact.

L S : *You have said you feel that the great filmmakers are the writers and that in
your own consciousness of filmmaker as story-teller, that really means being a
writer.*
G L : Unfortunately, even though I'm working on a screenplay right now,
I'm not a good writer. It's very, very hard for me. I don't feel I have a natural talent for it—as opposed to camera, which I could always just *do*. It
was a natural. And the same thing for editing. I've always been able to just
sit down and cut.

But I don't have a natural talent for writing. When I sit down I bleed on
the page, and it's just awful. Writing just doesn't flow in a creative surge
the way other things do.

L S : *I've been teaching film writing at San Francisco State, and the question of
how long a film should be in script form is very relevant. How long—how many
pages—does a writer figure he's going to have to go? I have said that a good*

screenplay length is between 100, 115 or 120 pages. Roughly it works out to a
minute per page.

GL: It's amazing how closely that formula applies. I've done a lot of
research on that, and I've discovered that the screenplay and the length of
the screenplay are essential not only to a well-planned production, but to
a good movie. *Citizen Kane*, for instance, was a 120-page script for a 119-
minute film—almost exactly the same!

I know filmmakers who have had serious problems when the screenplay
was too long, like I had on *Graffiti*. Yet I knew it going in. I said, "A 140-
page screenplay is too long. It's never going to work. The musical numbers
will make it longer; it will never play!"

Most studios like a picture to come in between 100 and 110 minutes
because a theater likes to run a 2-4-6-8 schedule. They get more bookings
out of it and make more money that way. So the studio will always fight to
get a picture down under 110 minutes—unless of course you're a $10 mil-
lion-dollar block buster, and then they let it run longer because it seems to
make it more important. But I think 100 to 110 minutes is just right for
most feature films—it's an enjoyable length of time to watch. If it goes
much longer than that it gets to be too long sometimes.

But you face it on the set. With *Graffiti* I knew it, and I could have cut
it down, but I just wouldn't do it for various reasons. I just wasn't in the
mood. It takes something to go in and start chopping things you really
like out of a movie. To me, it seems easier to do it at the end when you're
in that process of cutting it down and are mentally set up for that. When
you're creating the thing, to go in and say "Cut this out! Cut that out!" is
very hard. But what happens is you find that the screenplay and its length
are very important.

Granted your first screenplay usually comes out to 130 or 140 pages, but
if you can start cutting it down then—if you can get that discipline at the
screenplay stage, so the structure and everything works then—well, you
don't have to worry about it later. But most people wait until later and try
to figure it out then.

LS: *Back to that old interview. We discussed the concept of filmmaker as artist*
or technician. At the time you said you had gone with Francis Coppola to a con-
ference where George Cukor spoke, and he was adamantly opposed to the idea of

filmmaker as technician and considered himself an artist. Two things about that now seem to be interesting: Cukor was an actor's director, and bad as it is to categorize, he was more that than some of the other action directors; his films are more concerned with character. Graffiti *is concerned with character. Do you see this as a creative progression in you, the filmmaker?*

G L :   First, George Cukor isn't a filmmaker, he's a director. He directs people and he directs a production—and he really does it! In the studio system as it was in those old days people were more compartmentalized, and it worked very well. They could make a lot more movies—as opposed to somebody like me who can only make a movie every two or three years.

Also, I came out of film school, so I really was a *filmmaker—which means doing it all.* I didn't just have the actors to deal with; I did everything. I think of myself as a filmmaker still. I'm writing a screenplay now. But then a lot of those guys you think of as directors also wrote their own original stories and screenplays. In a sense they were filmmakers too—William Wellman, for instance, made movies from start to finish.

In my mind, I guess, you're a filmmaker when you write an original screenplay, not a work from a book you've found, but something out of your own brain which you then make into a movie—and you have control over the editing and the camerawork. Some directors do have control over the camera and some have control over the editing, but it's hard to do everything. I think that thing before about filmmakers was just my attitude more than anything else. I like making movies—I like the physical act of filmmaking.

For me it's like sculpture or painting. I come up with an idea that I think will make a great image or a great scene and then I go out and I make it happen. I do it partially because I think it will be good for the story; and I do it partially because I want to see that scene re-created from what was in my head; and I do it partially just from enjoyment. For instance, I enjoy cars, and the result is a lot of cars in *Graffiti*. It's not necessarily an intellectual idea, but my own thing I like to work with.

L S :   *For you the step between cars and filmmaking was painting. Is what we're talking about the integration of a personality?*

G L :   Back then Cukor compared filmmaking to watch-making, which means putting things together physically, and I enjoy that. But another reason I made *American Graffiti* is because I love the music. I love rock 'n' roll. Making *Graffiti* I could sit down at my Steenbeck and play all this rock 'n' roll all day; that was my job in editing. The editors were cutting the scenes and I was putting in the rock 'n' roll, saying, "Wow, that's really great!" It's like carving something; it takes shape, and it's a lot of fun. It's a kind of therapy.

L S : *I had the impression that you put the idea of artist down — as opposed to technician, that is.*

G L : My thing about art is that I don't like the word *art* because it means pretension and bullshit, and I equate those two directly. I don't think of myself as an artist, and I don't think I ever will. Even when I was a painter I didn't think of myself as an artist. Art is for critics, for somebody back in New York who spends his time figuring it out and doesn't really do anything else. Well, that's for them; I'm a craftsman. I don't make a work of art; I make a movie. If it does what I want it to do then somebody else can come along and figure it out. Art is very controversial. After all, people make their living just arguing about it. But I make my living making things. If other people want to call it art, or just want to call it movies — that's their problem.

L S : *Then you make your films for an audience? Or, to put it another way, if the audience loved your film but the critics hated it, what would your feelings be?*

G L : Well, the "San Francisco Chronicle" put *Graffiti* down. But their review was so irrational it's hard to believe they ever saw the movie. That bothers me because it's so irrational. And it, by the way, was the only bad review we got. Of 385 reviews it was the only bad one. We got some mixed — for instance, Pauline Kael in the "New Yorker" re-reviewed it and said it was a male-chauvinist-pig movie. That's her opinion, and she brought up some interesting points which are valid. Basically, she liked the movie and thought it was interesting and well-made, but she objected to the treatment of women in it. That's a valid, intelligent, rational viewpoint. But, as opposed to the "Chronicle," I have never met or heard of anybody who hated the acting and the actors or thought they were unattractive people. Why? They're nice warm kids.

So 80% is for me and what I like. The rest is where I get crazy, but then — hopefully — I say: "Well, most people won't like that." So sometimes I modify my crazy enthusiasm in deference to the general viewing audience in order to let them enjoy it more. It's a business and they are paying their money to see the film.

But I don't see that as compromising. Rather I see it as being realistic. I get very crazy notions once in a while, and sometimes you have to be realistic about that. But at least 80 or 90% of a movie is just me, and I hope everybody else likes it. If they don't then they don't—if they do, then they do.

L S : *The film is usually described in reviews from a nostalgia point of view. That's defined as: "a longing for the experiences, things, or aquaintanceships belonging to the past." And it's not only in film these days, but in all the arts. What are your feelings about that term in relation to* American Graffiti—*is it enough to say it's a "nostalgia genre" film?*

G L : Well, the "nostalgia genre" film is something which has just become a genre—which is amazing. When John Ford made his nostalgia films they were called westerns, and Raoul Walsh's were called gangster films. But they were still nostalgia films, like *Graffiti*. I didn't have the west or gangsters or anything, so I used what I grew up with. I'm doing what filmmakers have always done. After all, *Citizen Kane* was a nostalgia picture. It's just that now they've made it a classification, so any time you do a film that's five years in the past it's a nostalgia film.

Originally I didn't think about it as nostalgia, even though it took place in 1962. The film is about teenagers; about teenagers moving forward and making decisions about what they want to do in life. But it's also about the fact that you can't live in the past, which is part of that same idea. You have to move forward, things can't stay the same; essentially that's the point of the film. No matter how much you want things to be the same, they won't and can't; everything is always changing, and you have to accept change. So a movie about accepting change is called a nostalgia film, even though you're dealing with change and the past, present, and future. *Graffiti* is partially a nostalgia film, partly a film about teenagers, and partly a film about the future.

L S : *Some people who describe nostalgia say it's a harking back to a simpler time, a time when the problems that we face today weren't so evident.*

G L : *Graffiti* is about that too. It's about a period of transition in history in America where in one year you had a President that a lot of kids admired, were proud of; you had a certain kind of rock 'n' roll music; a certain kind of country where you could believe in things. You were also a teenager, 18 years old, going to school, living at home. You had a certain kind of life. But in the next two years everything changed: no longer were you a teenager, you were an adult going to college or doing whatever you were going to do. The government changed radically, and everybody's attitude toward it changed radically. Drugs came in. Although it had always been there, a war surfaced as an issue. The music changed completely.

Graffiti is about the fact that you have to accept these changes—they were on the horizon, and if you didn't you had problems. You know, the brittle bough breaks. The willow bends with the wind and stays on the tree. You try to fight it, like John did, and you lose. You're not going to remain 18 forever.

LS: *At the end of the film John says: "you beat me." So he is forseeing his own future?*

GL: Right. He knew he couldn't beat it. That's in his character. Steve, on the other hand, is in to it when he stays and doesn't live up to his potential.

LS: *I think there's some truth to the idea that we're interested in nostalgia because it was a time that was more simple, but in the current definition is a concept of sentimentality. Your film is not sentimental at all—it's very realistic. Granted there is sentiment in it, warmth and human feelings, but it's not a sentimental film about a period of time. Did you have that feeling when you were writing it, or did it evolve in the making?*

GL: In my life that was a very strong time. It's very much like the movie. My high school years had a big impact on my life. When I made the film I knew I wasn't going to make fun of it. Like the music—I liked and still like that kind of rock 'n' roll. As a result I didn't treat it like they do in *Grease*. They make fun of it! Well, it was kind of crazy, but it had charm; something about it was really quite nice. And there was respect for it, which I still have. Just like I still have respect for cruising, for being a teenager.

Part of that stuff about innocence and a different time has to do with being a teenager; things are much more innocent. Even now—today—we are more aware of the pressures than a teenager is. I talked to a lot of them in the process of doing *Graffiti*—in the interviews, in the making, in the screening of the finished film. A lot of teenagers today are just like we were when we were teenagers, but when you grow up you forget. You become aware of the world around you. You realize all these things about life. You forget when you were a teenager how you sort of knew about it but you didn't really care as much. What you cared about were a lot of things that you would now call petty — like kissing a girl and all the other stuff in the movie. But that's the time when those things should be important and you shouldn't have to be burdened with all the problems of the world; when you should worry just about girls, and cars, and homework — all that kind of stuff. When you hit college is time enough to confront the other aspects of life.

LS: *And you still think that operates?*
GL: I still think it operates to a degree. Obviously today teenagers are infinitely better educated, know a lot more, are aware of more. Of course they are living in a much different world than the one we lived in, but a lot of the problems are still the same. Ultimately I don't think their energy and concern is much different than ours was. After all, we cared about a lot of things. Remember, the film is about 1962. A lot of people say it's a 50s movie — the innocent 50s. What it's about is the end of the 50s. 1962 was not 1957 — there's a big difference between those years; but people forget, lumping it all together. The film is about the end of an era, not the end of one particular year.

LS: *One of the most criticized aspects of the film has to do with those titles at the end.*
GL: Controversial is the word for that. Half the people love it and half the people hate it. But they were designed to put the film in perspective: the film is about change, and it says that things change, even though you already knew it. The real criticism of it has always been the fact that it's an overstatement and it's not necessary. But, as I said, half the people hated it and half thought it was the greatest thing in the movie. So the half who don't like it are ultra-sophisticated film people or ultra-sophisticated intellectuals who don't like overstatement, and they are offended by it. But for a lot of people it was enjoyable; it was a re-affirmation of something.

In making a film you have a wide range of intellect and sensibilities to appeal to and it's hard to find a medium ground to appeal to all. The film was designed for kids, for teenagers; that's who was meant to see it. But everybody went. The studio thought it was for the people out of college—between 25 and 30. But it was designed for people between 16 and 20, and then everybody from 10 to 60 went to see it—and everyone seems to be able to relate to it in one way or another. In Los Angeles the teenagers are going; in New York it seems to be getting the 25 to 30 crowd. It's amazing—the different audiences who are going to see the movie.

LS: *So those titles were designed as an original part of the movie; they weren't an after-thought?*
GL: Right—those titles are in the script. By the way, the largest real criticism about that has been that we didn't tell about the girls. But Women's Lib has really evolved since the film was finished a year ago January. It was going on, but it wasn't as militant then.

LS: *That's also coming out of left field. The film is about those 4 guys, and you, the creator, can't include everything.*
GL: True. And it's also being consistent for a film about 1962. In 1973 you would put those things in, but sensibilities have changed very radically, and most critics deal with today, not with the fact that this script was done in 1971, when that title card was put on there.

LS: *You said the film was made for teenagers but that people from all age groups have seen it and found something in it. Do you feel the reason the film is such a good picture of that time—not that time in history but that time in life which your one night depicts—has to do with your attitude about being a teenager?*
GL: Obviously my feelings about that time and my perceptions of it have a lot to do with the way the film turned out. It's very much stamped on the movie. I'm not condescending about it; I'm proud of it. I'm glad I was a teenager; I enjoyed being a teenager. I don't hang my head and say, "Well, we were just a bunch of dumb kids then." We weren't; we were just kids, and being a kid is great!

LS: *Despite the travail, the frustrations, the misconnections, the film evinces a tremendous joy. Were you into all that joy, or did it come out of the actors?*
GL: It was out of the actors, but it was really out of everyone. It was a lot of fun. We shot at 5 o'clock in the morning, and after that you're a little crazy. A lot of the joy is just the joy of the making of it.

Also, it has a certain ring about it because it's true. In order to do it, we lived all night. For 28 nights we went out and cruised and hung out. And the kids—they weren't 29 or 30 years old, they were kids, most of them teenagers. They were having fun, like kids have fun, playing reality.

L S : *What about the adult figures, the authoritarians, the parents? It's wrong to say that they were defeated because it's not that simple—and yet they always are. They don't come off as being very good at what they're doing, as being authorities.*

G L : The whole film is essentially a teenage fantasy. It's not really the way it is. That one night is really a year's cruising. It's purposely done that the kids get the better of the authority figures. That's part of a teenage fantasy. How often do you really get the better of an adult when you're a kid?

L S : *After that scene when the cop comes and stares down at John through the window of his car there's a tremendous release in the theatre when the rear end is ripped out of the cop car.*

G L : Yeah. It also has to do with one of the reasons the film was made—as opposed to *THX*, which was about real things that were going on and the problems we're faced with. I realized after making *THX* that those problems are so real that most of us have to face those things every day, so we're in a constant state of frustration. That just makes us more depressed than we were before. So I made a film where, essentially, we can get rid of some of those frustrations, the feeling that everything seems futile.

L S : *Roger Greenspun wrote about Curt's dream, the girl in the T-Bird—the metaphor. I must admit I didn't see it until I read his piece and saw the film a second time. Then it really clicked! How aware of that were you—in the writing and in the making?*

G L : It was an integral part of the structure. Ultimately we hung the film on Curt, said this is a film about Curt and his friends, as opposed to a film about John and his friends. The problem we had with Curt was that he didn't really do anything. His only problem just came down to deciding whether he was going to leave town, and that's an awfully thin idea to hang a movie on—especially when you have these other dynamite things going. So I invented the girl as a metaphor.

The reality of cruising is that you do it ultimately because you are hoping to find that one girl, the dream girl you've always wanted to meet.

That's why you keep doing it every night. And there's always the element of chance. It's like gambling; sooner or later she's going to come along, and you're going to meet her, and that's going to be it—even though it never seems to happen.

So we made that girl a sort of literary device. It's the most literary device in the film, but I thought it would be worthwhile to see if we could make it work—a realistic visual film with a literary idea in it. She was really quite controversial. She was originally designed as the siren in the town who would lure him back, keep him there. People have interpreted his following her all over while she eludes him as the reason why he finally leaves. So, interestingly enough, when you do something like that everybody interprets it in his own way.

LS: *That's OK because that's really what a metaphor is all about. And once you start talking about a metaphor, you destroy it. In one of the last shots in the plane, down below on the road is the car; it really works in the film. She also drives the perfect car.*

GL: Right. And she is in white. She is a dream. Nobody knows who she is; everybody thinks she's somebody else. She's a fantasy; she doesn't exist. Something I wanted to do (but didn't because everybody thought I was crazy, and it also would have been expensive and technically difficult) was to superimpose that girl driving through the empty drive-in, ghostlike. Since it would have been the first image in the film people wouldn't have been aware she was a ghost; it would have appeared real. But we didn't do it because you wouldn't really know whether it was a bad optical or what. Anyway, it's an example of how I was getting carried away by the idea.

As for the white T-bird being the "right" car, a lot of the material in the film comes out of the material of the times. Just like a lot of it comes out of the Beach Boys' music. If you listen to them, there are about 5 songs that relate directly to the film. The T-bird is one of them: "Fun, Fun, Fun" is about a girl who rides around in a T-bird doing exactly what the girl in the film does—until her daddy takes the T-bird away.

LS: *That's fascinating. Although the film is super-realistic, that's a fantasy. You never know whether she's real or a figment of his imagination. That's what film can do; there's a real photograph of a T-bird, but it's a fantasy in his head and in the heads of the audience. How do you explain how that works?*

G L :   It's the style of the film. The *style* of the film is realistic; it's not that
the film is realistic—and that's an important distinction. The actual film,
as I say, is a myth. For instance, some friends of mine did that to a police
car, but it didn't come off like that. The car just sort of went clunk, and it
was really very undramatic. But in the film it comes off. The hoods are
another example. There are groups like that, but they're not really like
that. It's been mythized so that it's easier to take and more fun. The fact
that it's shown in a very realistic style makes it believable.

You can get away with a lot of crazy things, like the girl in the T-bird, if
the style is strong enough to offset it. If it isn't strong enough it and rings
phony most of the time, then you can never get away with tricks like that.
When it's strong you accept it because everything is strong; it pulls it
down into its own realism.

L S :   *Curt flies off on Magic Carpet Airlines. Was that real, or did you paint it
on there?*
G L :   We painted it on, but actually it's semi-real. The people who gave us
the airplane were Magic Carpet Travel Service. We searched all over for an
old prop plane, but they're not easy to find anymore. Finally we found a
couple of airlines who would give us a plane if we used their name. I had a
choice between Air West, Air California, and Magic Carpet. I decided to
use Magic Carpet, but it wasn't written in the script. I thought it was
appropriate, and that's one of those things that when fate gives it to you,
you make the decision.

L S :   *How long a schedule did you plan, and how long did you actually shoot?*
G L :   It was planned for 28 days, and that's what we shot.

L S :   *6-day weeks?*
G L :   No, 5-day weeks—or rather, 5-night weeks. We could only shoot
from 9 at night until 5:05 in the morning when the sun came up. There
was just no way after that because the film was 80% exterior night, and
there was no way to fake it. You know, the other way, you just put up
some arcs and shoot for another hour. But in this case, when the sun came
up that was the end of it.

Working on a tight schedule like that I would shoot the meat of the
scene—the close-ups and the dialogue—then save the long shots and the

drive-bys till last. I figured if I didn't get them I could pick them up on 2nd Unit.

L S : *Did you have a* THX-*type 2nd Unit? (Note: 2nd Unit, in ordinary motion picture parlance, is defined as literally another crew and director shooting at the same time as the main unit. 2nd Unit, as the term is used here, was an innovation in the production of* THX, *and it means a smaller crew, more flexible because of size, less burdened by heavy equipment, shooting after the main part of the production, usually those scenes which don't require actors and sound.)*

G L : Eventually, yes, we did — for one day, for two reasons: first, it was stuff like long-shots or cars that we didn't get; second, the original screenplay for the film was 140 pages, which is too long, and the original film, because of that and with all the cars and the music in it, came out to 160 minutes. We knew it couldn't be that long because the contract said 110 minutes. So we had to figure out a way of cutting out 50 minutes of film.

The first cut was really amazing; it was one of those rare instances where the first cut works and is great. The only other time I've seen that happen was with *Finian's Rainbow.* That's it — what are you going to do? Just trim it, clean it up, send it away. If you wanted to change it you couldn't; it works the way it's going to work and that's it.

Graffiti worked the way it was going to work from the start. It was paced very nicely and it had a good flow to it. After that all of our editorial efforts were in cutting almost an hour out of it but keeping the same pace that was in it originally and keeping the stories in balance.

So, getting back to 2nd Unit, I cut two scenes from the beginning which were essential to the exposition. I took those two scenes — about 5 minutes — and condensed them into a 1-minute scene. We re-shot that, and that was part of the 2nd Unit.

L S : *Technically, then, you directed 2nd Unit?*

G L : Yes, it was like *THX* where I counted the last two weeks for the cars as 2nd Unit. Just pick-ups, with no actors or anything like that.

L S : *How did you work with the actors?*

G L : I'd sit them down before we started and discuss their characters and everyone would read through his part.

L S : *Did they read against each other, or individually with you?*

G L : I did them in twos — the boy and the girl from each group came in and read together. And, in certain cases, the hoods read together. And, in certain cases, the hoods read together. Whoever had the meatier parts would come in and read together. But there were small groups — only two people at a time. Actually, I did have one day when everybody came, but with 10 or 12 actors in one room, sitting around and drinking coffee, you don't get much in the way of a real situation — especially with kids. So, we didn't do a really out and out playing-the-part rehearsal because I frankly didn't think they needed it.

L S : *The business of an actor working right has to do with picking the right actor for the part, of course. The people here were basically unknown. How did you sense that they would work? How did you go about finding the right actors?*

G L : It's tricky; it's something that either you can or can't do. We spent 4 months, 6 days a week, 12 to 14 hours a day interviewing people, and I personally interviewed everybody for 5 to 10 minutes. We literally saw thousands and thousands of kids between the ages of 12 and 25 in the Los Angeles and San Francisco area.

I'd see them and put down a check mark next to the names of those I was interested in. Then we ran those people back to read a scene. Then we went back and took the top 5 or 6 from each of those groups and shot video tests of them. Then we rotated them around, trying them in the different characters — this Steve with that Laurie — in videotape scenes. For the 10 leads in the film there would be 5 or 6 for each part — so that's 50 or 60 kids to worry about. I picked 2 or 3 in each category that I really thought were good, really perfect. Then Haskell Wexler and I went down and shot 16mm screen tests. Then we looked at those on the screen and made our decisions. Each time they were actually doing scenes from the movie.

L S : *Why did you shoot a film test after you had already done a video test? Didn't you consider tape good enough?*

G L : Well, there's something that happens on film, a quality difference — the color, seeing it on a screen, the way it's supposed to be as opposed to seeing it on a little television set. For the screen test we even had them dressed, had their hair done. They were as close to the part as we could get them.

There's just something that you can get on film that you can't get on tape. Tape gives you a record, gives you a chance to reflect. Just seeing a scene done in front of you, after 3 times your mind starts to go crazy. So tape gives you a chance to sit for a couple of days and study it, ponder it, decide on it. But a screen test shows you what you're actually getting, what you're going to get in the end. It really made a difference in a couple of the parts—and our decisions.

L S : *Did you want unknowns, or was it a money problem?*
G L : It really didn't make that much difference, and I didn't really care. When you're dealing with kids that age you're most likely to get unknowns because there aren't that many knowns. Besides, I wasn't really interested in those few knowns who were available.

L S : *And what about the training of the actors? Were they trained or where they fresh off the street?*
G L : Some of them were. Mackenzie Philips who played Carol and Paul Le Mat who played John had never acted before. Rick Dreyfuss who played Curt was primarily a stage actor who had done a little television, but this was his first feature film. Ronny Howard (Steve) spent 15 years as a television actor; Cindy Williams (Laurie) was essentially a feature film actress. There was a wide variety of backgrounds so one of the real problems in directing was trying to make sure that everyone stayed even.

L S : *That's what I was about to ask you—what about the differences in perfor-mance; how much work did you have to do with those who were inexperienced?*
G L : Well, the thing was trying to keep everybody's style consistent. And part of that had to do with the characters—making sure the acting style fit the character. It was cast that way, and the thing I worried about was mak-ing sure that the acting styles were consistent.

L S : *As an aside, did you ever consider shooting this film in Super-16?*
G L : We thought about it, but rejected it because we needed the speed of the film. We would have had to shoot with EF, and we felt the quality wouldn't be good enough to make it work.

L S : *What about the future?*
G L : Yes, I'd shoot in Super-16, but it would have to be the right kind of movie.

I like Super-16, and I think it's the way people are going to make movies, but you obviously can't do a big flashy musical in it. We wanted *Graffiti* to be in wide-screen, so that was one of the factors. The other was that we just didn't think the available 16 film would be fast enough or have enough latitude under extremely difficult conditions. If it had been a day picture, not in wide-screen, I might have done it.

L S : *What do you think about* Graffiti *now?*
G L : I've never seen *Graffiti* in the theatre because the previews we had were so ecstatic. I've heard that in a theatre it's even better.

L S : *So you've closed the book on it?*
G L : Yes, because I've been working on this new film. I've always wanted to go down and see it in the theatre. I did with *THX*, and it was really a great experience. But I just haven't had the time.

L S : *Would you like to talk about your new film?*
G L : Well, it's science fiction—Flash Gordon genre; *2001* meets James Bond, outer space and space ships flying in it.

L S : THX *was a kind of "process" film and* Graffiti *an autobiography—is the new film hooked to you personally?*
G L : I'm a real fan of Flash Gordon, and this is a much more plotted, structured film than the other two. *THX* is a *milieu* film, and *Graffiti* is a character film, but the new one is plot-action-adventure. Since I've never done that before, it's hard to say exactly what it is. Take the first two and combine them with another side of me that hasn't been seen yet and you get this new film. But where it comes from I don't know.

Finally, you know, *American Graffiti* wasn't that hard to write. I did it in 3 weeks, but I've been working on this one for 6 months—it hasn't been easy at all. Maybe that has to do with having to make it up.

I'm doing it myself, like last time, but then I'll look at it and if I'm not entirely satisfied, I'll hire somebody to do a re-write. I discovered something on *Graffiti,* having re-written it twice myself: your mind gets locked into something and it's hard to break loose, to get new ideas, a fresh point of view. It pays to have somebody come in with fresh enthusiasm and a new look.

George Lucas: The Stinky Kid Hits the Big Time

STEPHEN FARBER/1974

GEORGE LUCAS'S AMERICAN GRAFFITI is the surprise block-buster of the year. Made for $750,000, it has already earned over $21 million; Universal is predicting that it may even outgross *Airport*. When he first conceived the film, Lucas could not have guessed that it would be released at the height of the nostalgia boom.

Although actually set in 1962, *American Graffiti* is the quintessential fifties nostalgia movie—a comprehensive recreation of the world of sock hops, drag races, cherry cokes, and Eisenhower complacency. The remarkable thing, however, is that the film recaptures the past without sentimentalizing it. A comedy with unexpected resonance, *American Graffiti* is neither a glorification nor a mockery of the period; it summons up the deeply con-flicting feelings that we all have when contemplating our own youth and the primal experience of leaving home.

Dressed like one of the characters in the movie—Ivy League shirt and T-shirts, chinos, sneakers, and white sox—George Lucas could have stepped out of a time capsule; his beard is the only incongruous touch, a hint that he combines some of the irreverence of the sixties with the square earnest-ness of the fifties. Either way Lucas has little in common with most of Hollywood's chic superstar directors. In fact, he lives a long way from the studios—just north of San Francisco, in San Anselmo, in a spacious,

beautifully secluded house that may remind him of the farm he grew
up on.

American Graffiti is probably as close to an autobiographical film as a
studio-financed Hollywood product will ever be. Lucas, like his characters,
grew up in Modesto, California, and graduated from high school in 1962;
he spent most of his teenage years on the main drag, cruising. He says, "In
a way the film was made so my father won't think those were wasted years.
I can say I was doing research, though I didn't know it at the time." Most
of the incidents in the film "are things that I actually experienced in one
way or another. They've also been fantasized, as they should be in a movie.
They aren't really the way they were but the way they should have been."
For example, there is a hilarious scene in which the hero demolishes a
police car. "Some friends of mine did that one Hallowe'en night," Lucas
recalls, "but all that really happened was that the car drove off and went
clunk. It wasn't so spectacular. It just doesn't happen that way in real life."

The movie follows four main characters: Steve, the superstraight class
president dating the head cheerleader; John, the dragstrip champion who
models himself on James Dean and drives the meanest deuce coupe in the
valley; Terry, the dumb, creepy kid who only drives a Vespa but finally gets
a chance to play the stud; and Curt, the most sensitive and introspective
of the group, who chases a mysterious blonde in a white T-bird, and reluc-
tantly boards a plane out of town in the morning—the only one of the four
to break free. Lucas says he is, in a sense, a composite of all four characters:
"I started out when I was young as Terry the Toad, and I think everybody
sort of starts out as Terry the Toad. And I went from that to being John; I
had a hot car, and I raced around a lot. Finally I got into a very bad accident and almost got myself killed, and I spent a lot of time in the hospital.
While I was in the hospital, I became much more academic-minded. I had
been working as a mechanic, and I decided to give up cars and go to junior
college, try to get my grades back. So for the next two years, while I was at
junior college, I more or less was Curt. I was thinking about leaving town,
and I had a lot more perspective on things."

It was his car accident that eventually led Lucas into film-making. Unlike
many of today's young directors, he had no special passion for movies as a
child. "Modesto was a small town, and there were only a couple of theaters.
When I went to the movies, I really didn't pay much attention. I was usually
going to look for girls or goof off." However, he had always been interested

in graphic arts, and after his accident, he began working in photography—taking stills of sports cars. By chance he met the superb cinematographer (and director of *Medium Cool*) Haskell Wexler, who is a sports car enthusiast himself. Lucas happened to be working for the mechanic hired to build one of Wexler's race cars, and they became friendly.

The encouragement of Wexler and his own growing interest in photography brought Lucas to the University of Southern California's film school. "When I finally decided that I was going to be a film-maker," Lucas remembers, "all my friends thought I was crazy. I lost a lot of face because for hot rodders the idea of going into film was really a goofy idea. And that was in the early sixties. Nobody went into film at that time. At USC the girls from the dorms all gave a wide berth to film students because they were supposed to be weird."

For the first time he began seeing movies compulsively. "In a way movies replaced my love for cars. Since I was about 12 or 13 I had had this intense love relationship with cars and motorcycles; it was really all-consuming. After my accident, I knew I couldn't continue with that, and I was sort of floundering for something. And so when I finally discovered film, I really fell madly in love with it, ate it and slept it 24 hours a day. There was no going back after that."

Since then his obsessive devotion to movies and his fierce, sometimes dogged determination have kept him going even through the most difficult waiting periods. "When I got to film school, the other students said, 'You really can't make movies here. They don't give you enough film, they don't let you keep the camera for very long.' Well, I made eight films at USC, ranging from one minute to 25 minutes. It was difficult, and there were lots of barriers, but it wasn't impossible. I came up against the same discouragement when I left film school: 'You'll never get into the industry. Nobody ever does.' But, you know, I did it because I didn't believe what they said. You just have to be stubborn and bullheaded, and move forward no matter what you're up against."

Lucas managed to find work as a grip, then as cameraman and editor. A futuristic short he made at USC won the National Student Film award and a lot of attention; his first feature was an extension of that short. *THX-1138*, which made very inventive use of existing technology and architecture to create a chilling future world, came and went quickly. Although it found a cult following, it did very little for Lucas's reputation in the industry.

When he developed the script for *American Graffiti*—before the fifties nostalgia craze was in full swing—he submitted it to a lot of unsympathetic readers. He wrote the screenplay for United Artists, but they considered the project too risky and dropped it. He spent another year hawking the screenplay to every studio in town before Universal finally agreed to gamble on it.

Despite all the rejections during that period, Lucas stubbornly refused to abandon the project. "We were in dire financial straits, but I spent a year of my life trying to get that film off the ground. I was offered about three other pictures during that time. They all turned out to be duds. One of them was released at the same time as *Graffiti*—it's called *Lady Ice*. I turned that down at the bleakest point, when I was in debt to my parents, in debt to Francis Coppola, in debt to my agent; I was so far in debt I thought I'd never get out. Everybody in Hollywood had turned down *American Graffiti*. Universal had already turned it down once. And they offered me $75,000 to do *Lady Ice,* which is more money than I'd made in my entire life. And I said no. I said, 'By God, I've got a movie here, and I'm going to get it made somehow.' And I did."

The deciding factor was the commitment of Francis Ford Coppola as producer. At the time that Universal was debating whether or not to make the movie, *The Godfather* was released, and one executive suggested to Lucas and his producer Gary Kurtz that if they could involve Coppola on *American Graffiti,* that might swing the studio. His name finally clinched the deal.

Lucas can thank Coppola for many of his lucky breaks over the last several years. The two met approximately six years ago, when Lucas was on a six-month fellowship at Warner Brothers, and Coppola was shooting *Finian's Rainbow* on the lot. Lucas was assigned to observe Coppola work, and they immediately struck up a friendship. "We were like the only two people on the set who were under 50," Lucas recalls, "and we were also the only two people on the set who had beards." Lucas then worked as Coppola's assistant on *The Rain People,* and Coppola was able to get Lucas his deal to direct *THX-1138* for Warners.

Their working relationship is an unusual one. Lucas says, "Francis is involved on all my pictures, and I'm involved on all his pictures. We more or less work together as collaborators. What we do is look at each other's scripts, look at the casting, then at the dailies, at the rough cut and the fine cut, and make suggestions. We can bounce ideas off each other because we're totally different. I'm more graphics-film-making-editing oriented; and he's more writing and acting oriented. So we complement each other, and we trust each other. Half the time he says I'm full of shit, and half the time I say he's full of shit. It's not like a producer telling you that you *have* to do something. Francis will say, 'Cut that scene out, it doesn't work at all.' And I may say, 'No, you're crazy. That's my favorite scene. I love it.' And he'll say, 'Okay, what do I care? You're an idiot anyway.' Actually, he calls me a stinky kid. He says, 'You're a stinky kid, do what you want.' And I say the same thing to him. It works very well, because you really need somebody to test ideas on. And you get a piece of expert advice that you value."

Coppola and Lucas once hoped to set up an alternate film studio in San Francisco, where a group of maverick directors could work in a congenial, stimulating, noncompetitive atmosphere. They formed American Zoetrope in 1969. Encouraged by the success of *Easy Rider,* Warners agreed to back a whole series of films under Coppola's sponsorship. A few months later the "youth market" vanished as suddenly as it had appeared, and Warners pulled out of Zoetrope. Lucas recalls, "Francis was developing about seven screenplays—they were all interesting, adventurous scripts. But then Warner Brothers decided not to finance any more youth-oriented, adventurous, crazy movies. They went back to hard-core entertainment films. For them it was a good decision because they made a lot of money on that decision. But they sold us completely down the river."

Zoetrope still exists as a facility—and rents out its equipment to other film-makers—but not as a full-fledged studio. Nevertheless, Lucas believes that an alternate film community may still emerge in San Francisco. "Slowly but surely, a film community is being developed here. Michael Ritchie lives up here now, John Korty lives up here, I live up here, Francis lives up here. They are all close friends of mine, and we are continuing to make movies up here. We sort of support each other. My wife worked as an editor on *The Candidate,* and she's also worked for John Korty to get us through these little tough spots between movies. I hired Michael's wife on my picture. Just recently Phil Kaufman (*The Great Northfield Minnesota Raid*) moved up here, and a couple more of my friends are thinking seriously about moving here. So there is a community here, a very small one, and we all exchange ideas. It's not something you can create overnight.

You have to get the environment right for it, and then let it grow very slowly. Unfortunately, we have a lot of problems with the unions up here, but we're surviving in spite of it all. At certain times it's a drag to be so far from LA, but I definitely want to stay here."

Over just two movies Lucas's artistic development has been remarkable. *THX-1138* was a dazzling technical achievement; it revealed Lucas's control of all the resources of film — sound as well as image. Unfortunately, it also exhibited the most common failings of the science-fiction genre: the ideas (drawn from Orwell and Huxley) were rather stale, and the whole movie was cold and arid; the zombie characters could not really stir our sympathy. *American Graffiti* has the same technical flair, but Lucas's work with the actors reveals a new talent; this film has a depth of feeling missing from *THX-1138*. Lucas claims that he wanted to surprise his critics with his new movie: "After I finished *THX*, I was considered a cold, weird director, a science-fiction sort of guy who carried a calculator. And I'm not like that at all. So I thought, maybe I'll do something exactly the opposite. If they want warm human comedy, I'll give them one, just to show that I can do it. *THX* is very much the way that I am as a film-maker. *American Graffiti* is very much the way I am as a person — two different worlds really."

Nevertheless, Lucas is quick to call attention to the themes that the two films share. *THX* concerns one man's escape from the monolithic technological society. At the end the rebellious hero THX emerges from the underground prison, into the sun; it is an ambiguous conclusion, both liberating and a little frightening. *American Graffiti* also ends with one of the teenage boys breaking out of his cocoon, leaving home and escaping the enclosed, insulated world of the fifties. And he has the same mixed feelings that THX experienced on his escape — exhilaration at the new sense of possibilities, a pang of regret on leaving the safety of the familiar world. Lucas says, "I've always been interested in that theme of leaving an environment or facing change, and how kids do it. When I was 18 or 19, I didn't know what I was going to do with my life. Where was I going to go, now that I was more or less free? What was I going to become? You can do anything you want at that age. And the kids who don't believe that are wrong. Both *THX* and *American Graffiti* are saying the same thing, that you don't *have* to do anything; it still is a free country."

Beyond the obvious autobiographical impulses in *American Graffiti*, Lucas says the film reflects his interest in sociology and anthropology: "When I was in junior college, my primary major was in social sciences.

I'm very interested in America and why it is what it is. I was always fascinated by the cultural phenomenon of cruising, that whole teenage mating ritual. It's really more interesting than primitive Africa or ancient New Guinea—and much, much weirder."

The American obsession with the car is intensified in California. The kids in Modesto still cruise, and they still cruise in Petaluma, where much of *American Graffiti* was actually shot—Modesto having changed too much in just ten years. For that matter, Lucas points out, "They still cruise in Los Angeles, and it's bigger than it used to be. Van Nuys Boulevard is a big cruise street. We went down there one Wednesday night, which they call Club Night, and it was just bumper-to-bumper cars. There must have been 10,000 kids down there. It was insane. I really loved it. I sat on my car hood all night and watched. The cars are all different now. Vans are the big thing. Everybody's got a van, and you see all these weird, decorated cars. Cruising is still a main thread in American culture."

Lucas's interest in early rock music is another strong influence on the movie. Excerpts from the radio—41 pop songs and fragments of Wolfman Jack's monologue—accompany most of the action in the film. "I have a giant rock and roll record collection—78s and 45s," Lucas reports. "Mainly old rock, pre-Beatles, though I love the Beatles. I was always very interested in the relationship between teenagers and radio, and when I was at USC, I made a documentary about a disc jockey. The idea behind it was radio as fantasy. For teenagers the person closest to them is a fantasy character. That's the disc jockey. It's like younger kids who have make-believe friends. A lot of teenagers have a make-believe friend in a disc jockey, but he's much more real because he talks to them, he jokes around. Especially a really excellent disc jockey like Wolfman Jack. He's part of the family. You listen to him every day, you're very close to him, you share your most intimate moments with him."

Lucas remembers listening to Wolfman Jack when he was growing up in Modesto in the late fifties and early sixties. "When we were cruising, we could get Wolfman Jack from Tijuana. He was a really mystical character, I'll tell you. He was wild, he had these crazy phone calls, and he drifted out of nowhere. And it was an outlaw station. He was an outlaw, which of course made him extremely attractive to kids."

The 41 songs in *American Graffiti* were actually written into the script. When it came to editing the film, Lucas found that some songs he wanted to use were either unavailable or too expensive, so he had to make substitutions and shift some songs around. Even so, he spent $80,000 purchasing music rights, probably a record sum. "Walter Murch did the sound montages, and the amazing thing we found was that we could take almost any song and put it on almost any scene and it would work. You'd put a song down on one scene, and you'd find all kinds of parallels. And you could take another song and put it down there, and it would still seem as if the song had been written for that scene. All good rock and roll is classic teenage stuff, and all the scenes were such classic teenage scenes that they just sort of meshed, no matter how you threw them together. Sometimes even the words were identical. The most incredible example—and it was completely accidental—is in the scene where Steve and Laurie are dancing to 'Smoke Gets in Your Eyes' at the sock hop, and at the exact moment where the song is saying, 'Tears I cannot hide,' she backs off, and he sees that she's crying.

"In a way you could trace the film through the Beach Boys, because the Beach Boys were the only rock group who actually chronicled an era. We discovered that you could almost make a whole Beach Boys album out of just *American Graffiti* songs. The blonde in the T-bird is from 'Fun, Fun, Fun.' 'I Get Around' is about cruising. You listen to the words of that and think of the movie. It wasn't intentional, but they were chronicling that period so true that when we came back and redid my childhood the way I remembered it, their songs blend right into the movie. 'Little Deuce Coupe' could be about John and his deuce coupe. 'All Summer Long'—which is sort of the theme song of the film—talks about T-shirts and spilling Coke on your blouse. '409' is about dragging. 'California Girls.' I always loved the Beach Boys because when we'd cruise, we'd listen to their songs, and it was as if the song was about *us* and what we were doing. It wasn't just another song about being in love. They got more specific."

Although *American Graffiti* is a highly personal film, it was not a one-man show, and Lucas is quick to point out the important contributions of his collaborators. His co-writers, Willard Huyck (whom he met at USC) and Huyck's wife Gloria Katz (a graduate of the rival film school at UCLA), worked with Lucas on the original treatment and on the final draft screenplay. "I'm really quite lazy and I hate to write," Lucas confesses. "Bill and Gloria added a lot of very witty dialogue and wrote all the scenes that I couldn't find my way to write. In my script, the characters of Steve and Laurie didn't work at all, and I couldn't make them work. The Huycks saved that. And they brought a lot of character to the hoods. My screenplay was much more realistic, and they added a lot more humor and fantasy to it, and improved it a great deal." (The Huycks have just sold their own original screenplay *Lucky Lady* to 20th Century-Fox.)

An equally important collaborator was Haskell Wexler. The entire movie was to be shot at night, and that created unusual difficulties. Lucas explains, "We'd start at 9:00 at night and end at 5:00 in the morning. In a regular movie, if you don't get what you're supposed to shoot one day, you can just throw up a few arc lights and shoot for another hour. On *Graffiti,* when the sun came up, that was the end of the ballgame. We couldn't get one more shot. It was very hard on the crew. Nobody gets any sleep, so everybody's cranky. And it was very cold—like 40 degrees. We had to shoot it in 28 days, and sometimes we'd do as many as 30 setups in one night. So we had a horrendous problem." Lucas had originally asked Wexler to shoot the film, but Wexler did not want to work in widescreen. However, the two cameramen Lucas hired could not find the visual style he wanted, and Wexler finally agreed to come to his aid. Lucas pays tribute to Wexler: "He's really, in my estimation, the best cameraman in this country. Essentially he was working in a medium he hated—widescreen. He hated Techniscope because it's very grainy and doesn't look very good. I wanted the film to look sort of like a Sam Katzman beach-party movie, all yellow and red and orange. And Haskell figured out how to do it. He devised what he calls jukebox lighting. He has his own company in Los Angeles that shoots commercials, and he was working at the time. So he'd fly up here to San Francisco every night, shoot the picture all night, sleep on the plane down to Los Angeles, shoot all day on commercials, then fly back up here. He did that for almost five weeks. It was just an incredible gesture, and he did a fantastic job. The movie looked exactly the way I wanted it to look—very much like a carnival."

Almost everyone grants the technical triumphs of *American Graffiti*—the achievements in cinematography, editing, and acting. But some critics protest what they think the film is saying. They interpret the movie as a simple celebration of the fifties, and they fear that because it is so popular, it may feed the indifference and complacency of a young audience eager to forget today's social problems. How does Lucas answer that charge? "Well, the main thing I would say is that there is going to be complacency whether I encourage it or not. That's because kids in the last ten years have been beating their heads against the wall, and their brains and their blood are all over the pavement."

Lucas also points out that the film is about moving forward, not backward: "The film is about change. It's about the change in rock and roll, it's about the change in a young person's life at 18 when he leaves home and goes off to college; and it's also about the cultural change that took place when the fifties turned into the sixties—when we went from a country of apathy and non-involvement to a country of radical involvement. The film is saying that you have to go forward. You have to be Curt, you have to go into the sixties. The fifties can't live."

At the same time, Lucas admits that he is hoping to revive some of the values of the fifties: "Everybody looks at the fifties as complacent, but I look at the fifties as optimistic. Well, the film isn't really about the fifties anyway. It's about 1962. The Kennedy era is really when I grew up, and that was an era of optimism, not complacency. It was the era of Martin Luther King.

"I realized after *THX* that people don't care about how the country's being ruined. All that movie did was to make people more pessimistic, more depressed, and less willing to get involved in trying to make the world better. So I decided that this time I would make a more optimistic film that makes people feel positive about their fellow human beings. It's too easy to make films about Watergate. And it's hard to be optimistic when everything tells you to be pessimistic and cynical. I'm a very bad cynic. But we've got to regenerate optimism. Maybe kids will walk out of the film and for a second they'll feel, 'We could really make something out of this country, or we could really make something out of our lives.' It's all that hokey stuff about being a good neighbor, and the American spirit and all that crap. There *is* something in it."

Lucas's early success at accomplishing the goals he set for himself may explain his belief in the American ideals of optimism and initiative. "Now everybody says, 'The country's rotten. We've fought for change, but it doesn't work. It's hopeless.' Well, life isn't that way. It wasn't that way for THX, it wasn't that way for Curt Henderson, and it isn't that way for me. When they said I could never get into the film business, I said, 'Well, okay, but I'll try anyway.' Anybody who wants to do anything can do it. It's an old hokey American point of view, but I've sort of discovered that it's true."

Lucas hopes to do more experimental work in the future, but he is amused that many people think of him as an arty director. "Francis is really the arty director," he comments wryly. "He's the one who likes psychological motivations, Brecht and Albee and Tennessee Williams. I'm more drawn to Flash Gordon. I like action adventure, chases, things blowing up, and I have strong feelings about science fiction and comic books and that sort of world." It is the process of making films that thrills him most: "Some of my friends are more concerned about art and being considered a Fellini or an Orson Welles, but I've never really had that problem. I just like making movies. I was at a film conference with George Cukor, and he detested the fact that everyone called us film-makers. He said, 'I'm not a film-maker. A film-maker is like a toy-maker, and I'm a director.' Well, I'm a film-maker. I'm very much akin to a toy-maker. If I wasn't a film-maker, I'd probably *be* a toy-maker. I like to make things move, and I like to make them myself. Just give me the tools and I'll make the toys. I can sit forever doodling on my movie. I don't think that much about whether it's going to be a great movie or a terrible movie, or whether it's going to be a piece of art or a piece of shit. I never thought of *Graffiti* as a really great movie. I thought of it as a goofy, fun movie."

Despite his disclaimers, Lucas has the most important characteristic of an artist: integrity. He makes movies on his own terms, and fights any kind of interference. On both *THX* and *American Graffiti,* a few minutes were cut by the studio, and Lucas felt the cuts—relatively minor though they were—as a painful violation of his vision. "There was no reason for the cutting," he declares. "It was just arbitrary. You do a film like *American Graffiti* or *THX*—it takes two years of your life, you get paid hardly anything at all, and you sweat blood. You write it, you slave over it, you stay up 28 nights getting cold and sick. Then you put it together, and you've *lived* with it. It's exactly like raising a kid. You raise a kid for two or three years, you struggle with it, then somebody comes along and says, 'Well, it's a very nice kid, but I think we ought to cut off one of its fingers.' So they take their little axe and chop off one of the fingers. They say, 'Don't worry. Nobody will notice. She'll live, everything will be all right.' But I mean, it *hurts* a great deal."

Even though Lucas has now had a major success, he anticipates more of the same battles with studios, adding, "Every time you have a successful film, you do get a few more things in your contract. The film I'm writing now, *The Star Wars,* has been turned down by a couple of studios already, but now we're finally getting a deal because they say, 'Oh, he's had a hit movie. We don't really know about the idea, but he's a hot director, so let's do it.' They don't do it on the basis of the material; they do it on the kind of deal they can make, because most of the people at the studios are former agents, and all they know are deals. They're like used-car dealers."

His next two projects are more obviously "commercial" projects than his first two films. He describes *The Star Wars* as "a space opera in the tradition of Flash Gordon and Buck Rogers. It's James Bond and *2001* combined— super fantasy, capes and swords and laser guns and spaceships shooting each other, and all that sort of stuff. But it's not camp. It's meant to be an exciting action adventure film."

After *Star Wars* he wants to try a slapstick comedy—"Woody Allen, Laurel and Hardy, Abbott and Costello, Harold Lloyd, Buster Keaton all rolled into one. It's been a long time since anybody made a really goofy comedy that had people rolling in the aisles. It's very hard to do, which is why nobody does it, but it's a challenge; it's like climbing that mountain."

While hoping that a couple of strong commercial successes will give him more options in the future, Lucas does not feel he is compromising in making more straightforward entertainment movies. He is honestly drawn to the pop-kitsch world of space comics and slapstick comedy. His intensity and his bold visual flair are sure to give an emotional charge to any project he tackles. George Lucas's movies begin with images: "I always see images flash into my head, and I just have to make those scenes. I have an overwhelming drive to get that great shot of the two spaceships, one firing at the other as they drive through the space fortress. By God I want to see it. That image is in my head, and I won't rest until I see it on the screen."

George Lucas Goes Far Out

STEPHEN ZITO/1977

GEORGE LUCAS IS ANGRY.

The unit publicist on *Star Wars* advises two commercial artists to leave because Lucas refuses to see them that day. One complains that they have an appointment. It doesn't matter—Lucas is out of sorts. When Lucas gets mad, he doesn't yell and shout. He Sulks, Pouts, Refuses to Talk to people. Sometimes he takes to his bed.

The screening of the dailies doesn't improve his humor. Several of the special effects shots need to be redone, putting the production of *Star Wars* another day behind schedule.

It's a hell of a day to do an interview. Lucas wants to return to his home in San Anselmo, just outside San Francisco. He for sure doesn't want to break bread with a writer from the East. We drive to a local hamburger place in Van Nuys, weighted down by silence. The choice of restaurant is typical of Lucas—no frills, no pretensions, just plain old American junk food. He doesn't grandstand in the Polo Lounge. Lucas jealously guards his privacy—he was once recognized in a restaurant and has never returned.

George Lucas is a contradictory man. Short and slight, he has the presence of a bigger man. Young by Hollywood standards at thirty-two, he is the kind of guy you just might entrust with $8 million of your stockholders' money to make a science fiction movie. In a very public business, he is a very private person. He lives as far from Hollywood as he can and com-

From *American Film*, April 1977, pp. 8–13. Reprinted by permission of the American Film Institute and the author.

mutes there as if it were some kind of leper colony. He is, quite simply, a man who wants to have everything his way.

Lucas claims to be shy of the press but he is a good talker. Yet, he tells you nothing by accident, doesn't let you into his life.

He is one of the most successful of a new breed of Hollywood filmmakers—the bright young man out of film school who jumps into the industry without the seasoning once required of directors. Others of his generation include Francis Ford Coppola, John Milius, and Steven Spielberg.

Movies are clearly far more than a means of livelihood; they are his life. He is, first and foremost, a *filmmaker* who got into the Hollywood studio system by becoming Francis Ford Coppola's assistant on *The Rain People*. Coppola taught him a lot about writing and acting, produced Lucas's first film, *THX 1138*, and lent his name so that Lucas could obtain financing for *American Graffiti*. *THX 1138*, the expansion of a college-made film, was a modest critical success, a box-office failure, and something of a cult favorite. *American Graffiti*, well-received by the critics, became one of the largest moneymakers in the history of film.

What happens when you direct one of the all-time box-office smashes? Well, everything. You can write your own deal, do what you want, spend what you please, get your own way. Even up old scores. What a director does with this freedom tells a lot about the man. Some sink into self-indulgence, others into conspicuous consumption of movie budgets. George Lucas has used the success of *American Graffiti* to make an $8 million animated comic strip called *Star Wars*.

One cynic, in advance of its completion, has called it *American Graffiti* in outer space. The story, as reconstructed from the Lucas script and the tacky sci-fi novel which bears his name, concerns the adventures of Luke Skywalker, a bored young man who lives with his aunt and uncle on a remote farm on the desert planet of Tatooine, somewhere in the universe. Luke's narrow, confined life is shattered by a message from a kidnapped rebel princess that sets him off on a series of adventures. He soon falls in with a bizarre collection of companions—an old wizard, two robots, a daredevil space freighter pilot, and a giant *Wookie*.

If this sounds like the stuff of Marvel comics "sword and sorcery" plots, well, it is just that. (Marvel will even release the story in six installments this spring.) There is a lot here to charm the preadolescent mind—rebellion, interplanetary wars, doomsday machines, space pirates, black knights, magic and sorcery, death stars, mystical happenings, sophisticated torture devices, medieval weaponry, and a savage air battle above the gray surface of a killer satellite.

George Lucas does nothing to disguise the fact that *Star Wars* is for the schoolboy in us all. "I decided I wanted to make a children's movie, to go the Disney route," Lucas explains in his distinctively nervous manner. "Fox hates for me to say this, but *Star Wars* has always been intended as a young people's movie. While I set the audience for *Graffiti* at sixteen to eighteen, I set this one at fourteen and maybe even younger than that."

George Lucas, who wrote the screenplay for and directed this story, found his inspiration among the debris of American popular culture. He *believes*, truly believes, in his boy's own adventure plot, and approaches the pulpish narrative with a sense of wonder and with naive enthusiasm. His original impetus came from the work of Alex Raymond.

"I loved the *Flash Gordon* comic books," Lucas confesses between bites of his hamburger. "I loved the Universal serials with Buster Crabbe. After *THX 1138* I wanted to do Flash Gordon and tried to buy the rights to it from King Features, but they wanted a lot of money for it, more than I could afford then. They didn't really want to part with the rights—they wanted Fellini to do Flash Gordon.

"I realized that *I* could make up a character as easily as Alex Raymond, who took his character from Edgar Rice Burroughs. It's your basic superhero in outer space. I realized that what I really wanted to do was a contemporary action fantasy."

George Lucas, an avid reader and collector of science fiction literature and art (including a number of Alex Raymond originals) has been greatly influenced by other adventure and fantasy science fiction writers as well. "As a kid, I read a *lot* of science fiction," Lucas recalls. "But instead of reading technical, hard-science writers like Isaac Asimov, I was interested in Harry Harrison and a fantastic, surreal approach to the genre. I grew up on it. *Star Wars* is a sort of compilation of this stuff, but it's never been put in one story before, never put down on film. There is a lot taken from Westerns, mythology, and samurai movies. It's all the things that are great put together. It's not like one kind of ice cream but rather a very big sundae."

Such recent science fiction movies as *Silent Running, Marooned,* or even *2001: A Space Odyssey,* are heavily science oriented, constructed in accordance with what we know or can formulate about current hardware and technology. The characters are boxed in by probability, logic, and common sense. Not so *Star Wars*. The story is set in an alien galaxy with neither temporal nor spatial proximity to our solar system. It takes place in a land of fantasy. This is not *our* future realized: Lucas severs all ties with our solar system.

Lucas also cuts himself off from science. "It's very surreal and bizarre and has nothing to do with science," he says of what he mockingly refers to as the film's subtext. "I wanted it to be an adventure in space, like *John Carter of Mars*. That was before *science* fiction took over, and everything got very serious and science oriented.

"*Star Wars* has more to do with disclaiming science than anything else. There are very elaborate, Rube Goldberg explanations for things. It's a totally different galaxy with a totally different way of thinking. It's not based on science, which bogs you down. I don't want the movie to be about anything that would happen or be real. I wanted to tell a fantasy story."

When Lucas and I talked about *Star Wars,* there was no way to judge how successful Lucas had been in making this newmovie—which comes out sounding like *American Graffiti* meets *THX*. Not only does Lucas have control over the final cut of the movie, he controls merchandising and publicity as well. Only a handful of the people working on the film, and a couple of key studio executives, had seen the almost-finished film. Part of this secrecy is designed to protect the innovative special effects work, but it is also the result of George Lucas's intense need to control and to personally oversee every aspect of his movie. He is the total filmmaker, a self-styled auteur obsessed with hot rods, disaffected adolescents, and the glitter of low culture.

If Lucas's labors over the past four years result in a marvelous children's adventure to stand beside movies like *Forbidden Planet* and *This Island Earth*, it will not have been easy. As we finished our lunch, Lucas tells me that he is suffering from bouts of exhaustion, depression, and disgust. "I didn't realize it was going to take so long or be so big or take so much of my life," he says with the manner of someone on whom fate has played a dirty trick.

All of the four years of *Star Wars* have been difficult for Lucas. This has been his first experience of working on a big-budget picture with a large cast and crew, in which the director must be more than a filmmaker. He must be a diplomat, field marshal, and nursemaid as well. Perhaps the biggest problem for Lucas has been that, despite the high budget, there has never been quite enough money. "Although it costs a lot of money," Lucas says of *Star Wars*, "it's still a low-budgeted picture. So it's on the same intensity level as a Roger Corman movie only a hundred times bigger. We *still* don't have the luxury of a big movie—time, doing things right. Everything is compromise, cutting corners, not doing this or that. You suffer. You say, 'I can't do this,' or 'That looks terrible, but we'll go with it,' which you are normally doing on a $700,000 picture where you're saying, 'Get it done!' We're doing that, only it's taking four years. The hard part is, once we started production—which will be two years in May—it's been almost relentless, seven days a week, sixteen hours a day. That's all right for a couple of months, but when it goes on for over a year, it really gets to be a drag."

Lucas candidly admits that his problems on *Star Wars* were the result of his chronic inability and unwillingness to delegate authority and responsibility. He wants to do it all himself—write, direct, produce, supervise, edit, shoot. He has a hard time letting go. "I come up from the filmmakers' school of doing movies, which means I do everything myself," Lucas explains. "If you are a writer-director, you *must* get involved with everything. It's very hard for me to get into another system where everybody does things for me, and I say, 'Fine.' If I ever continue to do these kinds of movies, I've got to learn to do that. I have a lot of friends who can, and I admire them. Francis [Coppola] is going through that now, and he's finally learning, finally getting to the point where he realizes *he* can't do it all. He's getting into the traditional system: 'Call me when it's ready, and it better be right, and if it's not, do it again and spend whatever it costs to get it right.' But you have to be willing to make *very* expensive movies that way. You can't make cheap movies.

"If I left anything for a day, it would fall apart, and it's purely because I set it up that way and there is nothing I can do about it. It wasn't set up so I could walk away from it. Whenever there is a leak in the dam, I have to stick *my* finger in it. I should learn to say, 'Somebody else go plug that up.'"

The principal photography on *Star Wars* was completed last summer on location in Tunisia and on forty-five sets spread over eleven sound stages in England. The intervening months have been spent in editing the 340,000 feet of live-action footage and marrying it with the special effects shots being created for Lucas at the two-story warehouse in Van Nuys,

which serves as the headquarters for Industrial Light and Magic, an organization of technicians specifically formed to supply *Star Wars* with special
effects. The effects work for *Star Wars* has been expensive and painstakingly
difficult. Most of the work was done by young and relatively inexperienced
effects people rather than by such acknowledged masters of the art as Lin-
wood Dunn and Douglas Trumbull. The reason for this choice of staff was
characteristically pragmatic on Lucas's part. With his young staff, he has
more control over the special effects than if he had employed an established
special effects director with a style, approach, and hardware all his own.

"If you hire Trumbull to do your special effects," Lucas explains, "*he*
does your special effects. I was very nervous about that. I wanted to be able
to say, 'It must look like this, not that.' I don't want to be handed an effect
at the end of five months and be told, 'Here's your special effect, sir.' I
want to be able to have more say about what's going on. It's really become
binary—either you do it yourself, or you don't get a say.

"Technically, you always compare things against *2001*. If you took one
of our shots and ran it on the light box and set it next to one of Kubrick's
shots, you would say, 'Well, his are better.' But there is no way, given the
time and money we've had, that Kubrick could do any better. He was striving for perfection and had a shot ratio thirty times what we have. When
you spend that kind of time and money you can get things perfect. We
went into this trying to make a cheap, children's movie for $8 million. We
didn't go in and say that we were going to make the perfect science fiction
film, but we are gonna make the most spectacular thing you've ever seen!"

The "we" to which George Lucas occasionally refers includes Gary Kurtz,
the producer of *Star Wars* and, like others on the movie, an old and trusted
friend of Lucas's. The truth is that Lucas doesn't have many new friends—
he is a hard man to know. One of Kurtz's jobs is to function as an unofficial
consigliere—limiting access to Don Lucas, granting favors and interviews,
fixing messes, pouring oil on the troubled waters. He is friend, confidant,
interpreter, hatchet man. When Lucas talks, Kurtz listens. Only after Lucas
returns to San Anselmo do Kurtz and I have the opportunity to talk. He
explains that he and Lucas work together with a tense kind of harmony.

"It's a casual arrangement. If you want to categorize the function of the
working producer, it is to provide all the tools so the director can do everything he wants, or, at least, everything within the limits you are trying to
work. I also function as a sounding board to discuss everything that comes

up. *Star Wars* is more formally arranged than *Graffiti* was. We made *Graffiti* with eighteen people, but by the time *Star Wars* is finished we will have employed nine hundred people. The larger the picture, the less time you have to deal with detail. On a small picture, you can do everything yourself."

The burden of coping with production problems in England and Tunisia fell largely to Kurtz. He was responsible in large part for the selection of the British crew: Gil Taylor, the cinematographer who shot *Dr. Strangelove, A Hard Day's Night,* and *Frenzy*; John Barry, the production designer from *A Clockwork Orange*; and John Spears who was in charge of production effects and explosives. It was not always the happiest of crews. Lucas feuded with Taylor, and even fired an editor with whom he didn't get along.

Lucas never really adjusted to making the movie in England. The British crews insisted on knocking off work promptly at 5:30, and he felt himself to be a stranger in a strange land. "We had several problems," Gary Kurtz recalls. "George wasn't happy there—he doesn't like to be away from home. There are a lot of little things that are bothersome—light switches go up instead of down. Everything is different enough to throw you off balance." Kurtz was often put in the position of mediating between the introspective Lucas and certain key members of the foreign crew. "All film crews are a matter of chemistry," Kurtz says. "George is not a particularly social person. He doesn't go out of his way to socialize. It takes him a while to know somebody, to get intimate enough to share his problems with them. It's easier for him to work with people he knows."

George Lucas is, in many ways, most comfortable with what is known and familiar. He is marvelously adept at the manipulation of the styles and artifacts of the cultural past. Lucas and Kurtz function in many ways like a couple of pack rats. *Star Wars* is literally constructed from bits and pieces of the usable past. During postproduction, model makers at Industrial Light and Magic were busy cannibalizing model kits in order to make spaceships. They used fragments of Kenworth Tractors, Kandy-Vans, Panzer Kampf-wagens, and even Ford Galaxy 500 XLs to make their spaceships.

This wholesale recycling of the artifacts of the past is nowhere more apparent than in the final gigantic space battle that will take up the last twenty minutes of the movie. The scene is composed of a number of scenes right out of vintage World War II movies. Literally.

"Before the storyboards were done," Kurtz explains, "we recorded on videotape any war movie involving aircraft that came up on television, so we had this massive library of parts of old war movies — *The Dam Busters, Tora! Tora! Tora!, The Battle of Britain, Jet Pilot, The Bridges at Toko-Ri, 633 Squadron* and about forty-five other movies. We went through them all and picked out scenes to transfer to film to use as guidelines in the battle.

"We cut them all together into a battle sequence to get an idea of the movement. It was a very bizarre-looking film, all black-and-white, a dirty 16mm dupe. There would be a shot of the pilot saying something, then you cut back to a long shot of the plane, explosions, crashes. It gave a reasonably accurate idea of what the battle sequence would look like, the feeling of it.

Lucas and Kurtz showed the battle sequences to the special effects people and to the artists who transferred the ersatz movie to storyboards. "It's very easy to take your hand and fly," Kurtz says, making an imaginary loop the loop, "but it's very hard to convert that movement to what John Dykstra and the other special effects people had to do with the models.

The system that generated the special effects was created by John Dykstra, who received his training under Douglas Trumbull on *The Andromeda Strain* and *Silent Running*. Dykstra, who is the head of Industrial Light and Magic, oversaw the construction of a special computer-run system for making the more than 350 special effects in the film. The key to Dykstra's operation stands in a back room of the warehouse: a giant camera mounted on tracks and powered by high-torque motors under the command of a computer. Each shot is programmed in a computer and played back a number of times to accommodate the various model elements in the shots. The complex special effects system allows Dykstra to create special effects shots with models which approximate the effect of live-action shots.

Dykstra and Lucas didn't always see eye to eye. One of their biggest problems was communication. In special effects, there is always a gap between intention and execution, between conception and realization. Lucas sometimes became angry when the matted shots did not have the authenticity and pace he wanted for the movies. "Directors and special effects directors always disagree incredibly," Dykstra says, "because he conceptualizes one thing but *I* know what is capable of being produced. The major problem we encountered on this show was being able to apply what George started out with conceptually. From the day we met, we talked about World War II dogfight footage which involved lots of action, continuous motion, moving camera, streak, loops and rolls, and all of the things aerial photography allows you to do in live action. This has been difficult to do in special effects with multiple ships, planet backgrounds, and stars, because of the problems of angular displacement, matching shots, and depth of field.

"It's hard to explain that a concept won't work because of some technological thing, and this becomes a bone of contention. When a director shoots an exterior, he can see the lighting and the setup and the action and hear the dialogue, but when he comes in here, all there is is a camera running down a track about three inches a second photographing a model. So you have to be able to determine a spatial relationship without having to see the relationship in front of you or being able to compress in your mind's eye five minutes of motion into five seconds. It's more akin to animation than anything else.

"George has to trust me to be able to interpret the drawings and the black-and-white war footage, and that's really hard to do. I don't know if I could do that with somebody. That's one of the biggest problems there is."

Despite their differences of opinion, Dykstra respects Lucas for his single-mindedness, his obsession with getting things right, his love for every frame of *Star Wars*.

"The neat thing about George is that he has a sensibility. He is really involved in his movie, he is really attached. He's hardheaded about stuff, but, if he's wrong, he'll change his mind rather than say, 'I'm the director, I've made a decision and that's it.' He's got taste. He's got that gift for popular narrative. People like what he does: It's active; it's fast; there's humor in it. *Star Wars* is gonna be exciting all the way. The aerial battle that takes up the last reel of the film is going to be as exciting as the car chase in *The French Connection*."

During our lunch I had asked Lucas what he wanted from the movie.

"Rather than do some angry, socially relevant film," he answered, "I realized there was another relevance that is even more important—dreams and fantasies, getting children to believe there is more to life than garbage and killing and all that real stuff like stealing hubcaps—that you could still sit and dream about exotic lands and strange creatures. Once I got into *Star Wars,* it struck me that we had lost all that—a whole generation was growing up without fairy tales. You just don't get them any more, and that's the best stuff in the world—adventures in far-off lands. It's *fun*.

"I wanted to do a modern fairy tale, a myth. One of the criteria of the mythical fairy-tale situation is an exotic, faraway land, but we've lost all the fairy-tale lands on this planet. Every one has disappeared. We no longer have the Mysterious East or treasure islands or going on strange adventures.

"But there is a bigger, mysterious world in space that is more interesting than anything around here. We've just begun to take the first step and can say, 'Look! It goes on for a zillion miles out there.' You can go anywhere and land on any planet."

There can be little doubt that George Lucas has gone out on a limb. He has used the success of *American Graffiti* to put on film the dreams and fantasies of his childhood. He has spent $8 million in a genre where movies are usually done as cheaply as possible, resulting in shoddiness. The only question left about *Star Wars* is an old one, frequently asked since the Wright Brothers took their contraption to Kitty Hawk: "But will it fly?"

The Morning of the Magician: George Lucas and *Star Wars*

CLAIRE CLOUZOT/1977

HAS ANYONE HEARD STORIES about George Lucas? Has anyone read interviews with him in the French press? Actually, no one in France seems interested in George Lucas.

The year that he came to Cannes for *American Graffiti,* one French critic pursued him for an interview, but never managed to catch up with him. When Lucas says he has a phobia of press conferences, his sincerity is believable.

The best way to meet him is to go where he puts his feet up and plays with his world: his home in America. If well recommended, you stand a chance to meet him there.

That was my chance just before the release of *Star Wars* in California. One of the writers for Coppola's film *Apocalypse Now* gave me the key to his abode. This lost place some miles from San Francisco, this little Californian town named San Anselmo. There Lucas has established his studio, his residence, his ranch, his home. A sort of old colonial house which hides its treasures of American technology from the visitor's eye. "You'll recognize it," he told me on the telephone, "it's the only house that looks older than me." Indeed, it's very handsome, decorated everywhere with oak and antique furniture from a time long before *Star Wars.* Lucas lounges in a high-backed wicker armchair, his tennis sneak-

From *Ecran,* 15 September 1977, pp. 33–41. Translated from the French by Alisa Belanger.

ers resting on the table, his voice hardly audible. Miniature model cars, missiles, and tanks sit neatly organized on his otherwise empty desk—a man's toys.

This is the man who made the film that's breaking all of the records. Hardly one month after its release in 360 theaters, the film has already grossed over 20.5 million dollars. Its remarkable popularity among both children and adults is drawing ticket lines that circle entire city-blocks, as *Star Wars* toys inundate American households. Obi-Wan-Kenobi and R2-D2 are as popular as Batman. *Jaws* crushed! The magician behind the movie, Lucas can no longer hide himself; the *Star Wars* epic has forced him from the shadows where he once took refuge.

How long did you work on the screenplay for Star Wars?
It took me about three years to write the screenplay. I wrote four versions, meaning four completely different plots, before finding the one that satisfied me. It was really difficult because I didn't want [*Star Wars*] to be a typical science-fiction. I didn't want [it] to fall into the usual science-fiction film conventions. I wanted it to be a truly imaginative film. I had some good ideas in the first versions, but no solid storyline, which is a challenge for me because I hate "plots." The difficulty was managing to find an overarching theme. I always have a lot of trouble finding a framework with an ultra-simple base that can captivate me and captivate the public.

You wrote the screenplay all by yourself?
Yeah, it's terrible. It's painful, atrocious . . .

You didn't work with screenwriters?
At the end I had some friends come to England to do some last-minute rewriting when we were just about to shoot because I wasn't happy with the dialogue. I never arrived at a degree of satisfaction where I thought the screenplay was perfect. If I hadn't been forced to shoot the film, I would doubtless still be rewriting it now, as we speak.

But before that you didn't discuss it with anyone?
Well, yeah! We're all one group of friends here: Francis Coppola, Matt Robbins, Bill Heiken, Gloria Katz, and a friend I went to school with who

works in my production office here; we're all screenwriters. We read each other's scripts and comment on them. I think this is the only way for us to keep from writing in a total void. I respect the opinions of these friends; their comments are intelligent because they're into the same thing as me.

There are also those who, in addition to being screenwriters, are directors and friends of mine: Coppola, whom I've already mentioned; Phil Kaufman; Martin Scorsese; and Brian de Palma. I show them all of my footage, and they give me precious opinions that I count on. When you don't know people well, they either give you dishonest compliments or tell you how they would shoot it. And that's not what you're asking them for.

We serve each other as sounding boards to help at two crucial times in film creation: the first version of the script and the film editing. That's when you need a friend whom you have total confidence in, to tell you: here, you have to cut; there, you have to do this. Often, these are obvious things, but often, too, they're sections that you've spent months on, that you've worked on so long you can't see them objectively anymore.

Tell me a bit about how these discussions worked...
I wrote the first version of *Star Wars,* we discussed it, and I realized I hated the script. I chucked it and started a new one, which I also threw in the trash. That happened four times with four radically different versions. After each version, I had a discussion with those friends. If there was a good scene in the first version, I included it in the second. And so on... the script was constructed this way, scene by scene.

According to the case, I had this person or that person read it. Coppola read three versions, while the friends I invited to England to polish up the dialogue saw only the final version. Let's say it was the directors from San Francisco in particular—Coppola and Phil Kaufman—who followed everything, the ones I went to school with.

The princess and Alec Guinness's character, were they always in the script?
No, they evolved throughout the versions. The first one talked about a princess and an old general. The second version involved a father, his son, and his daughter; the daughter was the heroine of the film. Now the daughter has become Luke, Mark Hamill's character. There was also the story of two brothers where I transformed one of them into a sister. The older brother was imprisoned, and the young sister had to rescue him and bring

him back to their dad. But this posed some horrible problems. Nobody would believe it, it wasn't realistic at all . . .

Why are you concerned about "realism" when Star Wars *deals with an imaginary, inter-galactic war set in a future that doesn't even exist?*
Yeah, yeah, yeah . . . It all has to show impeccable logic and unflawed realism, even if it deals with a different galaxy and an era 3,000 years in the past or the future. Everything has to be reinvented from start to finish, the clothes, the customs, the silverware that they eat with, the culture of the Empire, of the Jedi Knights, etc. This can take years to do. And you have to pay attention to errors that can ruin the entire structure.

What kinds of errors, errors of internal logic?
Of logic, but also of taste. Knowing what has to be in the story and what has to be left out. I need to keep a "centered" view concentric with the universe that I'm constructing, so at every moment I maintain a general view of a multi-layered reality, having for every point of reference the mind of the inventor—that is, me. In films, you generally have a given culture, a given time-period, some social factors to which the film's story refers. I had nothing [to go on]. You can spend your entire life perfecting a new world when you create its every piece.

But, contrary to your THX 1138, *you're searching here for identification with the film?*
Star Wars *is a fiction film, but its key is taking hold of what's most realistic and possible inside the terms set by the fiction. Or more clearly, it must be as *credible* as possible. You have to be able to breathe the air on the author's planet—to be able to smell it. The film has to make us believe it really existed, that we've really gone to another galaxy to shoot [the film]. The success of the imaginary, it's to make something totally fabricated seem *real*. And that everything stays inside the invented system. *That everything be credible and totally fantastic at the same time.*

Do you like to read science-fiction, despite the "conventions" you just talked about? Which authors do you like?
Sure . . . I like Asimov, Clarke. I also like the perverse—Topor in particular—and the entire group of wacky young authors that currently exists. Beyond

that, I can't respond to this question any more than the question, "Who is your favorite director?" I like loads of authors...

So then what did you mean in saying that you dissociate yourself from science-fiction?
I didn't say that. I said that I wanted to do something other than science-fiction...

What I mean to say is that it's easier to write science-fiction than it is to film it. In literature, there are ways to leave shady areas and blurred outlines that you can't transpose in cinema because in a film *everything is visible.* Thus, a lot more difficult. You have to operate within specific limits, with characters working in a finite space, all within the bounds of realism. [The novels] *Dune* and *Lord of the Rings* are constructed using this model; they create an entirely new world. But when you try to transpose this world visually, it's much more difficult [to make them seem real].

You have to find the material texture of the world: objects, fabrics, vehicles, tools. And if you make a mistake about an object or a fabric, it'll betray you.

Since it was so difficult, what inspired you to write this type of screenplay? Were you looking for something that would please children of all ages, including yours?
When I was little, I really liked comic strips. I used to like *Flash Gordon.* I thought they were fantastic, which nobody does anymore. I wanted to make something like a comic strip, but I wanted it to be funny rather than idiotic. (I don't see why they have to be stupid...) Moreover, I tend to veer toward sci-fi or fantasy films because, for me, they're challenges. It's a great exercise of the mind, something exciting. A lot of work, but a lot of fun, because for me the really hard work...it's the most fun kind...

Did you already have a Star Wars *comic book and line of toys in mind before the film?*
You could say that followed from the general idea. I like comics and toys. I have a particular affection for games and toys; there's no doubting that I haven't grown up. All of this was a part of the film, the intention of launching toys in supermarkets, creating books and stuff. In the end, *Star Wars* is a great adventure for children.

It's curious that you can look to Brian de Palma, Scorsese and Coppola for help. Their vigorous return to conventional narratives shouldn't please you. Are you reconciled with classical narratives?

No, I come from experimental cinema; it's my specialty... My friendship and my association with Coppola compelled me to write. His specialty is "literature," traditional writing. He studied theater, text; he's a lot more oriented towards "play writing" than I am: mise en scene, editing, the structured film. He told me, "you have to learn to write, to structure." So it's because of him that I got into to it. He forced me.

THX 1138 was a non-narrative film, a film without a framework. *American Graffiti* was similar; it was a juxtaposition of different sequences rather than one coherent story. On the other hand, *Star Wars* is a classic story, an old-style narrative, even blatantly old-fashioned. I wanted to know if I could do it. I wanted to explore this creative field that I had consciously avoided. But it's against my nature.

That's the reason I had to write four versions. Actually, if someone tells me an interesting story, I can easily transform it into a screenplay. But to be the initiator of the idea, that's very difficult. It's really what I wanted to do: be the sole architect of a traditional story where everything was linked by cause and effect. In fact, I learned an enormous amount, more than from my "sequence" films. But now that it's done, there's no need to do it again. I want to go back to to more experimental films.

How do you explain that Alain Resnais wasn't able to make a Flash Gordon *film, but today there is a veritable boom in sci-fi and fantasy films?*

I don't know. What I know is that I didn't intend to make *Star Wars* such a large film, an expensive film, a big production. When I started the pre-production four years ago, the film had a 3.5 million dollar budget, and at filming time it had more than doubled. By the time it's finished, it'll cost just over 8 million dollars.

The cost of the film rose 25% per year, all because of the oil crisis. Salaries increased, transportation increased, carpentry, raw materials for the set construction, everything went up.

Were the Star Wars *special effects especially fun for you?*

Yes, I thought that they would be fun. Now the more I know about them, the more I find them difficult. The problem with special effects is that we spent a year experimenting with new cameras and various apparatus, and it's like the film became a test for them.

We made real technical discoveries on the matter. For example, the computerized camera that stores movements and actions in memory. This makes it so that you can take the film shot in this camera, load it in another one, and refilm [the scene] in a different set, on a different background, panning or zooming. This allows infinite variations, harmonizations of unmultiplied foregrounds and backgrounds.

It took us a year to perfect this system. We've just reached the point where it can be used for other films. In fact, when *Star Wars* is finished, all of the equipment will be available to others.

Did you work directly with the experts on special effects?
I put together a group here in San Anselmo and I brought in a guy, John Dykstra, who worked under Douglas Trumbull as the cameraman for *Silent Running*. Dykstra had come to Berkeley to do aviation research. He had started to create a system for pilot training with computerized cameras. From his theories, we constructed a camera, then two, then a third used by Doug Trumbull for Steven Spielberg's film *Close Encounters of the Third Kind*.

My company builds the cameras in a workshop, and I shoot [the film] at the studio in the other building. Half of us build the equipment, and the other half use it.

How much do you know about technology?
I don't know everything about special effects, but I started out in animation cinema, which is more or less the same thing. I made some credits with optical effects for Coppola. If you remember *The Godfather,* I did the montage of newspaper titles in the middle of the film. I worked as a cameraman, a specialist in the genre, like Saul Bass. But I know more about research optics than computerized cameras. I don't know how to build cameras—that's beyond me. As for the cameras that we're building here, they're specialized for shooting miniatures. We aren't going to mass produce them.

What's the difference between your filming and Spielberg's? Did you build sets?
We built sets. Spielberg used the same camera as we did, but he employed it differently. We both shot with scale models, but Spielberg only filmed

the foregrounds—people, actions, scenery, gestures—and refilmed in his model workshops. Strictly speaking, he only shot half of the film. For *Star Wars*, we filmed *everything* in sets, then we inserted the foreground special effects with the flying spaceships. It's the same technique used differently.

Why did you film in Tunisia? Because of the low cost of production there? And why Shepperton Studio in England?
Tunisia, that was for the countryside, [the natural rock formations] on the planet Tatooine. I needed the desert and the architecture, especially the architecture. I like the absurd houses in Djerba for the house of Luke Skywalker's uncle, they're totally futuristic.

England, that's because it was closer to Tunisia than here. And because of the devaluation of the pound, which was to our advantage. Rather than come back here, I finished the film in England. I didn't want to film in Hollywood where I don't feel comfortable. I made *THX 1138* there, though, because I needed an immense set, and you only find them there. But I prefer to stay here to make films in my studio.

You and Francis Coppola, do you share one or two production houses?
Together we used to—actually, in a certain way, we still do. American Zoetrope owns the equipment and would have worked well as a studio if Warner hadn't crushed us. Now we have each founded our own production houses: Coppola Film and Lucasfilm. I almost produced *Apocalypse Now*, Coppola's last film, since I'd had the initial idea and had written the first screenplay, but I wanted to make *Star Wars*.

Coppola produced his film with his two usual producers, and I produced *Star Wars* with Gary Kurtz. This means we each produce our own films now. Still, Coppola would give me anything I asked.

One of my dreams is to shoot films like before, when we could rehearse with the actors three months before shooting. That was impossible with *Star Wars*; Alec Guinness arrived only days before the shooting, like it's done nowadays.

You must really admire Alec Guinness to have chosen him for the part?
A lot...Moreover, on the set, I was the one who was impressed. He's huge and I'm so small. I didn't know where to put myself...

What is your production group going to do — produce your films?
I'm in the process of expanding. I want to produce other directors' films, to be just the executive producer and to shoot some films of my own that will be experimental instead of commercial. I want to try to do some films that no one has ever done, [regardless] whether they're watched, whether they're successful.

You'll be able to finance some experimental films now that Star Wars *is going to be a world-wide success? You're like Scorsese and de Palma, in the running...*
The cinema market might not like what I want to do, but luckily I'm not under pressure thanks to the success of *American Graffiti,* and maybe *Star Wars.* I can allow myself to do what I like. Scorsese and Brian depend on each production. As you know, films that fund themselves are very rare. Salaries are relatively low, and (since you own part of the film) if it works, you earn money. If not, nothing. I invested what I earned from *American Graffiti* without spending any of it. My production house can produce friends' films, films that will bring in good revenue, and I can make experimental films. And live relatively modestly, which Scorsese and Brian de Palma don't do.

I prefer playing with camera film over becoming the entrepreneur behind a gigantic operation. Tell people what they have to do, listen to their projects, approve them or disapprove them, yuck! I want to get away from all of that. Whereas Francis (whom I'm very close to) wants more and more power, I don't. Since he made money producing *Graffiti,* he's been exercising his power. When the idea took him to buy an airplane, he bought one for himself. I prefer miniature airplanes.

I had to direct 500 people on *Star Wars,* and I hated it. I accept the power to do whatever I like with my camera. But I refuse the power to command other people.

I found myself caught in the race for success, but it's not my thing. I like to be a cameraman, look through the camera lens, play with the lighting. I'm more of a technician or "artisan-cameraman" or editor, than a *producer-director.* I have more desire to use a [film editing machine] than my power. Making movies — that's really fun.

George Lucas

MICHAEL PYE AND
LINDA MILES/1979

MODESTO IS A SMALL country town that lives off its wine and its farms. Beyond its few streets lies the walnut ranch where George Lucas was raised. It has one little cinema on its main street. "Films by Jean-Luc Godard," George Lucas says, "do not play Modesto."

It follows that Lucas grew up away from the sophisticated influences that a major city would have offered. His adolescent passion was drag racing, the fine tuning of surreal cars until they roared into fast flight. He was one of the "Superkids," a member of the separate adolescent subculture that grew away from its community to form a mobile, affluent group on its own. He cruised the strip at night, chasing girls and listening to the blaring of the car radio. He was determined to be an auto mechanic and a racing driver, someone who had access to the marvelous, sleek machines that speeded, legally, on tracks instead of perilously on country roads. The dream left little time for schoolwork. He dropped out of high school with average grades of D1. He barely made junior college. There he took photographs for racers and thought of becoming a painter; his father was not enthusiastic. He also studied the sociology that was later to help him build his most spectacular success.

His interest in film came accidentally. He helped build a racing car for Haskell Wexler, the cinematographer; and he narrowly escaped death in a car crash. The meeting, and the accident, convinced him that he should

From *The Movie Brats*, 1979, pp. 113–39, published by Holt Rinehart and Winston. © 1979 Michael Pye and Linda Miles. Reprinted by permission of the authors.

use his visual talents rather than his mechanical ones. Painting seemed a
gamble, and photography was problematic. The simplest and easiest solu-
tion seemed to be film school. It was a period when nobody thought of
building a career on film school, but Wexler helped Lucas to get into USC.
"I got there on a fluke," Lucas says, "and coming from a small town with
one little theater I didn't really have that much of a background. Producer
and director were for me the same general category—the person who
made the movies."

His background in painting drew Lucas to the animation department of
USC, and the benevolent influence of Herb Kossower. From there, he moved
to cinematography; and, by the end of his film school days, he had become,
on his own admission, "an editing freak." The progression is logical. It left
him with a fascination for what he calls "visual film, the sort of thing the
French unit of the National Film Board of Canada was producing." It was
film as tone poem, film as metaphor, film divorced from narrative form;
he still feels uneasy with theatrical film and its need to push a story along.
That weakness often shows in *Star Wars*; Lucas makes a marvelous fireworks display, but finds it difficult to link the explosions and stars and
rockets together.

In school he quickly made up for the cinematic dearth he had experienced in Modesto. He found Truffaut and Godard; he learned to love the
sensuality of Fellini. He discovered the underground filmmakers of San
Francisco, the avant-garde directors like Jordan Belson. That was what an
"art film" meant to him. "Up there around San Francisco," he says, "it was
a whole different world."

Through friends like John Milius and Walter Murch, he began to
explore facets of cinema that otherwise might never have occurred to him.
"At USC we were a rare generation because we were open-minded. We had
guys there who did nothing but Republic serials and comic books. I was
being exposed to a whole lot of movies you don't see every day. I don't
know how else I could have learned so much in the time."

Lucas was a star, but not exactly a model pupil. He dominated student
film festivals with movies more sophisticated and accomplished than his
peers. But he constantly broke rules. He bought extra footage to make
films longer than class projects allowed. He used his first one minute allo-
cation of film to produce the animated short that won his first student
film festival prize. In all, he made eight films while an undergraduate. It

was a starry career, and his problems started only when he left school. "Everybody banded together to try to crack the industry," Lucas remembers. "But the door was still closed tight."

Lucas rushed through his undergraduate work because he expected to be drafted for the war in Vietnam. When his turn came he was classified 4F and given a medical exemption. He was unemployed and uncertain. For a time he worked as a cameraman for Saul Bass, the designer of movie titles and director of animated films. He made a living cutting documentaries for the United States Information Agency. "That," he says, "was when I decided that I really wanted to be a director." He went back to USC graduate school for a single semester, January to June in 1968. He was a teaching assistant; he trained navy photographers; and he assembled a formidable crew to make a science fiction short called *Electronic Labyrinth: THX 1138:4EB*. It was a simple, stark picture of some future, authoritarian society. Computers and electronic codes are set against a man running the length of a blind, white corridor. Every move is watched; reality is monitored by cameras and screens. It is powerful but simplistic, a metaphor rather than a narrative. When it was expanded later, its effect was blunted by greater length. What he had already created was a strong poem.

In this short Walter Murch played the voice of God; it was partly his script. But George Lucas was the director. The pair made "a blood pact like Tom Sawyer and Huck Finn," according to Murch. Both were up for a Warners scholarship to watch films being made in a studio. They had been collaborators throughout their college days and "we agreed," Murch says, "that whoever got the scholarship would turn around and help the other guy."

The winner was Lucas. He went to observe the making of *Finian's Rainbow*; and from that grew his partnership with Francis Coppola. The new alliance gave him a chance to bring Murch into the crew of *The Rain People,* while he himself served as "general assistant, assistant art director, production aide, general do-everything." On the side Lucas worked on a documentary about the making of Coppola's film, "more as therapy than anything else," he says. "I hadn't shot film for a long time." But his main occupation, between five and nine-thirty every morning, was work on a new version of the *THX-1138* script, a project originally devised with Murch and Hal Barwood. It was Lucas's first feature script; he thought it was "terrible." Coppola, when shown it, said simply: "It is. You're absolutely right."

"I wanted to hire a writer," Lucas says, "but Francis said: 'No, if you're going to make it in this business you have to learn how to write.' So he really took me out of my strong points." With Walter Murch, he prepared a new script; it became the first, and only, project of American Zoetrope as a studio.

The making of *THX-1138* was like a film student's dream. There was money enough to work properly, but the studio chiefs in Los Angeles never saw rushes or dailies. Warner Brothers saw no material at all until the rough cut was taken down from San Francisco for their inspection. Only Coppola, their friend and patron, had immediate influence on the operation; and he was, in effect, one of its architects. Working with friends allowed unorthodox methods. Murch allowed the intricate sound track to grow along with the images that Lucas himself was photographing, directing, and editing. The sound montage was an organic part of the film, not a decoration imposed afterward. The tiny crew, with the actors shaven-headed, could travel to locations in a single minibus. George Lucas was out on his own.

His THX-1138 is an individual man who lives in a drug-soothed, bleached-out, nightmare future where sexuality is banned, where all heads are shaven, where ruthless and literally heartless robot police keep order in a subterranean world. Passion, will, love, and lust have all been abolished. As in Truffaut's *Fahrenheit 451*, television has become a surrogate for sex. Only THX-1138 and his roommate called LUH have, for a moment, failed to take their tranquilizers. They find love together and decide to risk the almost inevitable charges of drug evasion. But SEN, a middle-aged man, has lost his roommate and he has decided to rig the computer to allow him to live with THX. Between the discovery of love and sexuality, the wiles of SEN and the risk of certain exposure as a drug evader, THX-1138 goes on the run. He breaks from his prison, a white void, with a hologram who always wanted to be real; and he makes for the surface of the world, past the stinking, dwarfish shell-dwellers and up a final chimney to the surface of the Earth. Below, bathetically, the chase after him is suspended because it has gone over the predetermined budget. THX stands against a giant, desert sun. A bird flies by. That is the substance of the story.

The film works at a near-abstract level. Its premise is classic in science fiction: an individual asserting himself against the social machine. Its first sequence is a quote from a Buck Rogers serial, with Our Hero "exploring the wonderful world of the twenty-fifth century." Its theme encompasses the same crushing of identity that is central to William Cameron Menzies's *Things to Come*. But Lucas works by different methods. The camera is often literally distanced from the action, to establish the weirdness and aridity of the underground world. Only for lovemaking does the camera close in on individuals; and then, it is in soft focus. The paraphernalia of the future world is voyeuristic, full of cameras that pry, screens that show, observers heard casually asking for tighter close-ups on THX as he is stunned into passivity. Its technology is as closely observed as the machines in *Star Wars*. Brisk, brash jet cars escape down endless tunnels, just as in the later film Luke Skywalker takes his jet car across the deserts of Tatooine. Electronic gauges show the robot police closing in on THX-1138 as he speeds for freedom; they resemble electronic games boards or the computer displays used in the attack on the Death Star. The delicate, spun probes that examine the body of THX are like the robot probe that threatens Princess Leia in her cell. Parts of *THX-1138* have the same guts, panache, and vigor as the later film; they resemble a dress rehearsal. "But it's just not that entertaining," Lucas says. "It's not that commercial a movie." One central trouble common to both films is the lack of character development; but at least in *THX-1138* the premise of the plot is that individuality has been suppressed, that the workers conform in shuffling herds like the geometric processions in Lang's *Metropolis*. Only two individuals are presented, because anonymity is the essence of the underground world.

THX-1138 plays off language in a way that is highly curious. Murch and Lucas evidently wanted to warn their audience of every possible route to nightmare, since the bland voices which control this bleak society are given a set of apparently conflicting clichés to recite. The constant, unfinished question of the authorities is: "Are you now, or have you ever been..." It echoes, obviously, the House Un-American Activities Committee at work. Yet an omnipresent voice also offers "the blessing of the State, the blessing of the Masses;" and the eye of God follows monklike figures who have power through faint suggestions of Catholic orthodoxy; there are confessionals where stand pictures of a face like Christ's, and there is a system of repentance and absolution. There is even a constant reminder—"Buy, Be Happy!"—that an affluent, consumer society has dangers too.

Under this wordgame, *THX-1138* is about a particular form of individualism. Lucas calls it the Horatio Alger myth "that if you want something bad enough, you can do it. We are living in cages with the doors open." He finds the same theme in *American Graffiti*; there the cage is life in the small California town, which anyone with initiative can escape. He is sufficiently committed to the idea to see its roots in his own film school days. "Most students sat around and grumbled 'I can't make movies. They won't let me make movies.' I managed to make eight or nine films while I was at school. And I still find the same attitude. I have a friend who works in commercials, and I found him sitting with a hundred thousand feet of film and a full crew and he was saying that what he really wanted to do was to make a feature. And I said: 'What's to stop you?'" Lucas firmly believes that "if you're good, you'll make it."

That facile attitude explains why the full-scale *THX-1138* fails. It is not enough of an idea, a theme, to carry a full-length film. And it is not quite so obvious a proposition as George Lucas likes to think. If he had not been the white, middle-class son of a California businessman, he might well have found it hard to escape his "cage." Many others are not as fortunate. Brute economics keep them trapped. *THX-1138* is committed, paradoxically, to the ideology of plenty—the idea that the constant supply of material goods makes class irrelevant, that will is enough for success. Lucas himself is not a brash man; he is determined rather than arrogant, shy rather than overassertive. But this self-confident ethic allows him to paint only a shallow, tepid picture of his future society.

The day Warners saw *THX-1138* the American Zoetrope dream was dead. Worse yet Warners recut *THX-1138*. "I don't feel they had the right to do it," Lucas says, "not after I had worked on that thing for three years for no money. When a studio hires you, that's different. But when a filmmaker develops a project himself, he has rights. The ludicrous thing is that they only cut out five minutes, and it really didn't make that much difference. I think it's just a reflex action they have."

The film was not a commercial success, although it found a steady audience in universities around the campus circuit. When, seven years later, it was rereleased in the form George Lucas had originally intended, it still did not take off. Even the fact that it came "from the makers of *Star Wars*" could not make its cold vision into something popular.

It was while Lucas was cutting *THX-1138* that Gary Kurtz came to visit him. Kurtz wanted to discuss the problems and virtues of the Techniscope process, but the talk ranged wider. Together they speculated about the idea of a rock 'n' roll film set in the late 1950s or the early 1960s, in the days before the Beatles and the killing of President Kennedy and the war in Vietnam. Over the next years Lucas distilled his own adolescence in Modesto into a script. He worked with Willard Huyck and Gloria Katz, USC graduates who had married after a suitably romantic meeting at a lecture by Roger Corman. The project was constantly stalled and shelved. Huyck and Katz were offered a chance to make a film of their own, a horror project called *Messiah of Evil,* later advertised as from "the makers of *American Graffiti.*" George Lucas and Marcia Lucas, exhausted by the horrors of the Zoetrope collapse, set off for a long vacation in Europe with packs on their backs. *THX-1138* was showing at the Cannes Film Festival, uninvited, in a back street cinema, but the trip to Europe was mainly an escape.

When they returned, Lucas found that United Artists was prepared to put up a little development money for the *American Graffiti* idea. With his other collaborators out of commission he decided to hire a writer. He found, quickly, that he should have stuck to Coppola's advice. The script was professional but disastrous. It was not authentic. With distaste Lucas says: "The man had put in playing chicken on the road instead of drag racing."

"That was my life," Lucas explains. "I spent four years driving around the main street of Modesto, chasing girls. It was the mating ritual of my times, before it disappeared and everybody got into psychedelia and drugs." He had no intention of allowing the film to be inexact. He wanted to recreate the years when there was, apparently, innocence; the years of transition, before Vietnam, corruption, drugs, and time changed everything. The time he lived was a vital part of our fantasies. It is in the lyrics of the great rock 'n' roll numbers. Europeans who knew nothing of cruising, surfers, or going away for the summer and crying until September; who did not have cars or high school rings; who never wore Chantilly lace; we, too, shared the world of rock 'n' roll.

The tension between our dreams and Lucas's life is what makes the film work for so large an audience. The low light filming, with its curious, golden radiance, becomes a dream. Time is collapsed. All the central characters are confronted with a turning point in the course of a single night. Yet that night could be placed anywhere within a decade. Cars and music span ten years, an era rather than a date. The slogan for the film—"Where were you in '62?"—makes the setting seem fixed in time, but it is not. The reality, the underpinning, is the music; and that goes from the start of Eisenhower's second term to the end of Kennedy's more golden years. "George wrote the script," Walter Murch says, "with his old forty-fives playing in the background." From the beginning, the group—Kurtz, Huyck, Katz, and Murch, as well as Lucas—discussed which tune best went where. They open the film on a giant amber light; as the camera pulls back we realize it is the marking on a radio dial. The structure of the film comes from the radio program, the songs that disc jockey Wolfman Jack plays. Characters take cues from the music. And Wolfman Jack is the unseen center of it all, father figure as much as circus master.

The Wolfman's howl, his wild rock and his wilder phone calls, are part of California mythology; this is long before the time when the Wolfman was found in television commercials. In reality, the Wolfman broadcast from Mexico. "His voice would drift all over the West," Gary Kurtz says. "He would come and go over California on the whim of the weather. While you were listening, he would suddenly fade away; it was a strange, ethereal feeling. And he got the most outrageous phone calls." There were always rumors about him: that he broadcast from an ever circling plane, that his taste for rhythm and blues proved he must be black.

But within the film the Wolfman has another dimension. Like a father, he resolves problems, calms fears, and arranges for meetings that would otherwise be only longings. The one character who ever comes close to him is Curt; after confronting him, it is Curt who can escape the town, while the others stay fixed in their past. Curt is the would-be cynic with a romantic spirit, frightened of catching the plane to go away to college. He spends the night of the film's action, against his will, with a gang of punks. He catches a glimpse of a wonderful blonde girl in a white T-bird, sailing past him on Third Street. The Wolfman is his only means of contact with his golden vision. He finds the courage to drive out to the radio station, enter the corridors, and face the station manager through a maze of reflecting glass; the sound track, in precise counterpoint, plays "Crying in the Chapel." The manager assures him the Wolfman is not there, the Wolfman is only on tape; but as Curt leaves, the manager puts back his head and lets out a Wolfman howl. In that moment of realization, Curt finds the power to face an outside world. On the surface we are watching a meticulous reproduction of the real teenage culture of California in the early 1960s. Beneath the surface is, in terms of Freudian psychology as

developed by Jacques Lacan, something as strong and basic as the resolution of an Oedipal complex—that is, Curt learns to repair his sense of loss
at separation from mother's earliest warmth. The force of *American Graffiti*
comes from the fact that its dreamlike quality also contains reference to
the real force of dreams.

American Graffiti is also funny; and it backtracks to the situations and
shots of movies in the late 1950s. There are echoes of *High School Confidential,*
of *Rock Around the Clock,* of Nicholas Ray's template for the high school
film, *Rebel Without a Cause.* The film's climax, a drag race in which the
sympathetic John Milner is forced to realize that he has been beaten by yet
another generation that overtakes him, is visually close to the chicken run
in *Rebel.* The difference is the quality of nostalgia, the knowledge of time
passing. Milner is a child of twenty-two, with a memory that goes back
five years; he is getting old, and he feels that "the strip is shrinking all the
time." Yet he is still played in the image of James Dean, kindly lit, allowed
his dignity; his "piss-yellow deuce coupe," barely a foot off the ground, is
allowed its splendor. Only when Milner knows he would have lost the drag
race if his rival had not skidded off the road is there a sense of pathos and
loss. The character is based on John Milius, an ardent surfer. "George told
me about it while it was going on," Milius says. "I guess he saw me in that
light because I was a surfer going past my time."

The values of the film come from its social background. The group of
teenage characters all have cars; and those who do not are outsiders like
Terry the Toad who must be loved despite their obvious material failings.
That is the message of dim, blonde Debbie's final commitment to the
Toad. Ranking is by possessions; college education is a chance for everybody; there is a sense of democracy among the kids. The love of
neighborhood and the profound sexism—the only characters whose fates
are described at the film's end are men—suggest the link with suburban
values that the film's context would lead us to expect. This is Middletown,
in its sunny, golden California version. Women are invisible because they
have given up their hard-won independence in wartime for the more stolid
values of homemaking. Material goods eliminate the problems of class and
aspirations; John Milner, car mechanic, has a machine of his own like Curt
Henderson, the would-be writer. The nostalgia in *American Graffiti* is as
much for social values that had lost their power by 1973 as it is for the
externals of the rock 'n' roll generation.

Ned Tannen was in trouble when the script of *American Graffiti* reached his desk at Universal. The screenplay had been rejected by United Artists, after its initial flush of interest; and it had been "turned down by every other company in town." But Tannen liked the idea. "God knows," he says, "I've made enough mistakes so I can say this wasn't one of them."

Tannen was at the end of a program of films made by directors who had not yet made money. Universal was voicing its corporate doubts about new talent programs. It worried about Dennis Hopper's project after *Easy Rider*, a film apparently lost in Peru on a diet of drugs, drink, and rumor; that project produced the extraordinary but unreleased *The Last Movie*, a fine film about filmmaking. Milos Forman had made his first American film, *Taking Off*, for Tannen; Douglas Trumbull, the creator of soaring space stations and visions of infinity for Kubrick's *2001*, had made a modest, marginally successful science fiction film called *Silent Running*. John Cassavetes made *Minnie and Moskowitz*, the film that helped Martin Scorsese stay alive in Hollywood by providing him with a job and cash. Frank Perry had contributed two films. The program contained quality and imagination. All it lacked was profit. "Really," George Lucas says, "Tannen's program had been cancelled."

"I was having a very difficult time," Tannen says, "persuading the company to let me make *American Graffiti*." Partly, it was a project that came to Universal at the wrong time. "Universal was a very conservative company," Gary Kurtz says. "It was making most of its money in TV, and gearing most of its theatrical film to an eventual sale to TV." The unconventional would not, Universal feared, attract a free-spending network. Moreover, the project arrived just as all the studios were preparing to clear away the debris left by the young directors so eagerly hired after the success of *Easy Rider*. "This community goes through a series of hot flushes when it believes some new messiah is on the horizon," Tannen says. "Those programs could be called the *Easy Rider* syndrome, and they produced some pretty staggering movies."

Then there was the problem of explaining *American Graffiti* to a board of directors. Samuel Arkoff later hit the perfect description: "It is," he said, "a beach picture *x* years later. Well done." But for Tannen, "it was just an idea. Nobody knew what it was. It wasn't based on some book that was a huge best-seller. It wasn't a special effects movie where you have all sorts of gyrations and people could say, 'Oh, boy! That's terrific!' It was a terribly personal, small story." There was no single line on which it could be promoted. "Pictures like *American Graffiti* have to be discovered. There's no way you can hype that kind of movie. What are you going to sell it on?" Even when the film was complete, Tannen says, "nobody in the company had any concept of what that film was. It's funny thinking of it now. It didn't seem funny then."

Universal made a condition for allowing the project to go ahead: find a big name. Lucas did not want stars. The only possible figure who could convince the all-powerful head of the studio, Lew Wasserman, was a producer—Francis Coppola. He was finishing *The Godfather*; he was established and known; he would do very well. Gary Kurtz remembers: "George and I went to Francis and asked him if he'd come into the project with us." (Ned Tannen remembers approaching Coppola himself.) The name proved enough for Universal to put $750,000 into making the film.

Evidently, the "name" they demanded was not enough to make Universal believe the project stood a chance of success. Lucas asked for $10,000 to buy the album rights to the songs he was planning to use on the sound track; Universal refused. When the film had been released, and its success was obvious, they had to pay $50,000 for the rights to the same material. While Coppola and Lucas were exiled from the lot by a strike of the Writers Guild, the studio altered the film. They refused to release the film in stereophonic sound although it had specifically been designed for stereo. And when they first saw a print, there were angry studio executives who believed the entire film was unfit to be released. It took a stormy outburst by Francis Coppola to save the film. Universal owes its gigantic earnings to Coppola's temper.

George Lucas intended the film to be his personal vision; and because he was an experienced cinematographer, he wanted to control precisely how it looked. When shooting began he pushed himself to the edge of his endurance, working twelve to sixteen hours a day. "I had shot my first picture myself," he says, "and I tried the same on *American Graffiti*. It was just extremely difficult." He had chosen to film on location, in two towns close to San Francisco, San Rafael and Petaluma, that had barely changed since the early 1960s. "We were using very low light levels and it was extremely hard for the operators to see what they were doing. We had two cameras going, and we were using lights of two foot-candles in some scenes when the usual low light level is about two hundred foot-candles. It just looked mushy." By the end of the second week of shooting, halfway through the schedule, it was obvious that Lucas was close to exhaustion. Coppola intervened and told him to ease up; it was simply not possible to be both cinematographer and director on a film that would have been hard to finish on time even with the help of a full crew. But Lucas was determined not to lose the elusive, radiant quality he wanted. "I was leery of bringing in some big Hollywood cameraman," he says, "because a cameraman is what I am, essentially. Francis told me to bring in a friend; and since I had worked with Haskell Wexler, and he had helped on *THX-1138,* I asked him for help." Wexler, one of the best cinematographers of his generation, had a generous habit of answering such appeals. "He was shooting commercials during the day, but he came up almost every night. He did it for free, as a friend. In the end I gave him some points in the movie, and Francis chipped in and gave him some points and he made money. But he came to help just out of friendship." Together Wexler and Lucas kept the soft, warm tone of the film; they devised the gold that surrounds its images of cruising the main street, in search of a dream, a good time, a girl.

Walter Murch came in to shape the sound when the visuals had already been assembled. Universal's skepticism about the project meant money was tight. That changed the scope of the sound and its relationship to the image. In two sequences the change was probably constructive. One is the scene where Curt has to prove his fitness to joint the streetwise Pharaohs by sabotaging a police car. The officers lurk in a used-car lot; Curt fixes a cable to the back axle of their car, and, as a speeding car screeches past, the officers drive off into midair, their back wheels anchored in the used-car lot and the body of their car smashed on the road. In the other sequence Terry the Toad has taken to the fields with Debbie and lost his borrowed car. As the couple walk through the dark woods, Debbie tells flesh-crawling stories of the Goat Killer, a homicidal maniac who leaves a severed goat's head beside his victims. "Both sequences would have had a score," Walter Murch says, "if there had been a budget for it. Since there wasn't, we made a score in sound effects." For the story of the Goat Killer, the eerie, elusive night sounds are more disconcerting than music could be; and, since the radios are far away from the action, the sound does not break the logic of the constant rock 'n' roll music.

That logic was changed by Universal's refusal to make sterco prints of the film. "Originally, we designed the film in stereo," Walter Murch says.

"The sound track was theoretically a radio show, with some tracks re-recorded to sound as though they were coming from the cars. As a car drove by, you would have the sound of music driving by. All through the film, people would be swimming in a soup of sound." In the film as it was originally released, that effect does not quite work; even the giant radio dial in the first shot is not quite enough to make the point. Numbers sometimes echo action or character very patly. In the stereo version that Lucas insisted was his condition for allowing a sequel to be made, there is complex crosscutting between speakers at the front and back of the cinema as well as from side to side. The effect is stronger. If you remember, we lived with the radio on; music frames and counterpoints the action.

The pain of Black Thursday came back on the night that Universal first saw the film. Lucas had put his life on the screen, in a film made by his company and largely at his risk. For three years' work he had taken $20,000, rather less than an average schoolteacher could hope to make. And now, in a crowded San Francisco preview, the studio pronounced its verdict. "This film," said one executive, "is a disgrace."

Ned Tannen saw the last of his films failing before it had a chance to start its life. "There was one man who worked in this company," he says, "who shall be nameless. But he was probably the senior editor in Hollywood and he has been in every film book on American cinema. He thought *American Graffiti* was totally unreleasable, and he wasn't unique." The studio's shock was compounded because they had not seen a foot of film before the preview. Like *THX-1138, American Graffiti* had been kept carefully away from Los Angeles, Hollywood, and the particular studio executives who had to decide its fate. Now they were assembled with an audience of a thousand to see the final form of their dubious project. "The audience loved it, and went crazy," Lucas says. "Then the lights came up, and the people were walking out, and this one studio man walked back to tell us what he thought of the film. He said it was an embarrassment."

That was when Francis Coppola lost his temper. "He just blew his top," Lucas says, "he was so mad." He bellowed at the studio man: "This poor kid has worked his ass off for you, making a really terrific movie the audience loved, and for no money at all. And you can't even say thank you to this kid, at least for bringing the picture in on schedule." In full flight Coppola reached for his checkbook. "I'll buy the picture back right now,"

he said. "I'll write a check now. I think it's a great film and I want it back."
The check won the point. Faced with this degree of passion, certainty, and
cash, the studio executives backed down.

Still, they recut the movie; and still, Lucas resents the fact. "It didn't
make the film shorter in a way the audience can feel or understand," he
says. "It's more a moral issue than anything else." *American Graffiti* lost
one sequence because Universal could not buy the rights to a song; "and
they had told us," Lucas says, "that they were so friendly with the copyright owners." Another went for reasons of length; Universal, in a fit of
unusual punctiliousness, insisted the film should run precisely the 110
minutes required by the contract. "That scene was one of the best in the
film," Lucas says. It put Steve, the central character of the film, against his
math teacher. "It really strengthened that character," Lucas says. "In the
film they put out, Steve is a nothing. The odd thing is, it was the second
most popular scene in the movie at the preview, according to the cards we
got back." Ned Tannen says that George Lucas agreed to the cuts, such as
they were; but Lucas, barred from the studio by the writers' strike, talks of
Gary Kurtz "trying to keep them from destroying the film. You spend three
years of your life on a movie, and someone comes along and puts a great
crayon mark along one side of it and it just drives you crazy."

When the final version was prepared, the studio still quavered and
dithered over its release. It might, someone suggested, be a suitable movie
for television. "There was a lot of last minute jockeying," Ned Tannen says,
"about where it was going to play and how it was going to be advertised."
Almost nobody in the studio could understand the title. Against this bland
hostility, Lucas and Kurtz took to guerrilla warfare. They rigged the audience for screenings within the studio. "Normally fourteen stodgy old men
sit in a room and that's it," Lucas says. "So, we said okay, we'll show them
the movie. But we want to show it with an audience of at least a couple of
hundred people — crazy kids, everybody's secretary. And after about seven
or eight of those screenings, they began to admit that maybe they did
have a movie after all."

What hurt most was the background of the men making this decision.
"They're people who have never made a movie in their lives," Lucas says,
"agents and lawyers with no idea of dramatic flow. But they can come in,
see a movie twice, and in those few hours they can tell you to take this out
or shorten that. The movie industry was built by independent entrepre-

neurs, dictators who had a very strong feeling about movies. They knew what they wanted and they made it happen. Now both *American Graffiti* and *Star Wars,* conventional as they were, also were totally off-the-wall projects. I believe a Jack Warner or a Darryl Zanuck would have said, 'Yes, it's a great idea, let's do that.' And it would have happened."

Star Wars began as fourteen pages of story. United Artists, entitled to see each Lucas project because of its interest in *American Graffiti,* refused it. "Universal never formally said no," Gary Kurtz says, "but I knew from talking to the people there that they were uneasy about the idea." As Kurtz and Lucas continued to build enthusiasm within the film world for their earlier movie, their new project for a space fantasy began to seem more plausible. It is a curious form of Hollywood logic: back winners, whatever they do. "If it hadn't been for that success," Kurtz says, "we would not have been able to get *Star Wars* made at any studio because they all had the same apprehensions."

This is how it worked. "We finished *Graffiti* at the end of January, and the answer print [the first full version of the movie] was ready in the first week of February," Lucas says. "That was when we had the arguments about the release dates. We made the deal on *Star Wars* on the first of May, and *Graffiti* came out in August. But the film was building before release. And it was really in Hollywood that it was beginning to build." All Twentieth Century-Fox promised in the May deal was the money to start developing a script. Like all Hollywood deals, this one moved step by cautious step. It did not guarantee the film would ever be written, let alone made. But by the second and third steps in the contract, *American Graffiti* was in release. "It did well in New York and Los Angeles, but it took a while to grow. It wasn't until well into October and November that we knew it was going to be an enormous hit," Gary Kurtz says. Neither he nor Lucas could control the marketing of the film or prevent Universal from selling off the rights in various states of the United States before exhibitors had a chance to see the film. Kurtz had planned to bide his time. "I thought we could go to theaters across the country and say, 'Look, the first week's take is good, the second week is good, book this picture.'" In fact, the second and third weeks of the release were what *Variety* calls "socko" and even "boffo." Mr. Wasserman, the head of Universal, intervened. He ordered his executives to scrap other bookings and made theaters bid again for the film. Mr. Wasserman is not lightly disobeyed.

Now, *Star Wars* was not some obscure science fiction project. It was the next film from the men who brought you the megahit, the superfilm, the most profitable film ever to cost less than $1 million to make. "Each week," George Lucas says, with a mock-rueful expression, "the figures would get worse and worse and more and more ridiculous." The absurdity struck him most painfully because he was still broke. "I was so far in debt to everyone that I made even less money on *Graffiti* than I had on *THX-1138*," he said later. He was living on $9,000 a year. The main prop of his and his wife's lives was Marcia Lucas's work as an editorial assistant. He had borrowed from almost everybody he knew, from his parents, from Coppola, and from his lawyers. He had also spent years working on the prospect of making *Apocalypse Now,* without studio backing or even the chance of it. Now, he decided to have a success.

Star Wars was manufactured. When a competent corporation prepares a new product, it does market research. George Lucas did precisely that. When he says that the film was written for toys—"I love them, I'm really into that"—he also means he had merchandising in mind, all the sideshow goods that go with a really successful film. From the start he thought of T-shirts and transfers, records, models, kits, and dolls. His enthusiasm for the comic strips was real and unforced; he owned a gallery selling comic book art in New York. His first film, *THX-1138,* begins with a suitable text from an old Universal serial. It presents Buck Rogers, and reminds the audience there is "nothing supernatural or mystic: take Buck, he's just an ordinary human being who keeps his wits about him." Star-struck audiences could take their cue from that line. The success of *Star Wars* was neither mystic nor supernatural; neither quality informs its brilliant, empty shell. George Lucas simply kept his wits about him.

From the start he was determined to control the selling of the film and its by-products. "Normally you just sign a standard contract with a studio," he says, "but we wanted merchandising, sequels, all those things. I didn't ask for another $1 million, just the merchandising rights. And Fox thought that was a fair trade." Lucasfilm Ltd., the production company George Lucas set up in July 1971, "already had a merchandising department as big as Twentieth Century-Fox has. And it was better. When I was doing the film deal, I had already hired a guy to handle that stuff."

Lucas could argue, with reason, that he was protecting his own investment of two years' research and writing; and he was also protecting his share of the $300,000 from *Graffiti,* which he and Kurtz used as seed money for developing *Star Wars.* "We found Fox was giving away merchandising rights, just for the publicity," he says. "They gave away tie-in promotions with a big fast food chain. They were actually paying these people to do this big campaign for them. We told them that was insane. We pushed and we pushed and we got a lot of good deals made." When the film appeared, the numbers become other worldly: $100,000 worth of T-shirts sold in a month, $260,000 worth of intergalactic bubble gum, a $3 million advertising budget for ready-sweetened *Star Wars* breakfast cereals. That was before the sales of black digital watches and Citizens Band radio sets and personal jet sets.

The idea of *Star Wars* was simply to make a "real, gee-whiz movie." It would be a high adventure film for children, a pleasure film that would be a logical end to the road down which Coppola had directed his apparently cold, remote associate. As *American Graffiti* went out around the country, Lucas refined his ideas. He toyed with remaking the great Flash Gordon serials, with Dale Arden in peril and the evil Emperor Ming; but the owners of the rights wanted a high price and overstringent controls on how their characters were used. Instead, Lucas began to research. "I researched kids' movies," he says, "and how they work and how myths work; and I looked very carefully at the elements of films within that fairy tale genre which made them successful." Some of his conclusions were almost fanciful. "I found that myth always took place over the hill, in some exotic far-off land. For the Greeks it was Ulysses going off into the unknown. For Victorian England it was India or North Africa or treasure islands. For America it was out West. There had to be strange savages and bizarre things in an exotic land. Now the last of that mythology died out in the mid-1950s, with the last of the men who knew the old West. The last place left 'over the hill' is space."

Other conclusions were more practical. "The title *Star Wars* was an insurance policy. The studio didn't see it that way; they thought science fiction was a very bad genre, that women didn't like it, although they did no market research on that until after the film was finished. But we calculated that there are something like $8 million worth of science fiction freaks in the U.S.A. and they will go to see absolutely anything with a title like *Star Wars*." Beyond that audience, Lucas was firm that the general public should not be encouraged to see the film as esoteric science fiction. "We sent them constant memos," he says. " 'Do not call this film "science fiction," it's a space fantasy.' "

The final plot line was concocted after four drafts in which different heroes in different ages had soared through space to worlds even wilder than those that finally appeared. It was a calculated blend. "I put in all the elements that said this was going to be a hit," Lucas says. He even put a value on them. "With *Star Wars* I reckoned we should do sixteen million domestic"—that is, the distributors' share in the United States and Canada would amount to $16 million—"and, if the film catches right, maybe twenty-five million. The chances were a zillion to one of it going further." Wall Street investment analysts, even after the film had opened, shared his low estimates. They felt it could never match *Jaws*. "It's my feeling," said one, "that the fear element draws a few more people."

Both makers and analysts were wrong. *Star Wars* was a "sleeper," a film whose vast success was in doubt until after it had opened for a while. Those doubts affected studio attitudes toward its budget. Only for a great "event," such as *The Godfather* or *Jaws*, will the studios be tolerant and relax their purse strings a little. Lucas and Kurtz had to do battle over budgets. The original sums were so tight that Kurtz told the board of Fox: "This will only work if everything goes perfectly. And it very rarely does." During shooting the designer of the monsters fell sick and he left his work for the sequence in a space tavern incomplete. The sequence did not work in its original form, but the studio would allow only $20,000 more to restage and reshoot the entire scene.

Compared with *2001*—Lucas calls Kubrick's film "the ultimate science fiction movie"—the special effects in *Star Wars* were cheap. Where Kubrick could allow his space stations to circle elegantly for a minute, Lucas always has to cut swiftly between individual effects. But that became part of the film's design. Where Kubrick's camera was static, Lucas and Kurtz encouraged their special effects team to develop ways to present a dogfight in space with the same realism as any documentary about World War II. As is usual in animation, they prepared storyboards, precise drawings of how

each frame was to look; but, unlike most animation, they based the drawings on meticulous study of real war footage. They looked for the elements
that made an audience believe what they were seeing. For Lucas it was a
return to his original interests at USC—the basics of film, recreated with
models, superimposition, paintings, and animation. "We used a lot of documentary footage," Kurtz says, "and some feature film footage. We looked
at every war movie ever made that had air-to-air combat, from *The Blue
Max* to *The Battle of Britain*. We even looked at film from Vietnam. We
were looking for the reason each shot worked, the slight roll of the wings
that made it look real."

John Dykstra, assistant to Douglas Trumbull on *2001*, retreated to a
warehouse in Van Nuys, California. There he developed a camera that
could move through any axis, to match real-life movement of wingtips or
fuselage, and he linked it with a computer which could remember the
movements and duplicate them exactly when a different model was before
the camera. That way two separate models, photographed separately, could
seem to do precise battle. The surrounding planets were on a painted background; the laser fire was added by animation. Superimposition brought
all the elements together. Developing the technique took most of the year
and the budget allocated to special effects. "The fact is that we didn't have
the money," Lucas said later, "and the key to special effects is time and
money. I had to cut corners like crazy. I cut scenes left and right. And I cut
out over one hundred special effects shots. The film is about 25 percent of
what I wanted it to be."

Arguably, the effects work to better dramatic effect than the spectacle of
2001. Lucas was invading the territory of Edgar Rice Burroughs, not a labo-
ratory. He was making a series of Tolkien episodes, with dragons, hobbits,
wizards like Gandalf, and dark forces with storm troopers like Nazgûl for
support. There is no respect for science, no residue of the onetime staple of
film—the menace of the atomic age. In this patch of deep space, giant
craft can thunder like jet airplanes, and the London Symphony Orchestra
can blast its romantic horns and violins. Mere physics says that space is
silent. And Lucas contrives his battles well enough to spare us any desire
to concentrate on the precise specifications of the craft involved.

But he does not tell a story. It is the basic failing of the film. It lacks true
narrative drive and force. It is a void, into which any mystic idea can be
projected; an entertainment, brilliantly confected, which is quite hollow.

Its only idea is individualism: that a man must take responsibility for others, even at great personal cost and peril. Its idea is, in classic form: "A man's gotta do what a man's gotta do."

The iconography is bizarre. Darth Vader, the dastardly villain, is black. That is common in science fiction. Even in the supposedly liberal *Planet of the Apes* series, the wicked and stupid gorillas are the military, and they are black. The honey-colored chimpanzees are the wise, good scientists. The closer to the color of a California WASP, the better the character; it is a fair rule of thumb. But Darth Vader's forces are storm troopers, armored in white. The wicked Grand Moff Tarkin lives in a gray green world, with gray green uniforms; he is clearly a wicked Nazi. Yet when our heroes take their just reward at the very end, there are images that parallel the finest documentary of Nazism, Leni Riefenstahl's *Triumph of the Will*. "I can see," Kurtz says, "why people think that. I suppose it is like the moment when Hitler crosses the podium to lay the wreath." Critical confusion is not surprising when there are allusions to Nazism as both good and bad. French leftist critics thought the film was Fascist-oriented; Italian rightists thought it was clearly Communist-oriented.

Nor is the vague pantheism of the film coherent. *Star Wars* talks much of the Force, a field of energy that permeates the universe and can be used for both good and evil. It is passed on, with a sword, just as the sword Excalibur is passed on in Arthurian romance; the influence of chivalric stories is strong. But when the Force is used by Luke Skywalker to help him destroy the monstrous Death Star, he is urged only to relax, to obey instincts, to close his eyes and fight by feeling. The Force amounts to building a theology out of staying cool.

Star Wars has been taken with ominous seriousness. It should not be. The single strongest impression it leaves is of another great American tradition that involves lights, bells, obstacles, menace, action, technology, and thrills. It is pinball, on a cosmic scale.

The true curiosity of *Star Wars,* beyond its clever artifice, is the ways in which public response was molded and stimulated. Publicity discussed the sources on which Lucas drew to construct his story. Indirectly that is a key point about the film. It does use film language that derives from the strengths of certain genres—the films about the Knights of the Round Table, the old moralistic Westerns, and the cheap serials that poured from

Poverty Row, in which Buster Crabbe was always a hero whether he appeared as Buck Rogers, Flash Gordon, or Tarzan. The story advances, not by any orthodox storytelling, but by telling the audience what to expect. It depends on their cine-literacy. "The real problem was exposition," as Gary Kurtz says. "We always saw the first movie as a kind of introduction to the environment of the characters."

It does not draw on the film grammar, strictly defined, of the films that share its conventions. "If you showed this film to an audience in the 1930s," Kurtz says, "they would not be able to follow what is going on, just because of how filmic language has evolved. The use of fades, dissolves, how things have to be organized was all a little primitive in those serials. We have the advantage of being able to jump over all that now."

But it does use cliché. Luke Skywalker pleads with his homesteading relatives to be allowed to be released from the harvest to join the space academy; it is the repeated theme of films by John Ford, the divide between the settlers and the wanderers. The only direct quotation from Ford in the film, and that a tenuous one, is the fact that the relatives die and their ranch is burned, as in Ford's *The Searchers*. But our experience of Ford's films, and others that use the convention, allows us to read the scene between Luke and his aunt and uncle in more depth than the scene itself would permit. The same mechanism works for the character of Han Solo, a cowboy braggart who blends cynicism with a potential heroism; it works for the duel between Darth Vader and Ben Kenobi, when the story requires Ben's sacrificial death; and it works when a monster tells Luke that it does not like his face. We can immediately read the start of a saloon brawl. Duly, that is what happens.

The cheap serials that poured from Gower Gulch used similar devices. There were conventions for how a proper villain and a proper hero would look. In Ben Kenobi, the hermit knight, we have a perfect equivalent of a Merlin. Lucas even filmed in Death Valley, a basic location for the filmmakers of Poverty Row. But what he takes from the serials is their morality. They always pitted good against evil, without equivocation. They used romantic dress, predictable stories; and "most of the stories," according to Gene Fernett, a historian of Poverty Row, "were glorified morality plays, much more acceptable to audiences as Westerns than were the old morality plays." Now that serials are dead, and Westerns have absorbed ethical relativism, *Star Wars* is left to inherit that tradition of moral certainty. It is

no accident that it should also have the romantic dress and the distant setting that absolute moral values now require: "a long time ago in a galaxy
far, far away." It offers the ultimate escape, withdrawal from complex questions of morality, and a display of magnificent fireworks as a bonus. It is a
holiday from thought.

On May 25, 1977, *Star Wars* went out on test release to twenty-five theaters.
In nine days it had grossed $3.5 million. Within two months it had
recouped its $9 million costs and its prints and advertising bill, and it was
in profit before its general release. Some cynics settled at Ma Maison and
the other Hollywood haunts, and they remembered the fate of other films
that had gone well on test release: *Young Winston, Hello, Dolly!,* and *Darling
Lili.* All had sunk without trace. But *Star Wars* was different, and the industry did not need to fall in love with amiable droids or cheer the heroic
Luke Skywalker to see why. The cost of the film was controlled, unlike the
runaway juggernauts that broke Hollywood in the 1960s; indeed, in real
money terms, *Star Wars* was made on a budget that would not have bought
a modest drama in the early 1960s if it involved overseas filming. Its marketing was directed, cleverly, at an audience that was known to exist—the
young in summer. It was released carefully, at ordinary ticket prices. Its
prospects had been properly researched. Most cynics, even at Ma Maison,
read the signs and bought stock in Twentieth Century-Fox as fast as they
could. As the share price soared, student groups justified the rise. Again
and again they returned to their favorite fantasy. And *Star Wars* received
the ultimate accolade which proved its appeal to the young of California;
the queues were joined by those dealing in loose marijuana cigarettes.

Twentieth Century-Fox waxed fat on the profits. It kept 60 percent of
the film's earnings. Neither Kurtz nor Lucas would talk of how the rest was
divided. Alec Guinness was said to be the richest actor in the world because
the producers had given him an extra half point in the profits. British tax
rates made that claim seem unlikely. But the real point of interest was the
attitude of Kurtz and Lucas to giving away profit in order to thank their
associates. "Some of the profit was obligated by contract to certain people.
Some of it wasn't," Kurtz says. "We used the uncommitted points to say
'thank you' to people for doing a good job. People tell me that's unheard
of in the movie business, but I really don't think so. It's a private contract.
People just don't talk about it."

George Lucas kept a sizable interest in any sequels that followed *Star Wars*. That was written into his original contract with Twentieth Century-Fox, at his insistence. The money will be the seed of his other projects. He still dreams of making personal films, concentrating on the poetry of cinema. Ned Tannen says: "The fact that *Star Wars* is the biggest hit ever made and that he doesn't think it is very good, that's what fascinates me about George. It's what I really admire about him, and I certainly think he is wrong."

The Empire Strikes Back and So Does Filmmaker George Lucas With His Sequel to Star Wars

JEAN VALLELY/1980

San Francisco's North Point Theater is packed with people, tension, anticipation. When the familiar strains of John Williams' Star Wars *theme finally rip through the theater, it brings smiles of relief and recognition to the expectant faces.*

"Oh, look," gasps a little boy in the second row. "It's Luke Skywalker!"

Sure enough, there's Skywalker, big as life. And Han Solo, Princess Leia, R2-D2 and C-3PO—the whole group. The adventure continues.

By the time the houselights come up, the audience is on its feet cheering. The Empire Strikes Back, *the long-awaited continuation of* Star Wars *has arrived. And it is wonderful.*

The Force behind both of these extraordinary films, as well as the cult classic THX 1138 *and* American Graffiti *makes his way through the crowd. Bearded, bespectacled, dressed in brown cords, brown V-neck sweater, checked shirt and tan sneakers, George Lucas, 36, looks more like a delivery boy than a man who is estimated to be worth more than $80 million. He tugs his wife Marcia's hand and the two slide out the front door, past the TV cameras and the reporters with microphones who are frantically looking for the stars of* The Empire Strikes Back.

Star Wars, *you may recall, not only captured the hearts and imaginations of millions, but also made millions. In fact, it's grossed more*

From *Rolling Stone,* 12 June 1980, pp. 31–33. Reprinted by permission of Straight Arrow Publishers, Inc., 1980.

money in film rentals than any other movie in the history of motion pictures—more than $400 million—that is, until The Empire Strikes Back. *Only God, in a galaxy far, far away, knows how much this film will rack up.*

The high wood fence that surrounds Lucas' house in San Anselmo, just north of San Francisco, is intimidating, as are the signs NO SOLICITING and BEWARE OF DOG. But just as Lucas' appearance is deceiving, so is all this. Behind the giant fence is a small, unpretentious wood house with a big front porch. And the dog that jumps up to greet me, an Alaskan malamute named Indiana, is about as vicious as Benji.

*The front door opens onto a comfortable living room, dominated by a jukebox that holds Lucas' extensive collection of vintage rock & roll records. Like these discs, Lucas is a product of the Sixties. He really does believe in all those Sixties things: art, sharing the wealth, one for all and all for one. He and his wife, a film editor (*Taxi Driver, New York, New York*), have been married for eleven years. They share a love of film (he attended the University of Southern California film school), of northern California (he was born and raised in Modesto), of the simple life (Francis Coppola calls them "country mice") and a distrust of Hollywood.*

Lucas settles into a roomy chair, crosses his legs, folds his hands on his lap and talks about his latest projects, his hatred of Hollywood and the movie system, how he hopes to beat that system, the tortures of trying to get a film made, his pal Francis Coppola and his dreams for the future—a place where George Lucas is much more at home than in either the past or the present.

Why didn't you direct The Empire Strikes Back?
I hate directing. It's like fighting a fifteen-round heavyweight bout with a new opponent every day. You go to work knowing just how you want a scene to be, but by the end of the day, you're usually depressed because you didn't do a good enough job. When I visited the set in Norway and saw all the problems and the misery that [director Irvin] Kershner was going through, wow, can you imagine being in the Arctic Circle at forty-five below zero? It's hard enough just to walk through it, let alone direct the actors, move the equipment. It was easy to let go of directing.

What did you do on this film?

I provided the story and technical advice, like, does a robot do this or that? They shipped me the dailies and I looked at them. There were some problems. They were a little over budget, over schedule. That concerned me, because I only had so much money and I was afraid if they used it all up, we wouldn't be able to finish the movie. But I knew they were trying to do the best job they possibly could, and I thought the stuff looked terrific. It's truly Kershner's movie.

Does that make you sad?

Well, it's still my story. I just didn't have to do all the work. [*Smiling sheepishly*] I feel Chewbacca is still my Wookie and R2-D2 is still my little robot.

How would you have made the movie differently?

Hard to describe. I look at a scene and think, "Gee, I wouldn't have done it that way." A lot of people have told me that *The Empire* is a better film than *Star Wars,* so whatever my disagreements were, well, Kershner was right.

Can you tell us how all this evolved?

[*Laughing*] Long, long ago in a galaxy far, far away, when I was in film school.... It's a very long story.

We have time.

Okay. I loved shooting *cinéma vérité* and thought I would become a documentary filmmaker. Of course, being a student in the Sixties, I wanted to make socially relevant films, you know, tell it like it is. But then I got this great idea for a rock & roll movie, with cars and all the stuff I knew about as a kid. And then I thought that what I'd really like to make is a big children's fantasy fairy tale. I won a scholarship to work at Warner Brothers for six months, and Francis Coppola took me under his wing. He offered to have me make a feature version of a film I made as a student, *THX 1138.* So being young and bearded, and Francis being young and bearded, I thought, "Well, he understands my concerns." But then he said, "If you're going to direct, you have to learn to write, and not only do you have to learn to write, but you have to get good at it." He forced me to write the script for *THX 1138,* and the first draft was pretty awful. Anyway, I worked for a year on the script. I just didn't think Francis was ever going to get this picture off the ground, so I started working on a screenplay with John Milius [*Dillinger, Big Wednesday*]. We both wanted to make a film about the war.

Was that Apocalypse Now?
Yeah. We were working on it when Francis not only got the deal for *THX* but for *Apocalypse Now,* and one to set up American Zoetrope [Coppola's film-production company]. It was exciting. We were going to be able to do just what we wanted. And then came Black Thursday.

Black Thursday?
Yeah. That's what we called it. Francis had borrowed all this money from Warner Brothers to set this thing up, and when the studio saw a rough cut of *THX* and the scripts of the movies we wanted to make, they said, "This is all junk. You have to pay back the money you owe us." Which is why Francis did *Godfather.* He was so much in debt he didn't have any choice.

What happened to you?
I was left high and dry. *THX* had taken three years to make and I hadn't made any money. Marcia was still supporting us, and I thought, "Well, I'll do the rock & roll movie—that's commercial." [*Smiling*] Besides, I was getting a lot of razz from Francis and a bunch of friends who said that everyone thought I was cold and weird and why didn't I do something warm and human. I thought, "You want warm and human, I'll give you warm and human." So I went to Gloria [Katz] and Willard Huyck and they developed the idea for *American Graffiti,* and I took the twelve-page treatment around.

And?
And it was turned down by every studio in town. The situation was pretty grim. Then I got invited to the Cannes Film Festival, because *THX* had been chosen by some radical directors' group. But Warner Brothers wouldn't pay my way. So, with our last $2000, we bought a Eurail Pass, got backpacks and went to Cannes.

But what about American Graffiti?
Well, I decided to stop in New York on the way to Europe and make David Picker, who was then head of United Artists, have a meeting with me, and I did. I told him about my rock & roll movie.

We flew off to England and he called and said, "Okay. I'll take a chance." I met him at his giant suite at the Carlton Hotel in Cannes and we made a two-picture deal for *American Graffiti* and *Star Wars*.

But United Artists didn't make American Graffiti.
I'm getting to that. Bill and Gloria had a chance to direct their own movie, so I hired an other friend to write the script. The first draft wasn't at all what I wanted. It was a desperate situation. I asked Marcia to support us some more. I was borrowing money from friends and relatives. I wrote the script in three weeks, turned it in to UA, and they said, "Not interested." So I took the script — remember, the story treatment had already been turned down by every studio — back to the same studios, which turned it down again. Then Universal said they might be interested if I could get a movie star. I said no. Universal said that even a name producer might do, and they gave me a list of names and Francis was on the list. See, *Godfather* was about to be released, and the whole town was abuzz. Universal, being what it is, was trying to cash in on this real quick. You could see the way they were thinking: "From the man who brought you *The Godfather*." Anyway, Francis said sure. *Godfather* came out and it was a hit.

And the rest is history?
Not quite. Universal wouldn't give us our first check. Francis came very close to financing *American Graffiti* himself. Finally, Universal mellowed. When I first screened *American Graffiti,* one of the executives from Universal came up to me and said, "This movie is not fit to show to an audience." That is what he actually said. Well, Francis blew his cork. In my eyes, it was Francis' most glorious moment. He started screaming and yelling at this guy: "How can you do this to this poor kid? He did this film for nothing, no money! He killed himself, and the first thing you tell him is that it's not fit to show to an audience. Couldn't you say, 'Thank you, you did sort of a good job. Glad you brought it in on budget and on time.'" Francis kept yelling and yelling and he said, "Well, I like this movie. I'll buy it. I'll give you a check for it right now."

Universal took the film, but we still fought and fought. They wanted to take five minutes out of it. Five minutes in a movie is not going to make a difference. It was nothing more than an exercise in authority; Universal saying they had the right.

Did anything good come out of this experience?
[*Laughing*] At the bleakest point in all this, I got an offer to direct. I was writing every day, which I hate, so there was a temptation, but I said no. It went on until the price was $100,000 and points. The most I had ever been paid to direct a movie was $15,000. I said no. It was a real turning point.

What was the movie?
Lady Ice, starring Donald Sutherland. It was a disaster. If I had done that movie, it would have been the end of my career. . . . I felt sort of proud of myself when I said no.

Then American Graffiti *went on and was a hit?*
Not quite. [*Smiling*] I told you it was a long story. It was January 1973. I had been paid $20,000 for *Graffiti,* it had taken two years, I was $15,000 in debt and Universal hated the film so much they were contemplating selling it as a TV Movie of the Week. I had to start paying back some of this money. So I thought, "I'll whip up that treatment, my second deal at United Artists, my little space thing." I did a fifteen-page treatment, showed it to United Artists. No deal. So I took it to Universal.

After what they had put you through?
I hated Universal, but I had to go to them. Part of my deal to make *American Graffiti* was that I had to sign my life over to them for seven years. That's the way they work over there. They owned me. They had first refusal on any idea I had. I showed it to them and they said no. I took it to Laddie [Alan Ladd Jr.] at Fox and he said he would take a chance. [*Laughing*] I was only asking for $10,000 to write the screenplay. In August 1973, *American Graffiti* came out and was a huge hit, and that sort of finished my financial woes once and for all.

What happened to Star Wars*?*
At that point, I was thinking about quitting directing, but I had this huge draft of a screenplay and I had sort of fallen in love with it. Plus, I was a street filmmaker. I had never done a big studio picture, so I thought, "This'll be the last movie I direct." I finally finished the script. I wanted to make a fairy tale epic, but this was like *War and Peace.* So I took that script and cut it in half, put the first half aside and decided to write the screenplay from

the second half. I was on page 170, and I thought, "Holy smokes, I need 100 pages, not 500," but I had these great scenes. So I took that story and cut it into three parts. I took the first part and said, "This will be my script. But no matter what happens, I am going to get these three movies made." [*Laughing*] When I made the deal to write and direct *Star Wars* at Fox, I obviously made it for nothing. All I had was a deal memo, no contract. Then *Graffiti* came out, was a hit and suddenly I was powerful. Fox thought I was going to come back and demand millions of dollars and all these gross points.

Did you?
I said, "I'll do it for the deal memo, but we haven't talked about things like merchandising rights, sequel rights." I said I wasn't going to give up any of those. Fox said fine. They were getting me for less than $100,000.

Did you know then that the merchandising and sequel rights were going to be so valuable?
Well, when I was writing I had had visions of R2-D2 mugs and little windup robots, but I thought that would be the end of it. I went for the merchandising because it was one of the few things left we hadn't discussed. I took everything that hadn't been discussed. All I knew was that I wanted to control the sequel rights because I wanted to make the other two movies.

What is your deal with Fox?
They have first refusal on every *Star Wars* film I want to make.

How many is that?
Seven left.

I guess you really do have reason to hate Hollywood.
They're rather sleazy, unscrupulous people. L.A. is where they make deals, do business in the classic corporate American way, which is screw everybody and do whatever you can to make the biggest profit. They don't care about people. It is incredible the way they treat filmmakers, because they have no idea what making a movie is about. To them, the deal is the movie. They have no idea of the suffering, the hard work. They're not filmmakers. I don't want to have anything to do with them.

But if you want to make movies, don't you have to?
That's why I'm trying to build the ranch.

The ranch?
Yeah, I bought 2000 acres in Lucas Valley, California [no relation] — to build a kind of creative-filmmakers' retreat. The idea for this came out of film school. It was a great environment; a lot of people all very interested in film, exchanging ideas, watching movies, helping each other out. I wondered why we couldn't have a professional environment like that. When you make a movie, it really is a fifteen-hour-a-day thing, and you don't have time to do anything else. If you do it year in and year out, you become a complete nonentity. You need an environment that gets people excited about things, and they don't do that in Hollywood.

What will the ranch look like?
I've always been interested in architecture. [*Smiling*] This is a way of being [an architect] without doing the work. There will be a main building, a big, simple farmhouse. Behind that, shingled outbuildings for the filmmakers and editors. There will be another big building off to the side, sort of tucked away on a hill, where there will be a screening room, recording studio, computer center and more editing rooms. And then, way over on the other side of the property, will be the special-effects building. There will be one other little section down by the road called the farm group, which is a little guest house for visiting dignitaries or whatever.

How much is this going to cost?
No way to project at this point, given the way the world is going. I figure it will take between five and six years and cost in excess of $20 million.

We know you're rich. . . .
That's way beyond my personal resources.

How are you going to do this?
We are taking the profits from *The Empire Strikes Back* and the next film, *Revenge of the Jedi,* and investing them in outside companies, then using those profits to build the ranch and maintain the overhead: It's just the opposite of how studios work. Basically, what we're doing is using the

profits of other companies to subsidize a film company, rather than a film organization subsidizing a conglomerate. My only interest in life is to make films, explore films and grow as a person—if I can just do that and break even and not be forced to make a movie this year, or if I can make a movie that is not commercial at all, not even releasable. Making a movie is very difficult and painful, and if someone comes along after you've done all this work and says you're a fool and an idiot, it's very hard to pick up and do it again.

What happens if The Empire *doesn't make enough money for your ranch?*
Well, if it doesn't happen with this one and the next, then that's the end. I'm not going to spend the next fifteen years of my life trying to make hit movies to get the ranch. If it doesn't, I'll fold up shop. I tried, I failed and I'll just make 16-mm movies and live the way I've been living.

Are you ever going to forgive Universal?
[*Smiling*] I hold grudges. When Warner Brothers cut *THX,* I held a grudge for ten years. After *Star Wars,* they apologized. I said, "Okay, I forgive you." I didn't want to be ridiculous. After *American Graffiti,* Universal tried to be nice to me, but I was really angry and I remain angry to this day.

Are there dangers in working with close friends like Steven Spielberg, who is direct-ing Raiders of the Lost Ark, *which you conceived and will be executive producer of? What if he goes over budget? Will that put a strain on your friendship?*
I don't think that's a problem. We all have large egos. We can be competi-tors and still help each other, respect each other. I try to work with only responsible directors, and Steve is a responsible director. He doesn't mean to go over budget. If you've got something that isn't working, the only way to really solve it is to spend more time and money getting it right.

I understand that your automobile accident when you were eighteen had a major effect on your life. Will you talk about it?
It was right before I graduated from high school and I should have been killed but I wasn't. I was driving a little sports car with a roll bar and racer's seat belt. I was hit, the car rolled, and for some reason the seat belt broke in one of the rolls, just before the car pretzeled itself around a tree. If I had stayed in the car, I would have been dead. When you go through some-

thing like that, it puts a little more perspective on things, like maybe you're here for a reason. [*Smiling*] Maybe I was here to do *Star Wars* and that's it. I'm living on borrowed time.

Coppola seems to have been another big influence on your life.
We respect each other, but at the same time we are totally different personalities. He says he's too crazy and I'm not crazy enough. Francis spends every day jumping off a cliff and hoping he's going to land okay. My main interest is security. It was great when we were together, because we complemented each other. I think we still have that relationship. The fact that he's always doing crazy things influences me, and the fact that I'm always sort of building a foundation, plodding along, influences him. But the goals we have in mind are the same. We want to make movies and be free from the yoke of the studios.

Are you having fun being head of Lucasfilms, a big corporation?
No. I don't want to be a businessman. My ambition is to make movies, but all by myself, to shoot them, cut them, make stuff I want to, just for my own exploration, to see if I can combine images in a certain way. My movies will go back to the way my first films were, which dealt a little more realistically with the human condition.

And how do you feel about the human condition?
I am very cynical, and as a result, I think the defense I have against it is to be optimistic and to think people are basically good, although I know in my heart they're not.

Oh, dear. Let's get back to The Empire Strikes Back *for a moment. In the movie, Ben says Luke is the last hope and Yoda says no, there is another.*
Yes. [*Smiling*] There is another, and has been for a long time. You have to remember, we're starting in the middle of this whole story. There are six hours' worth of events before *Star Wars,* and in those six hours, the "other" becomes apparent, and after the third film, the "other" becomes apparent quite a bit.

What will happen to Luke?
I can't say. In the next film, everything gets resolved one way or the other. Luke won the first battle in the first film. Vadar won the second battle in

the second film, and in the third film, only one of them walks away. We have to go back to the very beginning to find out the real problem.

What about the actors? Are they under contract?
Some are, but it doesn't matter. I am not going to force anyone to make a movie. [*Smiling*] I'm not Universal Pictures.

Do you have story lines for the seven Star Wars *movies left to be done?*
Yes, twelve-page outlines.

How can you think that far ahead?
[*Laughing*] Marcia says I either live in the past or in the future, never in the present. I'm always sort of living for tomorrow, for better or for worse. [*Shrugs*] It's just a personality quirk.

The George Lucas Saga

KERRY O'QUINN/1981

It was invigorating. The air was cool, and the Sun was warm. It was the kind of weather that gives people a reason to move to northern California.

I steered my car into the parking lot of the large brick building spread out in a quiet suburban community near the foot of a rugged chain of mountains. I stood outside for a moment and looked at the building.

Well, what did I expect? Maybe a flashing neon sign proclaiming, "You have arrived at Industrial Light & Magic — the special effects home of Star Wars *and* The Empire Strikes Back!"

What I actually found was no sign at all. In fact, no clue that inside these walls were the administrative staff, the artists and technicians who make the TIE's fly and Taun-tauns gallop. From the outside, everything looked totally unmagical.

Inside, surrounding the reception room, is a cluster of business offices, and down a long hallway behind locked doors are storyboard studios and rooms filled with model spaceships, miniature landscapes, matte cameras — all with such tight security that even the Los Angeles employees of Lucasfilm Ltd. cannot get inside those doors.

I identified myself: "I have an appointment with George Lucas." I was a half-hour early, so I sat down and began leafing through my notes. Suddenly I heard a bright "Hi!" I looked up. . . .

From *Starlog,* appearing in three installments in the July, August, and September 1981 issues. Reprinted by permission of the author.

Well, what did I expect? Maybe a John Williams fanfare—maybe a towering figure like Lord Vader—maybe the booming voice of a millionaire corporate executive—maybe the wise-cracking, sweet-talking jargon of a Hollywood moviemaker—maybe I expected a mighty handshake that I would still feel the next day.

What I saw was a man in his thirties, of modest build with a pleasant, smiling face and the familiar glasses, beard, jeans and sneakers I had always seen him wearing in photos. He seemed almost embarrassed by the occasion.

ILM's production manager, Tom Smith, was kind enough to loan us his office (George doesn't even have an office there) so, like everyone else, we could sit down behind closed doors.

KERRY O'QUINN: *Let me tell you why I wanted this interview. When I was growing up, Walt Disney was a very important person to me—not just because his movies entertained me and excited me about life, but because the man created his own world—built from nothing but determination and imagination. It was a wonderful lesson to me, and I think that you have that same sort of influence on today's youth. Not only your work, but you as a person. And yet you are not a well-known quantity to most people—certainly not to our readers. I'm here to get to know you as a human being. I want you to reveal yourself in any way you're willing and to say whatever you want. I'm interested in your soul and for you to share some of it with STARLOG.*

GEORGE LUCAS: All right, fine. I have to admit that I read STARLOG. Starting in 1973 I was very much focused on science fiction—the genre people, the conventions, the magazines, every fantasy thing I could get my hands on—to see where everybody's head was. And I've sort of continued it.

KOQ: *What are you doing these days?*

GL: I get up very early each morning and go to work writing the next *Star Wars*—*Revenge of the Jedi*—until early that afternoon. Next, I work on *Raiders of the Lost Ark*. I was editing the film, and now I'm helping with the special effects here—sort of checking in at ILM and letting them know what they can send to Steve Spielberg, who is directing *Raiders* in Los Angeles, and what needs a little more work. After that, I usually have to go to my office, read my mail and answer my phone calls and do all my business.

Then, usually around 6:00 pm is when I have any meetings I have to have. And that's about the way my life is today.

Next week I'm going to London to look for a director for *Revenge* and to listen to the score of *Raiders*. And it just continues like that.

KOQ: *So you're pre-producing and post-producing right now. It sounds like 12-hour days.*

GL: At least! I'm lucky if I can get a 12-hour day, and unfortunately, for the last few months, it's also been seven days a week. Although it's business, I count this (upcoming) trip to London as a weekend off—even though I'll be on an airplane most of the time.

KOQ: *Are you aware of the fact that you are a kind of cultural hero to a lot of today's youth—not to mention some of today's adults?*

GL: Yes, I'm aware of it. I get a lot of mail, and I get a lot of kids coming up to me on the street and in restaurants. I didn't get into the movie business with any anticipation of becoming famous. It happened despite my best efforts, and it's something I don't really want. It's something I have to go through, but ultimately I'm just someone who makes movies—like someone who builds buildings. I haven't any desire at all to have a spotlight focused on me, but unfortunately the success I have had has made me too visible.

KOQ: *Is it monetary success that draws the spotlight to you?*

GL: I think it's *all* monetary with *People* magazine and those kinds of things. They don't care about the movies. They just care about "Gee, this guy's real rich!" But I think the kids are interested because they *like* the film, they're amazed by it, and, therefore, impressed by me.

KOQ: Gone with the Wind *was big box office too, but it didn't make Victor Fleming a cult hero. Producers and directors are fairly invisible people. Generally, it's the stars that fans idolize.*

GL: As I said, when I became a director I assumed that I was going to be able to remain anonymous, but I got shoved into problems because of the monetary success; the fact that the film was the biggest hit in history made everything focus on me because it was an achievement—being "number one." If that hadn't happened, I think the kids still would have been impressed because *Star Wars* was designed as a film for young people, and very few films are being made like that today. It was done with all the energy and intelligence and thought that I could muster. It was *not* done like "Oh, this is just a kid's movie, so we don't have to worry about it." It was done like "This is going to be the best movie that can possibly be made under the circumstances." I think that because of that attitude *Star Wars* turns out to shine among all the other films that are done in the science-fiction genre.

KOQ: *The spotlight is on you, and you are not rushing toward it. Why? Is it a personal reluctance or is it a practical problem?*

GL: It's both. If I did all the interviews that are asked of me and answered all the letters that come to me, I wouldn't have time to do anything else—literally! I try to pick a few interviews to do each year, just so everyone doesn't think I'm a recluse and call me a hermit. But I am a very shy person. I don't do very well in large groups. I was terrible in speech class. In fact, the things that, for most kids, are the terror of their lives, were also the terror of *my* life—and still are. You always assume that when you become an adult you'll be able to speak at Rotary meetings and that sort of thing. It doesn't happen. At least with me it hasn't.

KOQ: *I've found that shyness turns out to be a very nice and often promising characteristic in young people. Perhaps the lack of social activity is replaced by more mental activity.*

GL: I think so. The advantage I had when I was young—younger than I am now—is that being shy, I was fairly quiet, being quiet, most people thought I was fairly smart. I listened a lot. You know, in Japan, if you don't talk, they think you're a genius. In this country, I think most people like to talk more than listen. So someone who listens is more easily liked by those who enjoy talking—because they have someone to talk to. I've discovered that most people who talk a lot make fools of themselves. So, if you don't talk too much, it makes you more intelligent than you really are.

KOQ: *When you were young—younger than you are now—what kind of things did you enjoy most?*

GL: One of my favorite things were Republic serials and things like *Flash Gordon*. I'd watch them and say, "This is fantastic!" There was a television program called "Adventure Theater" at 6:00 every night. We didn't have a TV set, so I used to go over to a friend's house, and we watched it religiously every night. It was a twenty-minute serial chapter, and the left-over minutes of the half-hour was filled with "Crusader Rabbit." I loved it. I read *Tommy Tomorrow* and, of course, lots of (other) comics.

KOQ: *What kind?*

GL: Mostly the DC comics—*Batman* and *Superman*. But I was also real keen on *Donald Duck* and *Scrooge McDuck* and that sort of thing. And I loved *Amazing Stories* and those other science-fiction pulps that were around at that time.

KOQ: *Any particular novels?*

GL: I wasn't a reader when I was young. I was more of a picture-oriented type of person. I read a few books like *Treasure Island* and *Swiss Family Robinson*—that sort of thing.

KOQ: *Certain people would think of those as rather un-profound influences. Does it bother you when critics say Lucas has created mental "junk food" or that* Star Wars *is nothing but an old-fashioned formula?*

GL: When you look at *Star Wars* it seems extremely simplistic, but it's like most successful creations: you struggle and you struggle and you struggle—for the obvious! You finally get there, and you say, "Why didn't I think of this six months ago?" But it requires quite a thought process to get down to the obvious. It's very difficult because it isn't that obvious when you start out.

Now, people look at *Star Wars,* and they say, "Oh, that's simple—there's nothing to it." They say it's like this movie or that movie. But the truth is, it isn't like any other movie. People have a tendency to think that it was just a formula—"Oh, he just took *The Wizard of Oz* and turned it inside out." But if you look at those two movies, they are totally different ideas. I mean, you can see certain similarities between almost any two movies. But coming up with a basic idea and developing it and making it work is very difficult and not to be underestimated.

Now, nobody likes critics. Stanley Kubrick told me he used to be concerned with what critics say. But he stopped getting upset when he realized that he spent three years developing an idea—working on it day and night—then somebody walks in and sees the film for two hours and spends a half-hour writing a review of it. So, the critic spends a total of 2½ hours on something that you spent three years on. Kubrick said that after he realized that, critics held no interest for him.

Critics are entitled to their opinions, and a lot of times what they say is true. It's just that they don't realize the effort and pain and struggling that went into something. A friend of mine made a film at the North Pole, and whether I think the film is great or not, I would say, "That is an achievement!" That's a very difficult thing to do. It's like the Alaska pipeline; it's something that was a lot of work, and you can't ridicule it and say it's nothing! The guys who made that film were up there in 50-below-zero, trying to make cameras turn-over and make polar bears do what they wanted them to do. And critics forget that.

KOQ: *In the case of* Star Wars—*forgetting the behind-the-scenes struggles that you know went into the making it—is the finished product an important film?*
GL: That's a hard question to answer....

KOQ: *Has the film changed lives?*
GL: I assume it has. I have my own personal feelings about what I think of the movie, but....

KOQ: *What are they?*
GL: I don't want to upset your readers too much, but it's just a movie. It's no big deal. From a technical point of view—my own point of view—I don't think it's altogether that well-made a movie, because I was working under extremely difficult conditions.

In film school, a student would show his workshop project, and someone would say, "Gee that doesn't make sense to me...." And the filmmaker would go into a dissertation of explanations, "Well, that day the sound man didn't show up, and the landlady came in and ran us out, and I just had time to get this one angle, etc." And the instructor would say, "Well, put it on a title card at the head of the film. Say 'This is why the movie is the way it is—because we had all these problems.'"

For what it was, *Star Wars* was made very inexpensively—a real low-budget movie—and it was very, very difficult getting things to work. The truth is that the robots didn't work at all. 3-PO works very painfully—and during the whole shooting of the picture I couldn't get R2 to go more than three feet without running into something. So you'll notice in the film that he moves very little. The 2nd Unit came back here to ILM and rebuilt the robot, and we took him out to Death Valley and actually got some shots of him going more than three feet. So in the beginning there are actually a few shots of him going somewhere. You get the impression that he moves through the whole movie, but he doesn't.

Everything was a prototype on the first movie, like "Gee, we're going to build this—we have no money, but have to try to make this work." But nothing really worked. On *Empire* we improved the size of the robot, and we managed to make things work a little bit better. We still had problems, but at least R2 could go down the road and his head would turn.

KOQ: *As long as you got the illusion across, how you really did it is just your concern. The audience was obviously not disappointed.*
GL: I'm sort of baffled by the movie, I have to admit. I mean, I expected it to be moderately successful film—like a Disney movie, or something like that. That's really all I expected of it. And the fact that it became such a popular film and appeals to people over 14 years old—it still amazes me!

KOQ: *So you weren't really expecting this kind of success. Is that why you ran off to Hawaii to avoid the premiere of* Star Wars?
GL: The main reason for that was that I worked on the film right up until the day it opened. In fact, I was mixing sound on foreign versions of the film the day it opened here. I had been working so hard that, truthfully, I forgot the film was being released that day. My wife was mixing *New York, New York* at night at the same place we were mixing during the day, so at 6:00 she came in for the night shift just as I was leaving on the day shift. So we ran off to grab dinner at Hamburger Hamlet, which, by coincidence, is right across the street from the Chinese Theatre—and there was a huge line around the block. I said, "What's that?" I had forgotten completely, and I really couldn't believe it. But I had planned a vacation as soon as I finished, and I'm glad I did because I really didn't want to be around for all the craziness that happened after that.

I think I'd do that on *every* film, because you don't want to be around for people to call and say, "Gee, what a terrible movie—what a disaster! Did you read what Vince Canby said about you . . . ?" And if it becomes a big hit, you don't have to put up with all the people calling with, "Oh, wow, I really loved your movie...." The people who usually call and say that, are really not the people you want to talk to.

KOQ: *So, your satisfaction comes not from the acclaim?*
GL: The satisfaction is in the movie. So far, every movie I've made is the movie I *wanted* to make, and I've been happy with it—*THX, American Graffiti, Star Wars, Empire* and now *Raiders*. I look at a film in the rough cut for the first time, and so far it's always turned out to be what I wanted the movie to be. I mean, I can argue technically about how well, or not, the film is made—about story points, ideas—but if I get an enjoyment out of it, then I say, OK, I'm happy. It does what I wanted it to do. And I don't really care about the premiere or the critics or all the rest of it....

KOQ: *Do you have any free time to goof off nowadays?*
GL: No, unfortunately.

KOQ: *Can't you take a vacation or go to the beach?*
GL: When I started out in film school, it was 24-hours a day, seven days a week—that was all I thought about and did. I didn't do *anything* else! Then when I started working professionally and got married, I *had* to work all the time in order just to get anywhere. And I didn't have a vacation until I finished my first film and went to Europe. I had a couple of bucks in the bank, and I said, "It's now or never." My wife had been bugging me. I'd been at it for four or five years straight, and she said, "You can't go on like this." That was in 1973. I didn't have another vacation until 1977—when I went to Hawaii, after *Star Wars*.

My wife likes to have vacations. She doesn't like not to be able to go anywhere, year in and year out. She'd like to be able to say, "Look, let's take off for two or three weeks and just cool out." So I *promised her* that after *Star Wars* every year we'd take two vacations—two to three weeks each year. That lasted for one year. Now, I try to get in one vacation a year, for a week or so, it always comes down to saying, "Next week. Just let me get past this thing...." By the time you get past this thing, there's always something else, and you can't leave. Now, 1983 is my goal; I intend to take off for a year, if I can, and just not do anything. And that is why I'm not planning any other projects.

KOQ: *How is the* Revenge *script coming?*
GL: It's coming. . . .

KOQ: *Is it easier than the last time?*
GL: No. They never get easier. They only get harder.

KOQ: *Is this trilogy going to wrap up a story?*
GL: Yes, definitely.

KOQ: *No cliff-hanger this time?*
GL: No cliff-hanger. The original idea kind of got segmented, and the fact that the story is a fairy tale kind of got lost, especially in the beginning, because the science fiction took over. I kept saying, "Don't call it science fiction!" I think that *Revenge*, for better or worse, is going to put the whole thing in perspective. I don't know whether people are going to like it that much, but the truth of it is, that's the way the film was originally designed. I think people have perceived it sort of different from the way it really is, and in this one it becomes obvious what it was all along—which, essentially, is a fairy tale.

KOQ: *Is it going to shift gears significantly?*
GL: It doesn't shift gears; it goes down the road, but what happens is, I should say, more obvious than most people think. It's not nearly as complicated. As I say, it started out as a simple fairy tale, and that's all it really is. It doesn't go off into some crazy . . . thing. It's really a little bit more controlled than you might think. When it comes out, people will say, "Oh, my God. How obvious! Why couldn't they think of something more interesting than that?" But I'm stuck with the way it was originally planned, and I can't suddenly go off on some tangent.

All I can do is make the movie, and people will either love it or hate it, and there is nothing I can do about it—because it is what it is. If a mistake was made, it was made six years ago. And it will be another two or three years before people find out about it.

KOQ: *Is there going to be character continuity among all three trilogies?*
GL: No—possibly the robots, but they weren't originally designed to go through the whole . . . nobody was designed to go through all three. I'd like to see the robots go through them, but I don't know whether they will.

KOQ: *What will provide the continuity then?*

GL: Well, the next trilogy—the first one—since it's about Ben Kenobi as a young man, is the same character, just a different actor. And it's the same thing with all the characters. Luke ends up in the third film of the first trilogy just three-and-a-half years old. There is a continuity with characters, in other words, but not with actors—and the look of the films will be different.

The first trilogy will not be as much of an action adventure kind of thing. Maybe we'll make it have some humor, but right now it's much more humorless than this one. This one is where all the excitement is, which is why I started with it. The other ones are a little more Machiavellian—it's all plotting—more of a mystery. I think we'll try, on the next one, to write all three scripts at once. Then they can come out every other year instead of every three years. Doing it the way we do it now, we race through one, and as soon as we finish one we race into the next one, and we go as fast as we can. We just barely get it done in time, and we race right into the next one. At ILM, they get six-month breaks between movies, but it's a non-stop race for me and for the main production people.

KOQ: *Here at ILM, you have formed a kind of repertory company—unlike most films, where people are hired free-lance for the duration of the project and they they leave and go on to another film.*

GL: Yes, it helps to have the same group of people that you work with because they know you. And in the case of *Star Wars*, the vocabulary is so unique that to bring someone in from the outside takes a long time to clue them in. If I say "Jawa," people here know what a Jawa is—they know how tall he is, what he looks like, how he talks. If I say we're going to have R2 do this and this and this, they know whether R2 can do that—as opposed to someone coming in from the outside who would just sit there and scratch their head and say, "Well, all right . . . !" The people here know what I like and what I don't like; it saves a lot of time.

KOQ: *Communication is important to all filmmaking, but especially in a series like* Star Wars. *The man at the helm really must get his ideas across to a lot of other creative people. Seems like that would be especially difficult for a shy person.*

GL: I am now in a situation where I have to do a lot of talking, and I am amazed that I do what I do—because it is alien to the way I am as a person. I would never have thought that I would end up being a director of films. When I was 16, if you had said I could do this—direct films—I'd have said, "Impossible—I can't communicate with people that well." I don't like being the General, but I ended up doing it. When you care about something, the idea and the talk automatically come. There's really nothing to talk about except what I want—whatever vision I have—and that's easy. Directing is a reaction to everything—I have to make at least a thousand decisions a day. A thousand people coming up to you every day—and this is not an exaggeration—saying, "Red or blue?" And you have to say, at that moment, with about 15 seconds to make up your mind, "OK, blue." And if they have reasons that it should be different, they say so, and you have another 15 seconds to analyze that. I guess that ultimately your level of success is how many of those are the right decisions and how many are the wrong decisions. If you can make the right decisions, you end up with a good movie. And if you make the wrong decisions, you end up with a terrible movie.

KOQ: *If, at 16, you had no idea that you could direct movies, what were you passionately interested in doing in terms of career?*
GL: I wanted to be a race driver at 16. I was a mechanic in a foreign car service, and my ambition was to be a race driver—sports cars, Formula One. That was it; that was my whole life. I lived, ate, breathed cars! That was everything to me.

> *Most of us don't realize it until we are mature adults looking back on our professional work, but from the first moment we are able to form concepts in our mind we are accumulating and recording experiences from our life. Everything that fascinates us, thrills us, frightens us— everything that we find exciting in life goes into that vast, complex storehouse in our head—the subconscious.*
>
> *As youngsters we are generally wide-eyed and eager for all life has to show us, soaking up everything in sight like a greedy sponge. If we are extremely perceptive in our observations—aware of fine details and emotional qualities—later we can retrieve our most memorable experiences and use them to form a picture of life that contains our own unique personal perspective.*

If we do this skillfully and the vision communicates objectively to others, we are called — artist.

We must never underestimate the value of our smallest, most off-beat experiences. The more doors we open in life, the more our subconscious is stocked with a richness of visions that may turn up in unexpected and surprisingly important places later in life.

K O Q : *That's a long way from* Star Wars! *What was the evolution? What were the steps?*

G L : I was in an accident the day before I was going to graduate from high school. I spent some time in the hospital, and I realized that it probably wouldn't be smart for me to be a race driver — especially after this accident. Before that first accident you are very oblivious to the danger because you don't realize how close to the edge you are. But once you've gone over the edge and you realize what's on the other side, it changes your perspective. I was in a club with a lot of guys who were race drivers — one of 'em went on and drove at LeMans — and he eventually quit too because of the same thing. You see what the future is there, and you realize that you'll probably end up being dead. That's where most of them end up; it's inevitable, because the odds are if you stay with it long enough that's what will happen to you. And I just decided that maybe that wasn't for me. I decided I'd settle down and go to school.

Meantime, I still had all my friends in racing; I was still interested in racing, so I started doing a lot of photography at the races — rather than driving or being in a pit crew. I had always been interested in art, and I'd been very good at it. My father didn't see much of a career in being an artist, so he discouraged me from that whole thing. When I went to junior college I got very interested in the social sciences — psychology, sociology, anthropology — that area. But it was really by a fluke that I ended up going to the University of Southern California and getting into the film business.

I had been interested in photography and art, and a very close friend of mine, who I grew up with ever since I was four-years-old was going to go to SC and asked me to take the test with him. I was going to go to San Francisco State and become an anthropology major or something like that. And he said, "They've got a film school down there, and it's great 'cause you can do photography." So I said, "Well, all right, but it's a long shot 'cause my grades are not good enough to get into a school like that." So I went and took the test and I passed. I got accepted!

At about that same time, I had been working on a race car for Haskell Wexler, and I met him, and he influenced me in the direction of cinematography—being a cameraman. So the idea wasn't that remote. I said, "Yeah, I know a cinematographer, and I like photography, and maybe that wouldn't be a bad thing to get into." But I didn't know anything at all about the movies at that point. Just what I saw on television, and going to the movies once a week, but I wasn't a big fan. I wasn't that much of a film addict.

K O Q : *Had you done any writing? Was that in your background in any way?*
G L : No. I was a terrible writer. I mean, I had taken some creative writing classes, normal English, and all the things you end up taking—and if I had gone to San Francisco State I might have become an English major. But I had no intention of becoming a writer. I was always terrible in English.

K O Q : *Were there courses in script writing or something of that sort along the way at USC, or how is it that you are a good writer now?*
G L : I don't think I am a good writer now. I think I'm a *terrible* writer. The whole writing thing is something I was very bad at—I can barely spell my own name, let alone form a sentence—and I struggled through English classes. I went to SC as a photographer—I wanted to be a cameraman—but obviously at film school you have to do everything: cinematography, editing and script writing. Well, I did terrible in script writing classes, because I hated script writing. I hated stories, and I hated plot, and I wanted to make visual films that had nothing to do with telling a story.

I was a difficult student. I got into a lot of trouble all the time because of that attitude. I felt I could make a movie out of *anything*; I mean, give me the phone book, and I'll make a movie out of it. I didn't want to know about stories and plot and characters and all that sort of stuff. And that's what I did. My first films were very abstract—tone poems, visual.

In film school I learned editing and I really got hooked on editing at that point, and that sort of became my whole life, and I loved what you can do with editing. After film school I went out looking for a job and I couldn't find one anywhere and I worked as a grip—you know a guy that carries things around—on a couple of independent productions. I worked

THX 1138, 1970

Maggie McOmie and Robert Duvall, *THX 1138*, 1970

Richard Dreyfuss and Bo Hopkins, *American Graffiti*, 1973

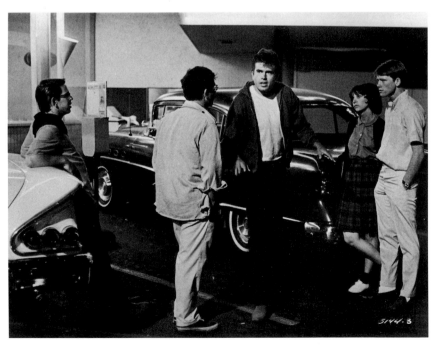

Charlie Martin Smith, Richard Dreyfuss, Paul Le Mat, Cindy Williams, and Ron Howard, *American Graffiti*, 1973

Mark Hamill, Carrie Fisher, and Harrison Ford, *Star Wars*, 1977

David Prowse and Mark Hamill, *The Empire Strikes Back*, 1980

John Rhys-Davies and Harrison Ford, *Raiders of the Lost Ark*, 1981

Carrie Fisher and Mark Hamill, *Return of the Jedi*, 1983

Howard T. Duck, *Howard the Duck*, 1986

Sean Connery and Harrison Ford, *Indiana Jones and the Last Crusade*, 1989

as a freelance cameraman for various people. I worked for Saul Bass on a film called *Why Man Creates*.

Then I got a job cutting, as an assistant editor, on a USIA project for President Johnson on his trip to Asia. Then I got moved up to being editor, and in the process of all that I decided that I wanted to be a director. I really didn't like people telling me how to do this and how to do that—you know, carrying out someone else's ideas that I really didn't think were so great. It was frustrating.

In the meantime I was also teaching at SC—a class in photography—and then I decided to go back to graduate school. I was there for one more semester and did many more movies, but still non-story-type films. I was interested in abstract, purely visual films and cinema-verite documentaries. I won a couple of scholarships at the end of that semester—one to watch Carl Foreman make *McKenna's Gold* out in the desert and make a little behind-the-scenes movie, and the other was a Warner Brothers scholarship in which you observe movie-making for six months.

After being on *McKenna's Gold* for a couple of months—well, it takes about a week of watching for you to get bored. After that you've seen everything you could possible see about making a movie. Watching does not teach you anything, so when I got to Warner Brothers I wasn't interested in watching them make movies, but they assigned me to *Finian's Rainbow*, which was the only picture they were making there at the time.

Francis Ford Coppola was directing *Finian's Rainbow*. I was there for a couple of weeks trying to get off the picture—saying I really wanted to go over to the animation department. But animation was empty; there wasn't anybody there except one guy who was sort of head of the department and he would just sit in his office and twiddle his thumbs all day. But I figured if I could get over there with all those cameras and stuff I could swipe some film somewhere and make a movie.

When Francis found that I was trying to get off the picture—I told him why—and he said, "Listen kid, you come up with one good idea a day, and I'll give you a lot of other things to do."

KOQ: *Did you know Coppola prior to that?*
GL: No. And the first couple of weeks on the set he saw this bearded kid wandering around—at that time in the film industry there were very few young people. Francis and I were about the only two on the film under 50

years old, and we'd both been to film school and both had the same kind
of background, so we could relate to each other.

KOQ: *How old were you then?*

GL: Let's see—I was about 22. Francis's main areas of expertise were directing actors and writing—and mine was primarily in camera and editing.
So we interfaced very well and complimented each other. I became his
assistant, and I helped him with the editing, and I'd go around with the
Polaroid and shoot angles, and that sort of thing.

In the meantime I was trying to get a movie off the ground, because
Carl Foreman had been impressed with the movie I'd made for him, so I was
talking to him about this other project I wanted to do which was based on
a short subject I did in school—*THX-1138.* So Francis heard about that too,
and he said, "Well, look, I'll do it for you." He said he'd get me a deal to
write the screenplay. I said, "I can't write the screenplay. I'm not a writer.
I can't possibly write it!"

And he said, "Look—if you're going to make it in this industry, you've
got to learn how to write. You can't direct without knowing how to write.
So you're going to sit down, and you're going to learn how to write!"

So they chained me to my desk and I wrote this screenplay. Agonizing
experience! It always is. I finished it, read it and said, "This is awful." I
said, "Francis, I'm not a writer. This is a terrible script." He read it and said,
"You're right. This is a terrible script." So he and I sat down together and
re-wrote it, and it still was a pretty bad script. I said, "Look, we've got to
get a writer." So we hired a writer to work on the project—a playwright
who'd written some stuff for films. I worked with him and gave him the
screenplay, and we talked about it, and he wrote a script, and it was all
right—it just wasn't anything at all what I wanted the movie to be. It was
a completely different idea from the type of movie that I was trying to
make—which was surreal and abstract.

You know, I had this idea and I just couldn't express it. I tried to express
it to the writer, and he tried to give it back to me, but his script was just
not what I wanted. It was worse than what I'd done. So after that experience I realized that if the script was going to be written the way I wanted
it, I was going to have to write it myself. So a friend of mine from school,
Walter Murch, sat down with me, and we wrote the screenplay—and it
was still pretty esoteric and weird, but it was good enough to make into a

movie—the one that finally got made—*THX-1138*. Francis talked Warner Brothers into going with it, and that's really how I got into writing.

My second project was *Apocalypse Now* which John Milius and I had been working on in school, and we got a deal with Francis to develop that project. So I said, "This is great; I love John Milius; he's a terrific writer." I was going to get a great screenplay, and I wasn't going to have to write it. Finally, I had somebody better than me. But we couldn't get it off the ground, and I wanted to do this rock 'n' roll cruising movie, but I didn't want to write it.

I had some good friends of mine, Bill and Gloria Huyck, to whom I told the story, and we worked on it and did a story treatment, and I peddled it around and tried to get money to have a screenplay written. This went on for seven or eight months, and I couldn't get anybody interested in putting up a very small amount of money to do a screenplay. Finally I went to New York and I talked to the head of United Artists and convinced him it was going to be a great movie, and they gave us a little tiny bit of money, and I called back Bill and Gloria, and they said, "Gee, we've got a chance to direct a film and we really don't want to write that now."

Actually, I was in New York on my way to Europe—*THX* had been included in a kind of off-shoot of the Cannes Film Festival....

KOQ: *Had* THX *opened here at that time?*
GL: Yes, it had come and gone. But I had been invited to a directors' part of the festival over there. Warners wasn't going to send me, and I couldn't get *American Graffiti* off the ground, and I'd never been out of the country—so my wife and I just put our backpacks on and took off and said, "What the heck!" We took our last $1,000 and split.

So I called another friend of mine from school, and he was funny and a good writer, and I said, "Hey, here's the story treatment. I'm over here in Europe, and I'm going to come back in a month, and I want to try to get going on this thing as quickly as I can." So I came back and read his draft of the screenplay, and, again, it wasn't badly written—it was just not at all what I wanted the movie to be. It was a totally different kind of movie—instead of drag racing, they were playing "chicken" and things that didn't relate at all to the way I grew up.

Given a story treatment that's fairly specific, it's amazing how completely different you can get a screenplay. You couldn't even recognize it.

So I said "Oh my God, I'm not going to make this script into a movie. For me, this is terrible." Well, I had already paid him the money I had to do the screenplay, so I was forced to sit down and write the screenplay I wanted. I mean I had to turn in a script to UA, but I didn't want to turn in this one because what if they liked it and wanted to do it? I sure didn't want to do it.

So, again, I was sort of forced into writing against my will—kicking and screaming. I wrote the screenplay to *American Graffiti* in three weeks—fairly quickly. I was in debt. As I said, we spent our last thousand dollars going to Europe, and we came back with absolutely no money, and I was borrowing from my parents and from friends and finally Marcia got a job as an assistant editor so that sort of sustained us through that period. It was a very rough time for me.

THX had come out and sort of done OK—but it didn't set the world on fire, and everybody in Hollywood thought I was this weird science fiction director and very cold. So I wasn't getting offered very many pictures. As a matter of fact I wasn't getting offered *any*.

I did get offered some weird off-the-wall project. When I think back on it it must have been some sort of test. They kept calling and offering a lot of money for me to direct it, and I kept turning them down. I was right in the middle of writing *Graffiti,* but they kept calling and saying they would up their offer. They had it up to $100,000 to direct this film. Now, I had made $10,000 to write *and* direct *THX,* and that took me three years, so I was used to making three or four thousand dollars a year and I was broke, and they kept offering me all this money, but I kept turning them down and I'm glad that I did because *Graffiti* was essentially the movie that I *wanted* to make. I would have been very unhappy just taking the job and taking the money and doing it because of a chance to direct.

When I finished *Graffiti* I took that screenplay around—United Artists turned it down, they said, "No, we don't want to do this movie." So I went around again to all the studios, and everybody turned it down again. And this was another six or seven months of beating on doors before we finally got Universal interested. They said, "We sorta like the screenplay, but we've got to get a name connected." So I got Francis connected to it, and it got made.

Star Wars was a little bit different, because by that time I'd decided that it was useless to try to get someone else to write my screenplays.

KOQ: *You finally gave up...*
GL: Yeah, I finally gave up!

KOQ: *And created* Star Wars.
GL: And struggled with *Star Wars* for about two-and-a-half years, it took me to write it. It was really awful. It was every day, five days a week, eight hours a day, sitting there writing. And I wrote draft after draft. I kept saying, "This is terrible," and I kept changing, trying to come up with the right story. . . .

KOQ: *Were you setting out to make an exciting adventure or deliver a message or what?*
GL: With my first film I wanted to show the mess we've made of the world and *THX* sort of got a following, but it wasn't a *big* successful movie, and it didn't move people very much.

KOQ: *But your motivation was largely a message?*
GL: Oh, yeah, wanting to change the world and trying to say, "Look, we've got to change the way we live." That film did not accomplish that at all. So then I said, "Well, maybe I'll take that message and wrap it up in a completely different guise." I wanted to do this rock 'n' roll movie about cruising, which at the time I described more as a sociological study of the American mating ritual that nobody had ever put on film before. I felt that no matter what the story was, at least we'd have a lot of good music that would keep me entertained.

KOQ: *So what was your motivation with* Star Wars?
GL: Well, *American Graffiti* was a rather horrendous experience for me. It was 28 days of shooting at night—very, very difficult conditions—and I'm not really a "night person" and making a film in that short a time with all sorts of cars—it was a very complicated thing. I found myself saying, "I don't really like directing that much. This is no fun!" What I really like is editing; that's what I can really sit and do and lose track of time and enjoy myself. Directing is very difficult because you're making a thousand decisions—there are no hard fast answers—and you're dealing with *people*, sometimes very difficult people, emotional people—I just didn't enjoy it. So I was going to retire after that. . . .

But when I finished *American Graffiti* again I was broke. I had got paid twice what I made for *THX* — $20,000 for *Graffiti,* but it took me two years to do it, so when you take taxes out there was not much left. So by the time I was finished, I was out of money again. My wife was working, and we were trying to make ends meet, so I said, "I've got to get another picture going here — just to survive." So that's when I decided that what I wanted to do was a children's film.

It was a very eccentric idea at the time. Everyone said, "Why don't you make another *THX*? Why don't you make some kind of *Taxi Driver* movie? Some kind of important movie." But I said, "No, no — I think I'll just go off in some completely different direction." My first movie had been made in the streets, using absolutely nothing, and I thought before I retire I want to make one real movie — you know, on sound stages with sets, the way they used to make movies.

I'd had this idea for doing a space adventure. In the process of going through film school you end up with a little stack of ideas for great movies that you'd love to make, and I picked that one off and said, "This space epic is the one I want to do." Like *American Graffiti,* it was such an *obvious* thing that I was just amazed that nobody had ever done it before. The closest thing that had ever come to it was, say, *Forbidden Planet.* But nobody had made this kind of movie, apart from the Republic Serials like *Flash Gordon.* So I said, "I'll make this because I'd like to see it, and nobody else is ever going to make it."

In the process of doing *American Graffiti* and getting so many letters from young people saying, "Wow, this film really changed my life; I finally figured out what being a teenager is all about," I realized that film had a far greater impact — and accomplished what I was trying to accomplish in my first film. I kept getting these letters saying, "Gee, I was lost, but now I know what I'm doing." And I thought, "Great!" So after that, when *American Graffiti* became a hit, it renewed my faith in *Star Wars.*

I said, "This is the kind of movie we need. There needs to be a kind of film that expresses the mythological realities of life — the deeper psychological movements of the way we conduct our lives that are evident in fairy tales." Nobody has been doing that. The more I researched it, the more I realized how important it was, and the more dedicated I became to actually pulling it off.

KOQ: *From what you're saying. I gather you had learned how to put something across that you could consider important, but that also had very strong entertainment values.*

GL: Yes. *American Graffiti* was not very traditionally plotted—it was a very off-the-wall sort of movie. No one had every really made a movie which was four or five stories, not told sequentially—nobody had tried to interweave four stories and jumble them all up. That was one of the problems that I had in getting this film off the ground. Everyone said, "This is crazy. This is a musical montage. This isn't a movie—it has no score, no plot, no characters." So I said, "My next film I'm going to do a real plotted movie just like everybody else does. I tell you I can do it!"

My challenge on *American Graffiti* was something Francis threw out to me. He said, "Look, everybody thinks that you are some cold science fiction guy—*a real cold fish.* Why don't you do something warm and human?"

So I said, "OK. I'll prove that I'm *not* what everybody thinks I am." So I did that, and then I said, "Now, the goal is to make a *real* movie—with a plot and characters, a story—all that stuff. So that is what I tried to do with *Star Wars.*

KOQ: *Do you think that the* Star Wars *saga is going to have an influence on the youth of today?*

GL: It's obvious that it's had some kind of influence, the same way *Flash Gordon* had on me. I don't know—maybe some kid will grow up and make a terrific science fiction film 10 years from now....

KOQ: *It'll have to be later than that, 'cause you'll still be going then.*

GL: Well, maybe 15 years. My feelings about *Star Wars* are not as awed as a lot of people. No matter what, it is a rather simplistic movie.

KOQ: *Do you think the importance of it is over-analyzed by some people in the same way it is underrated by others?*

GL: Yeah. The underrating and overrating are the same kind of reactions. The people who are saying "It's nothing; it's junk food for the mind," are reacting against the people who are saying "This is the greatest thing since popcorn!" Both of them are wrong. It's just a movie. You watch it and you enjoy it.

There were certain underlying ideas when I started: one was to tell a fairy tale, which is what it is—a fairy tale in space guise. The reason it's in a space guise is that I like the space program, and I'm very keen on having people accept the space program. We've grown up in what is the flowering, and maybe the apex, of the space program, and *Star Wars* was made during that time when everyone was saying, "What a waste of time and money." And that talk is still happening. And I was hoping—and still am hoping—that if, 10 years from now, it comes up for a vote that people will be a little more prone to saying "Yes, this is important and we should do it." Not necessarily for rational reasons, but maybe for totally irrational, romantic reasons that have nothing to do with "Yes, I see we can mine this stuff up on the Moon and can make a 15% profit if we do this and this and this...." People don't always make decisions that way. Sometimes they make them because "Yeah. It's exciting. Let's go do it!"

KOQ: *Then don't you think* Star Wars *is important in that respect—just on an excitement level?*
GL: If suddenly the space program gets a lot of money 15 years from now then I'll say, "Gee, maybe I had something to do with that. Maybe I helped in some way or another." But it's hard to tell at this point if *Star Wars* will have any effect or not.

KOQ: *But you know that as a kid some of the things that turned out to be very important elements in your life were things that somebody maybe dashed off and thought it was just a little folly that he spent a weekend doing—a comic book, a movie. The Republic serials that meant so much to you were pretty much thrown together.*
GL: Even a lot of the big movies were dashed off.

KOQ: *Right and yet they can have an impact and a power, no matter whether they were intended to be philosophically profound or have a message or an import...*
GL: It's just that people tend to take those things so seriously and get carried away when they should realize that it's just something you enjoy—like a sunset. You don't have to worry about the significance of it. You just say, "Hey, that was great."

KOQ: *Is there any* harm *in getting carried away with it?*

GL: No, not really. I think it might be harmful to let it become all-consuming in one's life, because there are a lot more important things in life than a movie. I think that if someone became completely consumed by it they would lose their sense of getting something accomplished in the real world. There is a danger there.

KOQ: *I want to ask you something overall about* THX 1138, American Graffiti *and* Star Wars—*the three films that you both wrote and directed. How do these represent* you? *What of you, personally, is in those films?*

GL: When you know filmmakers very well, and you see their films you realize how their personality is imprinted in the films. The director's personal weaknesses are the film's weaknesses. His strengths are the film's strengths. When you look at a *series* of films, you begin to see what those are, because the strengths are always the same and the weaknesses are generally the same—especially if you are a very personal director. If you're doing television it's hard to get your personality through, but if you're doing something where you write and direct—well, with my friends I can see this easily. But it's hard to see it in one's own films.

When I was doing *Star Wars,* Francis had a cameraman he wanted to see a print of *American Graffiti,* so I said, "Sure, come on over, and I'll screen it for him." I screened *Graffiti* that day, and that night I had to screen *Star Wars* (a rough cut), and I saw the films back-to-back. It was then I realized whatever unique quirk that I have that I don't think about and was not aware of until I saw the two films so close together. It's hard to describe in words, but the only thing I could ever come up with to describe the personal quality in my films is "a kind of effervescent giddiness."

That's obviously not the way I am as a person, yet somehow or another it came out in those two films—and it's even in *THX,* but most people don't see it. I mean, there's a whole lot of humor and craziness going on in that movie, but the film is so somber and serious and abstract that it goes right by most people. If you see the other films, and then you go back and see *THX,* you get a stronger sense of the humor. It was very slow-paced, while one of the strong elements in *Graffiti* and *Star Wars* was the fast pace, the humor and—whatever it is—the "heart."

That's on a purely *personality* level. Psychologically that's something I have absolutely no control over. It just happens, and I can't help it. And if I wanted *not* to do that I couldn't help but do it. On the *philosophical* level, there are ideas and themes that go through all the films—themes that I constantly use...

KOQ: *Is there a way you can briefly state your philosophy of life?*
GL: When you boil down philosophies, they become very personal. I've mentioned the philosophy that runs through the films a few times, and I've been criticized. One of the main thrusts in all the films is the Horatio Alger concept—the fact that if you apply yourself and work real hard, you can get what you want accomplished. Your only limitations are your own willingness to do whatever you want to do.

In *THX* that's expressed in the white limbo—the whole film, really, is the analogy that we're in cages and the doors are open. We just don't want to leave. That film is in three different parts and each part takes that theme and expresses it in a different way. The white limbo is the most abstract symbol; you can get up and walk out of there at any time, but you've got to have the will to do it and not be afraid.

American Graffiti is saying the same thing. The kids are growing out of a small town, accepting the responsibility of the fact that things change, and that you have to go out into the world and make something of yourself—no matter how frightening that is.

And it recurs again in *Star Wars* with Luke wanting something, but not wanting it enough to break the rules and say, "OK, I'm going to do it." The rules end up getting broken for him, but it's still that same theme. *Empire* is a little different, and *Revenge* is a little different too—it's the same thing but more *inward* than outward. More personal.

KOQ: *And obviously you believe this idea is true of your own life.*
GL: It's been a big factor in my own life. In growing up and going to high school and everything I was never the brightest kid in the world. Even in college I was aware of the fact that I wasn't as smart as everybody else was—or most of the class. I decided that if I was going to keep up with them, I had to work twice as hard, because I felt I was starting out with less. The goals I had set seemed totally impossible. First, I never even *dreamed* of going into the film business, and once I got into it I never dreamed I'd make

anything out of it, 'cause everybody said, "You go to film school, and you'll become a ticket-taker at Disneyland."

But I said, "I am determined that I will make it somehow." I made it into SC, which was a big achievement for me. I never thought I could get into a big university. I never had the grades, but I did it and I managed to go all the way through and *graduate*—which I also never thought would happen. Part of it is just determination.

When I was in film school there was a small group of us that were making films, while the rest of the class sat around and said, "Gee, we can't make movies—the teacher won't let us do this, or I can't do that, or you never get a break around here." While they were complaining about why they never got to make movies I made *eight* movies. And they're still sitting down there saying, "Gee, I can't get a job—and you can never make it in the film business, and when are they going to give me a break, and when is somebody going to let me make a movie?"

Nobody's *ever* going to let anybody make a movie. You have to go out and do it! And those who can figure out how to do it—do it. And nothing can stop them.

And that was my philosophy, that nothing was going to stop me. My goals were different then than they ended up. My goals were to make bizarre abstract movies, and I expected to end up a documentary filmmaker and work for a television station or something. I don't know if I'd have been completely happy at it, but I probably would have enjoyed it in my own way. I just sort of *overshot my target*—in a rather major way.

If you set your goals too high, then they are impossible to reach. You just get frustrated. So you set them as high as is realistic—not impossible but *very difficult*. As corny as it sounds, the power of positive thinking goes a long way.

So determination and positive thinking combined with talent combined with knowing your craft—which means a lot of hard work and homework—and a lot of *luck*. If you can generate all these other qualities, the luck will come eventually. That may sound like a naive point of view, but at the same time it's worked for me and it's worked for all my friends—so I have come to believe it.

Small dreams and short-term goals are relatively easy to achieve. They don't require that you change your whole lifestyle and give up lots of other pursuits. Little accomplishments require little efforts.

Grand dreams and long-range goals are another matter entirely. They not only require enormous effort, long hours, single-minded devotion over a period of perhaps years and years—but they also usually require that one exclude from his life activities that would drain time and dilute attention and energies.

A sudden success cuts the struggle short, and one can find—overnight—that life changes radically and completely.

With new-found powers, brought on by success, one must also learn to deal with new responsibilities and requirements. Some cannot handle the changes. The most trite example is the actor who, having worked for years climbing up the ladder toward stardom, suddenly becomes an "overnight" sensation and begins to fall apart emotionally—often ending with alcohol, drugs and even suicide—because he is not prepared for the "enslavement" of being a celebrity.

Others handle the changes quite easily—not without some regrets and yearnings—but with a calm, feet-on-the-ground realism and a broad perspective of what their success is "buying them" in terms of other, more personal goals.

Much as failure is torturous to deal with—success has its own revenge that requires as much of an individual as the climb upward did.

KERRY O'QUINN: *In terms of the business side of things, you are obviously going to keep a strong hand in the future* Star Wars *films, but what is your involvement going to be as a filmmaker? Are you going to stick with it for nine movies, or are you going to move on to other projects? I ask because your first three movies were in totally different directions, and that seems to indicate you enjoy variety in your work.*

GEORGE LUCAS: There are a lot of other movies that I would like to make. Right now I'm focused on trying to get *Revenge* finished, and once I can get this current trilogy out of my hair, and it's done, then I can start to think about the next one—plus all the corporate things: the company, the ranch, all the things I hope will be culminated by 1983–84. I'm trying not to take on anything else until that point. Then when the dust has cleared I'll be able to say "OK, this is the direction that we're going to take." Right now I'm just sort of winging it.

KOQ: *Do you have the whole nine-film series plotted?*

GL: Yeah, but it's a long way from the plot to the script. I've just gone through that with *Revenge of the Jedi*, and what seems like a great idea when it's described in three sentences suddenly doesn't hold together when you try to make five or six scenes out of it. So plots change a lot when they start getting into script form.

KOQ: *Do you think you're going to be able to turn the scripting over to anyone?*

GL: I don't know.

KOQ: *Would you like to?*

GL: I'd love to. But I don't think its going to be possible.

KOQ: *So at least as a writer you may still . . .*

GL: I may still have to be involved through all nine films. I'm hoping to find someone I think is very good—who understands it and can deal with it. You know we have lots of people who write to us and say they'd love to write a STARLOG . . . uh, *Star Wars.*

KOQ: *Just wait till this gets in print. You'll be flooded with writer resumes.*

GL: But finding a professional writer who's got a lot of experience and has good taste is relatively difficult. Someone who has never written a screenplay before could possibly do it—possibly—but that really isn't the kind of person I would go to write these films. I would go to somebody who would initially *not* want to write them—who was writing their own thing—and then try to get them to do something for *Star Wars.*

Anybody can write, but there are very few who can write well. And when you get into something like *Star Wars*, it has such a unique personality to it, that it's next to impossible to come up with somebody who can do it.

KOQ: *Do you ever plan to direct another* Star Wars *chapter?*

GL: I might one day, but I really don't have a strong desire to do it. I've *done* it, and if I did it again it would be because I had to do it. Finding a director is also very difficult, just like finding a writer. You need someone who technically knows what they're doing with extremely complicated movies—much more so than with any normal movie. I say that to people, and they don't really believe me.

Even Irv Kershner didn't believe me. I said, "You're in for a surprise on this one! I know you've been directing films for fifteen years, but you've never come across anything like this—believe me!" And he said, "Oh, yeah, don't worry George." It was the same thing I told Matt Robbins when he started *Dragonslayer* and the same thing I told John Milius when he started *Conan*. I got a message from John last weekend saying, "*I quit!* I'm going to retire, and you're the only person in the world who will understand what I'm talking about."

These films are not like regular movies. When you have that many special effects going on, and things have to be planned out so far in advance, and there are so many little pieces that have to fit together perfectly, and the chances of their doing that are very remote—it drives you crazy.

KOQ: *You mean it isn't true that you can fix anything in the editing?*
GL: (chuckle) No, it really has to be planned out much more than a normal movie.

KOQ: *You mentioned the ranch, and I've read a few things about this project and heard lots of rumors. I know you bought lots of land out here in the middle of nowhere and that you're doing major construction. Can you set the record straight and explain what it's all about?*
GL: There's a lot of confusion about the ranch. I said somewhere that I wanted to recreate the atmosphere that I had in film school, so everyone assumed that I'm building a film school. But I'm not. All we're really doing is building an office building. It's a bigger, better version of the office complex we've got now.

KOQ: *You mean the offices in Los Angeles?*
GL: No! L.A. is an abberation! Up here we have this big old white Victorian house where several of my filmmaker friends rent space and we make our movies. What we've done, essentially, is take that house and move it out to the country and make it bigger. We are pretty crowded right now, but we'll have a *giant* Victorian house with offices for everybody—a screening room, a library, a few other conveniences.

K O Q : *Descriptions I heard made it sound like a much more elaborate installation.*

G L : It's not. It has been blown completely out of all proportion. It's purely an office. I mean, my personal operation is me, an assistant and a secretary. That's my whole company. That was my company before *Star Wars*, and now I've got all these other companies going on all around it—the merchandising, the corporate thing, I.L.M. and all these other things—but ultimately *my* end of it is still just three or four of us.

K O Q : *All these various business concerns—do they involve responsibilities that are a big struggle for you—do they eat into your time and creative energies more than you'd like—is the business side of your success the hidden revenge of the boxoffice—or do you handle all that very happily?*

G L : No, I don't. I don't really like to do it. I do it because I have to, not because I want to.

K O Q : *It sounds like script writing all over again.*

G L : It is. Interestingly enough, my whole life is that way. I'm not really doing what I particularly want to do.

K O Q : *And yet, a lot of people say "George Lucas is in the* ideal *position—he has created a company and a situation in life that allows him the freedom to do anything* he wants to do."

G L : But the more wealthy you get and the more powerful you get, the more restrictions you have—and the *less* you can actually do.

K O Q : *But isn't the ranch an attempt to fight that in some way?*

G L : The ranch is a way of formalizing what we already have. I mean, before *Star Wars* I was going to restore the building we're in—which was sort of run down. Then when the film was such a success I realized we could do this the way the original dream was, which was the dream for American Zoetrope, Francis Ford Coppola's film company, which is also based up here in Northern California. Meanwhile, Francis decided he'd rather be in the city. His original idea was to build a film studio—but my idea was to build a group of offices where my friends, and other Marin County filmmakers, could have a close proximity with each other.

KOQ: *Is the ranch all filmmaking or are there any other arts involved?*
GL: Not at this point. It's just a few friends from film school that happen to be living up here making movies and sharing office space and, as a result, being able to go out and have lunch together and exchange ideas and what not. It's the way studios used to be a long time ago.

KOQ: *When the ranch is finished, what kind of films would you like to make?*
GL: I have a lot of ideas for movies—personal things—which is why I'm going about this whole thing, so I can get into a situation where I can make my own kind of movies which aren't necessarily commercial. If you take *THX-1138* as the pivotal point—you go way off in this direction to *Star Wars*, which is about as conventional as I can get—but I want to go in the *other* direction, which is into a more abstract kind of movie, without characters and without plots.

KOQ: *So—that desire is still bubbling in the back of your head?*
GL: Yes. That's still where my heart is, and I can't get away from it. Even *Star Wars* and *American Graffiti* got a lot of criticism for the fact that they were so abstract—not made the way a normal movie is made. And they aren't. *Empire* goes even further than *Star Wars* in terms of moving through an idea as quickly as one can possibly deal with it.

KOQ: *How are you going to approach this filmmaking? Are you going to finance your own films, and are you willing to lose money?*
GL: It goes beyond even that. I'm going to make films that are very *experimental*. They're not really theatrical films. They may end up being a hour or an hour-and-a-half—whatever. I want to spend time doing films and exploring ideas, with the opportunity to *fail*—which you don't have in the professional film business. You've got to win every single time, and it's very difficult because you end up making very safe movies: you know this works, so you do it. Since your career depends on it, you go with what you know works.

I want to try making some films that I'm not really sure will work or not. So it goes beyond the possibility of losing money—it goes to the point of my looking at a finished film and saying "Boy, was that a mistake..." putting it on the shelf and saying "Let's forget about that one!"

KOQ: *That's a very personal goal. Very personal. I mean, it's not even a* Lucasfilm *goal! It's a* George *goal.*

GL: It *is* a very personal goal. It's something that I've wanted to do ever since I was in film school. My friends who are making those kinds of movies struggle along on grants, and it's difficult because they have very limited resources. You can't make a living that way, and I realized that years ago, so I went into "regular filmmaking." I happened to fall into it with Francis. If I hadn't met him and he hadn't sent me along that line, I would have moved to San Francisco from SC, and I would have been up here doing films like that—but struggling with them.

KOQ: *Obviously your film school experience is quite important to you, not only because of the education, but because of the pool of people you met there—people with whom you have kept in touch and, in some cases, continued to work with. What kind of educational advice would you give* STARLOG *and* CINEMAGIC *readers—especially those interested in film careers?*

GL: I am a strong believer in going as far in your education as you can possibly go. If you want to get into the movie business, it's not absolutely necessary that you go to a film school, but if you do, you can learn so much in four years that it would take you fifteen years on the outside to learn. And when you come out of a film school, you are well rounded. Many film schools insist that you get your degree in some other field—science or chemistry or some other discipline—so that when you get into film you have some sort of feelings for what you want to make movies *about.* You have to have lived, and you have to have some sort of experiences in order to know what you want to make movies about. And the greater that exposure, the better you're going to be able to articulate your own perspective—sort of regurgitate it back onto the screen.

There are two ways of working in film. The school I came out of is—*you* create everything, you come up with the ideas, you write the screenplay, you are a filmmaker. The other school is being a hired hand—which is just as good. But even there, you must know your craft and must have broad experiences.

Very few people I know get hired into the film business without at least making it into college. It's tough getting into college, and it's tough getting *through* college, but no matter how hard it is, it's going to be *even harder* when you get out and try to make it into the film industry. There is no easy road. Nobody is ever going to hand somebody a movie and say "Here, direct this." It just doesn't happen. It will never happen. You have to fight all the way. You have to excel at whatever you can excel at to get that spotlight shining down on you. Once you start getting a reputation of being very good at doing whatever you do, then everything starts to follow. But it's always a struggle.

Whether you're a writer, a filmmaker, a director, a cameraman, whatever—if you stand out in your field—if you're the best—that's when you start getting offered jobs. I'm sort of a strong believer in that concept. In film school my friends and I were the best student filmmakers around. If you went to any international film festival we were always there winning the first, second or third prize. And it was that attention—especially one film festival where I wiped out every category—won first place in all categories—that led to some people saying "Hey, this kid's sharp."

It's never "Hey, you—the third kid from the left—we're going to let you do this movie," or: "We're going to let you do the special effects." All the people who work here at I.L.M. have excelled in their field, and that's how they came to my attention—not because they walked in and said, "Here's my resume; I've had some experience, and I want to learn about special effects." We hire people who have a reputation of being the best there is. They got that reputation by doing little things and showing that they know what they're doing—and not depending on anybody to give them that break. I'm a firm believer in the fact that you make your own breaks.

When you get up to bat, if you've done your homework, then you can hit that home run. But you only get up to bat a few times, so you've got to be sure you're prepared. A lot of people aren't; they may work their way into getting that opportunity, but they just aren't qualified to do it. And they fall flat on their face. Then the chances of their getting another opportunity are even more remote than the first time.

It's hard work, making movies. It's like being a doctor or a lawyer: you work long hours, very hard hours, and it's emotional, tense work. If you don't really love it, then it ain't worth it.

KOQ: *I get a tremendous amount of mail addressed to me, but really for you. I'm either going to start sending it to you or—here's your big chance to answer "the most-asked question." STARLOG readers want to know how to break into the film field and, more specifically, if there is any way they can work with you on an upcoming production.*

GL: My feelings about getting into the film business are that the best route is going to film school. The advantage of film school is not only the education and the experience in all areas, but it also puts you in contact with a lot of contemporaries who have some of the same goals, and you can trade information. It's also a chance to find out if you can excel at making films and to make a movie that you can take around and show people. It's in that environment that you begin to figure out how to get jobs.

Most of my friends who made it in the film business succeeded because they wrote screenplays that they kept showing around until someone finally said "This guy is good." The other way is to make a ten or fifteen-minute film that is so professional and so entertaining and so impressive that you get your break. That's how I made it.

That's how Steve Spielberg, and several other of my friends made it — they managed to get a movie together somehow, that was then seen by the studios, who said "This guy's good; let's give him a chance to direct televi- sion." And they moved from that all the way up.

Everybody can't be a director, and film school also gives you a chance to explore and see what you're good at and what you're not good at. Maybe you're not good at directing, but you're good at photography — or you're not good at photography, but you're good at sound — or great at editing, or writing. There are lots of areas in the film business. Film school is sort of the "test bed" of your career, because *there* is where you have the chance to make films and fail.

Once you get into the field, you can't fail.

The only real advice I can give is *work real hard* — harder than anybody else. And if you're talented, and if you get lucky, you'll make it. And if you work hard, and you're talented — sooner or later you'll get lucky.

Now, in terms of working with *me* . . . there just aren't enough positions to go around. All the people who work for me are experienced, accomplished people. We don't really have room for people who aren't professional. We're not big enough to have that kind of training program. We have to go for people who have *shown* that they are very good. And as for menial jobs — just hanging around on location — it may seem exciting, but it really is a waste of time. One would be much wiser to spend a day at Disneyland.

KOQ: *The kind of people you're talking about are really filmmakers—like you. But many who write to me are much more specialized in their skills and interests: they are modelmakers, costume makers, mask makers, robot builders. What they are dying to do is come around and show you their wares. I'm not sure film school is the place for them because their interests are not really in filmmaking—in a general sense.*

GL: Right. For people like that the best place to be is in Los Angeles. My situation up here in San Francisco is very limited because there isn't that much production going on. For instance, we have nine modelmakers when we're at peak, and we lay off maybe a third of those when we're not in major production. So our permanent staff of modelmakers is, say, six people—six people that we hired a long time ago, and we don't foresee any of them leaving.

In Los Angeles there's Trumbull and Dykstra and Hartland, in modelmaking—there's all those companies down there, and there's endless commercial houses. So if you can get yourself known down there to the Greg Jeins of the world, then when something comes up they'll say "This guy is good, let's use him."

The entire film industry is a very hard life—and the worst is for actors. They're lucky if they can work three days a year, and it's very hard to make a living that way. For modelmakers—if you can get on a project you may work for six months, but it may be two or three years before you get on another project. And these are guys who have *giant credits,* but when the film is finished they're *out*—hoping that something else will come along. It's a very esoteric and difficult business to try making a living at. You have to really be dedicated to it.

KOQ: *Here at I.L.M. you have almost three years between* Star Wars *films, yet you keep a permanent staff. What if in-between films like* Raiders *and* Dragonslayer *had not involved, for example, any modelmaking. How do you justify keeping the six people on staff?*

GL: That's a problem that we are trying to cope with. The overhead is just astronomical. So we're trying to bring in outside projects so between our own films we can keep everyone here working. The situation of having a permanent staff for special effects is very unique. In Los Angeles, for instance, there is no permanent modelmaker job. It doesn't exist. Maybe one or two, but I don't know of them. Basically, you're working from picture to picture and hoping something comes along.

There is a great amount of effort on my part, and everybody else's part around here, to keep this place going so that everyone here has a permanent job. The modelmakers around here can tell you more about that—how they lived before they got this job. Ask Dennis Muren.

KOQ: *How many people do you employ?*
GL: It's about 100—but it varies.

KOQ: *What sort of outside projects would you like to bring in?*
GL: Well, things like *Raiders* and *Dragonslayer*—projects that obviously fit into the special effects that we do. We've got a couple of special projects coming up. We're essentially in competition with Apogee and [Douglas] Trumbull, companies like that, so people either go to them or they come to us with their film.

All specials effects houses involve a lot of effort just to keep them going with work. Even in a big operation like this we're going from month to month—hand to mouth. You must know what that's like; it's like publishing a magazine. I mean, why don't you have 35 staff writers?

KOQ: *I know the answer to that one!*
GL: Well, it's the same here. The film world is not that unique. It's like a lot of other things. It's just not as permanent but it's more exciting. I guess that makes up for it.

KOQ: *In this exciting, impermanent field, you have brought your dream to life, in a way. What is there left for you, personally, to dream about? What is your secret desire?*
GL: Right now, my hidden desire is to do these rather abstract movies that I've been wanting to do for a long time. The ranch won't be finished until, say 1984, and then I'll get to start making my own movies. I don't know how long I'll be intrigued by that—maybe five years, maybe ten years, maybe the rest of my life.

KOQ: *Is there anything outside of the film world that you long to do? For instance, do you still want to paint?*

GL: No, I don't think so. If there's any interest outside of film, I'd say its architecture. I'm into architecture. And that's what the ranch represents.

KOQ: *Are you having a lot to do with the design of the ranch?*
GL: Yes. I spend a lot of time on it, and *that* I enjoy. That's what I do for a hobby—design buildings. I wanted to be an architect when I was a kid, because that was a way of combining my desire to do art with practical things. But I really couldn't get past the mathematics. Basically, I'm a very lazy person, and I have a tendency to take the path of least resistance. That's why I get chained to my desk at home and forced into things, because if I had my way I'd just sort of sit on the beach and do nothing. But, unfortunately, the more successful you get the harder that kind of thing is. Unfortunately!

KOQ: *I don't know what time it is, but do you realize that this is probably going to turn into a nine-part interview in STARLOG? I think we'll start with "Chapter Four" and end "Chapter Five" with a cliffhanger . . .* (laughter)
But seriously, you mentioned earlier that there is nothing being done nowadays like the Star Wars *films—nothing for that audience.*
GL: Well, there is *now*—but there wasn't when *Star Wars* was originally done. Now, obviously, a lot of people have followed along.

KOQ: *Yes, the same way a lot of new SF magazines have shown up on the newsstands since STARLOG started.*
GL: There are some very good films that have been made since then, but many of them are just bad copies that lack any real enthusiasm or intelligence. Actually if they had intelligence they wouldn't want to copy something. That's sort of a disappointment. I had hoped that the genre would open up and there would be lots of good new films.

KOQ: *Are there any films—or books or comics, for that matter—anything in the arts that you think are outstanding and worth calling to people's attention?*
GL: I'm reluctant to make a short list because then it sounds like these are the three films and three books that you should read. I think the arts are very personal. The best way is for people to read and watch films.

KOQ: *Well, a few years ago you were spending your last $1,000 to go backpacking in Europe. Things are a bit different today.*

GL: Yeah. If you'd asked me five years ago what I would be doing today, you'd never get the answers you're getting now. So I never predict where I'm going to be in five years. I can't say things are necessarily better, but they are different.

KOQ: *I'd say your life has been pretty good. I mean, you never had to dig ditches or wash dishes. Even when you ran off to Europe on the last of your money, you were doing what you wanted to do at that moment.*
GL: Right.

KOQ: *So that's pretty good.*
GL: Well, I've worked as a waiter. I can sympathize with that. And the one thing you can do with certain jobs is, at 5:00 you can run out the door and do whatever else you want to. You can completely leave it, but when there is responsibility on you, you can't walk out and have it all go away.

KOQ: *I know what you mean: you* never *leave it.*
GL: You wear it *forever.* And it gets bigger and bigger as you get more and more successful. That's a drag. With what is good, there is always some bad.

KOQ: *This has been interesting, George. It's been a long time since I conducted an interview, and I am consoled for my amateur standing at doing* interviews *only by the fact that you have a fairly amateur standing at giving* interviews.
GL: Well, this should be interesting to read...

KOQ: *Believe me, it will be.*
GL: I'll probably go into shock when I open up the magazine. To be very truthful, I always expect the worst. When you open a magazine to see what you've said, it's a rare relief when it turns out all right, and you can say, "Gee, that's makes sense and sounds intelligent. That's what I meant." A lot of articles either are wrong about things or they make up things. And when it's *Time* or *Fortune* everybody takes it as the gospel truth. Suddenly it become "resource material" and keeps cropping up over and over again. If I see the statement one more time that 2001 had only 30 special effects in it while *Star Wars* had 400, I think I'll die. That came from a *Time* article, but I don't know *where* it originated. You get sort of crass about this

kind of thing because most media types *demand* interviews—as if it's your obligation to society. It's *not* an obligation. What I'm doing is selling someone's magazine.

KOQ: *That's true, and I sincerely thank you for this whole, very special experience. It was a pleasure meeting you, and I hope your "giddy effervescence" never fades—for your own sake and for my own selfish pleasure—not to mention the pleasure you bring to our readers and the filmgoing people of the planet.*

Burden of Dreams: George Lucas

ALJEAN HARMETZ/1983

AT THIRTY-NINE, GEORGE LUCAS has become an institution. It is ironic that Lucas—who fled from Hollywood because he was afraid his art would be stifled by that town's commerce—is the sole owner of one of the most successful movie factories of all time. Of Hollywood's five box-office champions between 1903 and 1983, Lucas has had a share in three. He created, wrote, and directed *Star Wars*. He created and financed *The Empire Strikes Back*, and his company, Lucasfilm Ltd., produced it. He created the story for *Raiders of the Lost Ark*, also produced by Lucasfilm. It is almost inevitable that the third movie in his *Star Wars* trilogy, *Return of the Jedi*, will climb into the same financial stratosphere as its lucrative predecessors.

But a list of Lucas's successful movies—which would also include *American Graffiti*, currently among the top twenty-five box-office winners—comes nowhere near suggesting his impact on the movie industry. Physically and financially, he is almost completely independent of Hollywood. *Forbes* magazine has estimated his personal fortune at $50 million and his net worth, including Lucasfilm, at more than $100 million. Lucas must still use the major studios' distribution apparatus to get his films into American theaters, but he can demand his own terms.

Beyond Lucas's personal independence, he is creating and building tools—computer graphics, computer-assisted editing, digital sound—that

From *American Film*, June 1983, pp. 30–36. Reprinted by permission of the American Film Institute and the author.

will revolutionize the way movies are put together. A sprawl of converted warehouses in San Rafael, California, houses his six-year-old special effects company, Industrial Light and Magic, as well as his two-year-old research and development company, Sprocket Systems. Because it is a research company, Sprocket Systems has been losing $200,000 a year, but a recent deal by which Sprocket agreed to create and design video games for Atari should nudge the company into the black. Founded to do the effects for *Star Wars*, Industrial Light and Magic is now the premier special effects firm in the movie industry. *Star Trek II: The Wrath of Khan, Poltergeist,* and *E.T.* used ILM. So did *Raiders* and *Dragonslayer*.

Lucas is one of the three most visible members of the filmschool generation that began infiltrating Hollywood in the sixties. "Once we got our foot in the door, we took over," he says, and it's only a slight exaggeration, although—except for Lucas, Steven Spielberg, and Francis Ford Coppola— they have not cracked its higher echelons of power.

Hollywood was very different from what they thought it would be. "From my point of view, the film industry died in 1965," Lucas says. "It's taken this long for people to realize the body is cold. The day I won my six-month internship and walked onto the Warner Bros. lot was the day Jack Warner left and the studio was taken over by Seven Arts. I walked through the empty lot and thought, This is the end. The industry had been taken over by people who knew how to make deals and operate offices, but had no idea how to make movies. When the six months was over, I never went back."

Sitting in an unpretentious office adjacent to Industrial Light and Magic—which has been headquartered in San Rafael, four hundred miles north of Hollywood, for nearly five years—Lucas points south. "Down there, for every honest, true filmmaker trying to get his film off the ground, there are a hundred sleazy used-car dealers trying to con you out of your money. Going down there is like visiting a foreign country."

The creator of quintessentially Hollywood entertainments is a country boy from California's hot inland valley. Although he is still a shy person, enveloped in a privacy as tangible as brown wrapping paper, he has none of the rumpled, untidy look he had six years ago. With commercial success, Lucas has trimmed his graying beard and cut his hair. But the small-town California childhood that he put on the screen with loving care in *American Graffiti* still lingers in the rural twang of his voice—and in his choice of clothes. The green polyester pullovers, the blue-and-red checked shirts, the western shirts with pearl buttons, all seem fresh off the rack at K-Mart. He has always been painfully ill at ease among the deal makers in three-piece suits or designer blue jeans who muscle their way to success bearing "hot properties" and neatly wrapped packages of directors and stars.

Unlike the cosmopolitan Coppola, who has a gambler's passion for risks, Lucas is a cautious and frugal man. His personal life is austere and almost reclusive. "Francis accuses me of not knowing how to spend money," he says. "Francis is right." But frugality should not be confused with stinginess. Lucas has generously given "points" (percentages) of his movies' profits to key employees and has donated $5.7 million to his alma mater, the University of Southern California film school.

Coppola's creativity is unleashed by the threat of losing everything. But, says Lucas's wife of thirteen years, Marcia, "George is methodical and ritualistic. He loves to feel safe and secure. Any kind of threat would make him so uneasy and uncomfortable he couldn't work." Although he loves to play games, Lucas is too cautious even to play Monopoly well. The word most often used to describe him is "serious." "Even when he's silly," says Marcia, who won an Academy Award as one of the editors of *Star Wars,* "nothing is simply a fun moment. Everything gets logged." He has described himself as "not especially bright and not especially lucky," and credits his success simply to his diligence. It's no accident that his favorite fairy tale is "The Ant and the Grasshopper."

Until *The Empire Strikes Back,* George Lucas lived in northern California, but had to take the 9:00 A.M. Monday morning PSA flight south to make deals and do the postproduction work on his films. No longer. "The deal makers will come up here for George," says Michael Ritchie, another of the cluster of directors who live in northern California. "The rest of us still pay homage at the court of money."

With *Empire,* Lucas was at last able to cut the fraying ropes that bound him to Hollywood. In the summer of 1981, the last unit of Lucasfilm, the sales and marketing division, moved from its offices across the street from Universal Studios to San Rafael. Lucas had begun shedding his Hollywood clothing a year earlier. After quietly resigning from the Academy of Motion Picture Arts and Sciences, which had nominated him as Best Writer and Best Director for both *American Graffiti* and *Star Wars,* he tore up his membership cards to the Writers Guild and Directors Guild in the spring of 1981.

But then, he neither needs nor wants to write or direct his movies. (*Empire* was directed by Irvin Kershner and *Jedi* by Richard Marquand.) "I dislike directing," Lucas says passionately. "I hate the constant dealing with volatile personalities. Directing is emotional frustration, anger, and tremendously hard work—seven days a week, twelve to sixteen hours a day. For years my wife would ask why we couldn't go out to dinner like other people. But I couldn't turn it off. Eventually, I realized that directing wasn't healthy for me." The passion dissipates. He says simply, "I don't have to work for a living any more."

Together, *Star Wars* and *The Empire Strikes Back* have sold nearly $900 million worth of tickets. *Empire*, which cost $25 million, was completely financed from the profits of *Star Wars*. The $32.5 million *Return of the Jedi* was financed out of the $92 million in *Empire* ticket sales received by Lucasfilm. The company has earned another fortune from its share of the $1.5 billion in retail sales of products based on the two films' characters and artifacts. And the games and toys will continue to stock three or four shelves in every neighborhood toy store for years.

It would be a mistake to sneer at Lucas or accuse him of hypocrisy for railing at Hollywood's sleaziness while his own movies are spectacularly commercial. He is simply one of the lucky ones—like Alfred Hitchcock, Preston Sturges, and David Lean—whose vision, however lightweight, coincides with the inner needs and unspoken desires of his customers.

Lucas's first commercial movie, *THX 1138*, was not very commercial. Produced in 1971 by Francis Ford Coppola for $750,000 and filmed primarily in the unfinished BART subway tunnel in San Francisco, it was a longer version of Lucas's student film of the same name that won the 1967–68 first prize at the National Student Film Festival. *THX* was about a grim future, and it failed at the box office.

"After *THX*, I realized I had to make entertaining films or back off and release through libraries," Lucas says. "I didn't want to struggle to get $3,000. It was too limiting, like giving a painter one brush, a piece of hardboard, and tubes of black and white paint. You can do it, but...I didn't want to be a self-indulgent artist, and I didn't want my wife to support me forever. I started on the road to make a rock 'n' roll cruising movie, determined to master that trade."

The "rock 'n' roll cruising movie" was, of course, *American Graffiti*. Lucas may have intended to dash off an exploitation movie, but instead he created a film that evokes a time long gone and re-creates a lost innocence. "I was amazed when I saw *American Graffiti* and *Star Wars* together for the first time," Lucas says. "I thought to myself, Well, I have a certain talent at this. The two movies shared a certain nice effervescent giddiness."

His eyes fixed on the furthest wall, his body melting into his chair like some animal camouflaging itself in a tree, his voice as hesitant and soft as cats' feet, Lucas gives the impression of fragility. Diabetes, discovered during his army induction physical, kept him out of the Vietnam War. And there is about him at all times a sense of physical limits beyond which he is not willing to go. "Marcia makes him a tuna salad sandwich on white bread with the crust cut off, and he's under the covers at nine-thirty every night," says his friend writer-director Philip Kaufman.

Lucas cannot tolerate face-to-face confrontations and almost never shows his anger. He demands neither service nor obeisance, and his employees speak of his humility, but he can be ruthlessly arrogant about his values and priorities. "That he cannot be turned from the vision inside his head nor corrupted by outside influences is the key to his success," says one of his vice-presidents.

He resigned from the Directors Guild because the guild fined him for placing Irvin Kershner's directing credit at the end of *The Empire Strikes Back* (even though Kershner himself did not object). For *Return of the Jedi*, Lucas selected Richard Marquand, a little-known British director who does not belong to the American guild.

"The Hollywood unions have been taken over by the same lawyers and accountants who took over the studios," Lucas says angrily. "When the Writers Guild was on strike, I couldn't cross the picket line in my function as a director in order to take care of *American Graffiti* when the studio was chopping it up. I quit the Directors Guild because the union lawyers were locked in a traditional combat with the studio lawyers. The union doesn't care about its members. It cares about making fancy rules that sound good on paper and are totally impractical. They said Lucasfilm was a personal credit, not a corporate credit. My name is not George Lucasfilm any more than William Fox's name was Twentieth Century-Fox. On that technicality they sued me for $250,000. You can pollute half the Great Lakes and not get fined that much. When the DGA threatened to fine Kershner $25,000, we paid his fine. I consider it extortion. The day after I settled with the Directors Guild, the Writers Guild called up. At least their fine didn't all go into the business agents' pockets. Two-thirds went to writers."

In May 1982, just before the twentieth reunion of Lucas's Modesto High School graduating class, several of his classmates recalled him as a "nerd." Lucas remembers himself as a combination of *American Graffiti*'s inept, hapless "Toad" (played by Charlie Martin Smith); passionate drag racer (Paul Le Mat); and tentative, questing adolescent (Richard Dreyfuss). Only Ron Howard's serene and secure class president bears no relationship to George Lucas.

Lucas grew up on a walnut ranch, the third child and only son; his father owned a stationery store. "I was as normal as you can get," he says. "I wanted a car and hated school. I was a poor student. I lived for summer vacations and got into trouble a lot shooting out windows with my BB gun."

One day in his seventeenth year, on a country road outside Modesto, he encountered his moment of truth. "I was making a left turn and a guy ran into me. When I was pulled out of the car, they thought I was dead. I wasn't breathing and I had no heartbeat. I had two broken bones and crushed lungs. The accident coincided with my graduation from high school, a natural turning point. Before the accident, I never used to think. Afterward, I realized I had to plan if I was ever to be happy."

Is he happy? The answer, like the man, is not uncomplicated. "I took the day off yesterday," he says. "I saw dailies at 9:00 A.M., had a meeting from 10:00 to 12:00, saw more film, had another meeting. I worked from 9:00 to 6:00 on my day off."

A year ago, George Lucas said, "People have a perception that money will make everything wonderful. It doesn't make anything wonderful. You can live in a nicer house and choose what you want for dinner. But if your Mercedes-Benz has a dead battery, it's even more frustrating than a dead battery in your Chevy. When you're rich, everything is supposed to work."

One thing his money could not buy was the birth of a child. Finally, in 1981, after twelve years of marriage, the Lucases adopted a baby. "I was desperate to have a family," he says—a surprising admission, definitely out of character. "Yet I knew when I had a family I couldn't devote ninety-eight percent of my time to the company. Since my daughter, the focus has changed. Thirty percent of my time now, and in a year fifty percent, will be focused toward the family."

Saying he will extricate himself may be easier than doing it. "He is asked five hundred questions a day," says Sidney Ganis, vice-president of marketing for Lucasfilm. " 'Should we make the banisters in the ranch house mahogany or green?' 'Should we start this sequence with an over-the-shoulder shot of Harrison Ford getting off the ship?' 'Would it be OK to reveal a certain story point in the *Jedi* trailer?' When we were shooting *Jedi* in the desert and the winds blew and we couldn't work, we were depressed. Until George said, 'It's good luck. I always have a day like this on a picture.' Then we weren't depressed any more. When I worked at Warner Bros., Ted Ashley was my boss. But George is my leader."

Marcia Lucas is equally doubtful that he will cut back on work. "Some people are nine-to-fivers," she says. "George is a five-to-niner. He leaves home at five-thirty in the morning and returns at eight-thirty at night."

Nonetheless, George Lucas says, with just a tinge of desperation, "With *Jedi* I have finished what I began nearly ten years ago with *Star Wars*. When *Jedi* is launched, I'll take a couple of years off. The company was created to serve me, but it's turned out the opposite. I serve it. When I was in film school, I had a dream of having my own company of 100 people, to have facilities and talented people available to me so I could make the movies I wanted to make without considering the marketplace. The reality is that I have a company of 313 people depending on me. I've told them, 'I'm not going to make any more hit movies for you. I'm not going to carry this company on my back any more.'

"The original idea was to take the money my films make and put it into outside businesses—businesses like solar energy that don't pollute and aren't morally indefensible—and make money to fund more films. I wanted a financial base. I don't have it yet. Our profit of $12 million to $15 million a year is nothing. The big television producers—Tandem, Lorimar, Aaron Spelling—make more in one year than I've made in my whole career. 'The Jeffersons' outgrossed *Star Wars*. Pac-Man outgrossed *Star Wars*. If I really wanted to make money, I'd have been better off in the microchip business. The kid who started Apple has made ten times the money I have." He later adds, "I'm ready to have a different life, to go off and do different things."

Exactly how different that other life will be is a matter of debate. "That he will even consider taking a year off is an immense psychological change in George," says Marcia. "He grew up with the traditional American values of hard work, earning your own way, and more hard work. It doesn't do him any good to have the money to indulge himself if he never indulges himself."

His present project, now nearly half completed and projected to cost a total of $10 million, is a working retreat for filmmakers, a creative environment that he has offered to share with such writers and directors as Hal Barwood, Matthew Robbins, John Korty, Michael Ritchie, and Philip Kaufman. "A lot of rock groups build backyard recording studios because they like to work at home. I'm building a backyard film studio," he teases.

On the three-thousand-acre Skywalker Ranch, he has the luxury of building a world in which he finds it satisfying to live—an odd mixture of the nineteenth and twenty-first centuries. In an extraordinary coincidence, Skywalker Ranch is located in a valley north of San Francisco that was named Lucas Valley long before George Lucas was born. Driving down the winding valley road two years ago on a day so hot that the steering wheel was painful to touch, Lucas looked out at the yellow hills. "We have two seasons here—the green season and the yellow season," he said. "From the valley floor, we own everything in sight. Over ninety percent of the land will be kept in its natural state. It's a totally controlled environment, and it's designed so that no building will be visible from any other building. Four to six years from now, we'll have all the amenities for filmmakers— editing rooms, mixing rooms, automated dialogue recording, a film research library, and a place simply to sit and think."

Now the buildings are rising. Through a redwood forest, over a newly built wood bridge, is a Victorian village—octagonal buildings with casement windows and glowing stained-glass grapevines, tongue-and-groove oak paneling that can rarely be found in homes less than eighty years old, gables, cupolas, immense flagstone fireplaces, leaded glass doors—all of the quaint, eccentric buildings painted ice-cream white and blueberry gray. Inside, Victorian England seems to have been crossed with a lodge in the Adirondacks, and the huge, two-story rooms smell of fresh Douglas fir. Everything from the stained-glass field mice to the brass chandeliers has been designed and made in a Lucasfilm shop.

Below the lazy nineteenth-century landscape, in the basements of the quaint buildings, lie the conduits and wires, the circuits and computers of the twenty-first century. Those cellar computers will run the washing machines and irrigation system, sweep the three thousand acres with closed-circuit television, and control the electronically operated gates that keep out the curious.

If there is a touch of paranoia in his walled paradise, Lucas insists it is justified. "There are a lot of crazy people walking in the streets," he says. "Some guy came into our Los Angeles office claiming to be a Jedi Knight and pulled a knife on a secretary. Another real lunatic insisted he wrote *Star Wars* and came to pick up his $100 million check." Although Lucas's wife was ready to adopt a child several years ago, he hesitated because of his vulnerability as a person with "a well-known name."

George Lucas perceives film as a moral instrument. "Film and [other] visual entertainment are a pervasively important part of our culture, an extremely significant influence on the way our society operates," he says. "People in the film industry don't want to accept the responsibility that they had a hand in the way the world is loused up. But, for better or worse, the influence of the church, which used to be all-powerful, has been usurped by film. Films and television tell us the way we conduct our lives, what is right and wrong. When Burt Reynolds is drunk on beer in *Hooper* and racing cops in his rocket car, that reinforces the recklessness of the kids who've been drawn to the movie in the first place and are proba-bly sitting in the theater drinking beer."

"*Star Wars*," he goes on, "came out of my desire to make a modern fairy tale. In college I became fascinated by how culture is transmitted through fairy tales and myths. Fairy tales are how people learn about good and evil, about how to conduct themselves in society. Darth Vader is the bad father; Ben Kenobi is the good father. The good and bad mothers are still to come. I was influenced by the dragonslayer genre of fairy tale—the damsel in distress, the evil brothers, the young knight who through his virtue slays the dragon."

There will be another trilogy, of course, which takes place before the current one. It deals with the young Darth Vader and the young Ben Kenobi. The good and bad mothers will play their part, as will the robots—R2D2 and C-3PO—the only "actors" who will bridge the trilogies. At the end of the first trilogy, Luke Skywalker will be four years old.

How does Lucas see the future of motion pictures? "The technology of making movies," he says, "is getting more accessible. With a small, dedi-cated crew, you can make a movie with a very small outlay of capital. You can make a professional-looking film for quite a bit less than a million dol-lars. I think it's only a matter of time before one of the thousands of film school-trained guys goes back to Kansas City and makes a *Rocky* or an *American Graffiti*. The distribution system will be located in Los Angeles for quite a while before it breaks up. But even that will break up eventually as cable TV and cassettes and other markets open up. You can sell to cable TV by making five phone calls out of your house.

"I've been saying for a long time that Hollywood is dead. That doesn't mean the film industry is dead. But for one region to dominate is dead, although it will take ten or fifteen years to have that visible. The film-maker hasn't figured out that he doesn't need the agents and the studio executives. What is Hollywood? An antiquated, out-of-date distribution apparatus, a monopoly, a system designed to exploit the filmmaker. The system is collapsing because of new technologies. The movie companies are structured inefficiently. In good times, it doesn't show. But they won't be able to survive the bad times."

Lucas has made a point of using film crews from the San Francisco area even when they are not as skilled as Hollywood craftsmen. "I'd rather take the knocks of not quite as good a movie in order to train people," he says. "That way, eventually crews up here will be as good as crews in Hollywood."

He hopes that the films that come out of different regions of the United States "will be as different from each other as films from different areas of Europe. When filmmaking is diversified across the country, every film-maker won't be locked into thinking the same stale ideas. When you get film industries in Georgia, Texas, and Chicago, they'll stop copying Holly-wood product."

During his "year off," from the summer of 1983 to the summer of 1984, Lucas will have to make a major decision. Will he move Lucasfilm to the next logical plateau? Will he enlarge it into a movie production company that produces five or six films a year created by other filmmakers? "Do I hire somebody whose taste is compatible with mine and try to become a Ladd Company?" he asks.

He has no answer yet. He sits inside one of the concrete-block ware-houses that currently form his empire. On a shelf a few rooms away sit *Millennium Falcons* in all sizes down to one as small as a half-dollar. He has conquered outer space, and the stamp of *Star Wars* has shaped the deci-sions at every major studio for the last six years. It would be the ultimate irony if George Lucas, who argues fiercely for Hollywood's obsolescence, should be the mogul to replace it.

George Lucas

DAVID SHEFF/1987

You portrayed the prelude to the turbulent Sixties in American Graffiti, *which was set in 1962. The difference between the era you portrayed—cruising and hanging out at Mel's Diner—and just five years later is incredible. What caused the change?*
It was the culmination of a lot of things—the Vietnam War and Kennedy getting killed—as well as the fusion of foreign tastes into culture. It's impossible to identify exact cause and effect, but the combination of those things, primarily the war, had a huge impact. When I was growing up [in Modesto, California] around the time the film is set, cruising was the big thing. That scene represented an innocence that disappeared forever. Cruising and cars gave way to spacing out on drugs. That's why I made the movie. I felt that the phenomenon that meant so much to me may just drift off forever. The idea was to document that scene.

Was the Richard Dreyfuss character, who had graduated from high school and was getting ready to leave home, you?
All the characters were an amalgamation of me and my friends. That is the main theme of the movie: accepting the transitory nature of life. A line in the movie sums it up: "You can't stay seventeen forever." It became a great metaphor for what the country was going through at that point.

From *Rolling Stone*, 5 November 1987, pp. 241–44. Reprinted by permission of Straight Arrow Publishers, Inc., 1987.

How so?

Look at the music in the film as an example. There was the Elvis Presley era, which was simple, innocent, upbeat blues, basically. Suddenly, when these other influences—psychedelic music, the Beatles and the rest of the British Invasion—came in, the music became more sophisticated, more intelligent. And that's what happened in the culture. As with any change, you gained some things and lost some things, which is what the movie is about. It wasn't just us as individuals who were growing up. The country was going through a large life transition, and it was a very traumatic experience for those of us who went through it. It changed the way we look at the country, the way we look at ourselves.

How did you spend the late Sixties and early Seventies?

I was in college until '67, and then I began making movies. When you are making movies, you drop out of real life, so I was kind of on the fringe. I went through the whole draft process and ended up being classified 4F because I am diabetic. By the early Seventies, I was working with Francis Coppola at his new company, American Zoetrope. In a way, that was a microcosm of what was going on in general in the film business.

Meaning what?

It was very rebellious. We had a lot of very interesting projects and a lot of interesting people. We had very off-the-wall ideas that never would have been allowed to infiltrate the studios. Zoetrope was a break away from Hollywood. It was a way of saying, "We don't want to be part of the Establishment, we don't want to make their kind of movies, we want to do something completely different." To us, movies are what counts, not deals and making commercial films.

Was it a successful experiment?

Yes and no. The *no* is that we learned that the studios control the industry; there is no getting around it. It's the same problem that everybody had. Ultimately, all the radicals realized that you cannot break away from the system if you want to accomplish anything.

How did you hook up with Coppola?

After college, I went to [USC] film school for a few years and then moved to San Francisco. I had gotten some scholarships to watch other people make movies and to make behind-the-scenes films. Francis was making a road film called *The Rain People,* and I was hired as catchall production assistant. At the same time, I was writing *THX* [*THX-1138,* Lucas's first film]. After a long struggle, Zoetrope managed to get a studio to back *THX* and others that Francis wanted to make. This was about 1969. Another film I was working on was *Apocalypse Now,* with John Milius. In that package, Francis also presented *The Conversation* and a couple of other projects. When the studio finally saw *THX,* they were distressed at how odd it was, and they canceled the whole deal. We were really disheartened, and beyond that, Francis was in deep debt. That's why he had to make *The Godfather.*

Was your Apocalypse Now *different from the one Coppola eventually made?*
I was doing it much more as a documentary in the style of *Dr. Strangelove.* It was going to be shot in 16 mm. That's how John and I originally pitched it to Francis. Until he made it [in 1979], though, you couldn't do a film about the Vietnam War. That's what we discovered. No one would even have anything to do with it.

Why?
Vietnam films are fashionable now, but then, in 1971, in the midst of the war, no one would touch the subject. Most of the things in the film were things the public didn't know about yet. Nobody had any idea that people were taking drugs over there. Nobody had any idea how crazy it was. None of that had come out. The film at that time was vaguely an exposé, vaguely a satire and vaguely a story about angry young men. The country wasn't ready—it's barely ready now with movies like *Platoon.*

Since I couldn't get *Apocalypse Now* off the ground, I started writing *American Graffiti.* Even that took a year to get off the ground. We got turned down by every studio. They said it didn't make any sense, it was just a musical montage. They didn't get it. I didn't get it off the ground until after I took time out to work for Francis on *The Godfather* and, just as that movie came out and was a giant hit, Francis agreed to put his name on *Graffiti.* They felt Francis's name would make the film successful. The studios haven't wanted to make *any* of the films I have proposed, not *THX,* not *Apocalypse Now,* not *American Graffiti.*

Not even Star Wars?
Not even *Star Wars.* While the others were turned down at least once by every studio, [*Star Wars*] only got turned down by three or four studios. I

finally got it picked up, and only then because *American Graffiti* was getting extremely good previews from audiences. One man, Alan Ladd Jr. [then president of Twentieth Century Fox], thought that this might be a hot deal. And it wasn't like they were overenthused about the movie. All they gave me was ten grand to develop the screenplay.

Twentieth Century Fox got Star Wars *for $10,000? That was one of the better all-time deals made in Hollywood. Was the problem the budget? As proposed, was it as expensive a production as it turned out to be?*
At that point it was so vague I don't think anybody knew. It was a special-effects movie. Science fiction wasn't very big at that point—*2001* was the biggest science-fiction film, and everyone considered that a fluke, because it was made by [Stanley] Kubrick. We had no idea what this would cost. The budget finally was set at about $10 or $11 million, which is like $20 million now. The studio went berserk.

What does it take to get a film made in spite of the system?
Obstinacy. You just persevere. Even Indiana Jones, with Steven [Spielberg] involved, was difficult to get made.

Your track record doesn't give you carte blanche to do what you want?
It doesn't work that way.

Why? Don't they consider you a good risk, worth banking on?
They'll bank on Sylvester Stallone, but the films I make are very unusual films. We don't think about it now, but when *American Graffiti* was first presented, it was an extremely unusual film. It was very experimental. No one used music that way, no one cut movies that way. Now even *The Love Boat* is told that way, but then, telling separate stories and intercutting them was unthinkable.

Why did you choose to break tradition and insist on that?
I felt it was inherent in the story: different characters have completely different stories with no real connection except for the fact that they are friends. That is the way it is with cruising. It was just a group of friends loosely tied together. That was the way it had to be told. The studios are reluctant to try anything new. They want the tried and true.

Yet you got a studio to back Star Wars, *and it became one of the biggest movies of all time. What's your theory about why it was so successful?*
There have been a thousand different explanations for it. Ultimately, I think it's just entertaining and made people feel good.

Star Wars *has been called a space-age western. Do you buy that label?*
It has more in common with stories from mythology that go back to the Greeks and beyond. Most of the ideas came from ancient, timeworn tales.

Which you consciously updated?
Yes. I did a lot of research. It took two years to write, between what was coming out of my brain and the research I did in various mythological genres, which included fairy tales, folk tales and myths. You begin to understand how basic storytelling works when you immerse yourself in those genres. I was conscious about doing a modern fairy tale. It came out of one of the reactions to *American Graffiti.* After the movie came out, I got hundreds of cards and letters from preteenagers and young teenagers say-ing different versions of "Gosh, I didn't know that everybody has a tough time being a teenager." The kids were saying, "The problems I'm having are all the same problems the guys in the movies were having, and I guess they had those ten years ago."

It was easy to identify with those kids.
For a lot of people it basically said, "It's okay to be a teenager. You don't have to be some twenty-three-year-old groovy guy. You can be a fourteen-year-old nerd and still chase girls and have fun." The point was, you don't have to throw away your teenage years trying to be cool. That was liberating for kids struggling through that difficult period. Before *American Graffiti,* I was working on basically negative movies — *Apocalypse* and *THX,* both very angry. When I did *Graffiti,* I discovered that making a positive film is exhilarating.

How did this lead to Star Wars?
I thought, "Maybe I should make a movie like this for even younger kids." I realized that there are really no modern fairy tales. The western really was the last of the modern myths.

What was it you wanted to communicate to these younger kids?

When I made *Graffiti,* I was twenty-three years old. I was very aware of the changes taking place around me as I was growing up, and I loved it, but at the same time it was sad. I was kind of nostalgic for the loss of youth, I guess. But that's the point: things change, life goes on. Life is a constant transition, and you have to accept that fact. The film is all about the fact that you can't hang on to the past. The future may be completely strange and different and scary, but that's the way it should be. I thought that was one of the biggest challenges facing teenagers. I got to do what I wanted to do by not being frightened away by the future and the unknown, and I figured that was a good message to get across. *Star Wars* says the same thing in terms of technology, space flight and opening up the world.

So your intention was to make something more than pure shoot-'em-up entertainment?

The idea is not to be afraid of change. There are bad robots, good robots, aliens and monsters in all forms. *Star Wars* shows progression. You may be frightened—and it's sad because you are leaving something behind—but go forward. That's what life is about. You can either have a good attitude about change or a bad attitude about it. You can't fight tidal waves, you can only ride them. So the best thing to do is get your surfboard and make the best of it.

But in saying, "Accept the way things are going; there's nothing you can do about it anyway," aren't you encouraging passivity?

No. You must accept change so you can control it and make it work *for* you. People who fear that computers will take over the world are incapacitated. Those who realize that computers are here, and so you might as well learn how to make them work for you, are the ones who will have an advantage in the future—they will help determine how we use the new technology, how the new world is shaped. I think it's the people who realize this the fastest who can go in and subvert the system and direct it and have a far greater impact than the ones who try to throw bombs. I believe people learned that lesson in the Sixties.

A lot of people try to write off that period as insignificant because the tides have turned so dramatically. What do you think?

That period was definitely not insignificant. That little pockmark on history is going to go a long way. We swing in a different direction. The upheaval that occurred in that ten-year period will completely change things. Part of what we are going through now is because that period tarnished a lot. It poked a lot of holes in seemingly invincible facades. Culturally and psychologically, we haven't even begun to feel the impact of that. You can't have something as powerful as the Sixties and not have a consequence. Just because things appear quiet on the surface doesn't mean we are not in the midst of a completely new era. We don't know where it will lead, but the Sixties set us on a new course.

Did it set us in a progressive direction, or are we just more cynical?
I don't know. It will evolve, whether for good or bad. The point is that the period sent us spinning, changed our course forever. I feel fortunate that I happened to be there for that course change. I think there may be at least one more important course change in my lifetime. They come rarely, but their impact is huge. World War II was a course change. Wars have a tendency to be course changes, which is why it is dangerous for a society to get into a war—it shakes up the status quo. Vietnam is a perfect example. It was billed as a completely harmless war way over *there*; no bomb was ever going to fall on United States soil. But a *huge* psychological bomb landed on United States soil, and it changed it forever.

It's an ironic point: wars are often designed to maintain the status quo.
That's right. They are destroying the very thing they are supposedly trying to save. Before Vietnam, the United States was a very young country. It is like we turned eighteen or so in the Sixties. Now we're acting differently than when we were teenagers—for better or worse. Part of that is not for the better.

For example?
The system has not worked as efficiently as it used to. A culture operates totally on faith: if you can get a large group of people to believe something, then it works. If you can't, then it won't work. The Sixties shot the hell out of any shared vision we had for this place. It's going to be interesting, because it is going to lead to some new vision. It may take a hundred years to get there, but the fact is that eventually historians will look back and point to this period we are living in right now as a significant beginning.

Do you intentionally make movies with messages? Is that how you choose what you will make?

That is almost out of my control. I make films about the things I feel deeply about. I couldn't commit two or three years of my life to doing something just to make a living. Making a movie comes from a lot of complicated reasons, a lot of emotional and personal reasons. I create out of a need that I have to fulfill in myself. I don't have much control over it. Other than the movies I get involved in to support my friends' projects, I make movies that I have to make.

Is it just coincidence or luck that your passions happen to be incredibly commercial?

The fact that my particular talent connects on a level that a lot of people can relate to is just luck. I am also lucky to have a certain talent to make movies. I derive pleasure from storytelling. It is fun to sit around a fireplace and tell a story, and have everyone go "Oooh" and "Ahhh." That's what I'm doing with *Star Wars* or *American Graffiti*. In my current position, I can tell stories through large, epic, entertaining movies.

Do you get the same gratification from being a producer as you did from directing?

If I can get the right director, who thinks the way I think, it's the same thing. It is not as exciting as directing, but it is possible to do more this way.

If the perfect project came along, some grand idea that you were passionate about, would you consider directing it?

Oh, yeah. I will go back to directing one of these days. Most of the films I personally would like to explore aren't giant movies.

Do you feel that movies are simple escapism, or are they something more significant?

Movies are fantasy. People have fantasies, they have psychological needs. Films appeal to those needs. It is very easy to see why most exploitative movies work.

Are you speaking as a filmmaker?

And as a student of psychology. Filmmaking is a craft. Filmmaking is knowing how to communicate visually.

*So are filmmakers obligated to make socially constructive as opposed to exploita-
tive movies?*
The twenty-five percent of people that are using media in a responsible
way have enormous impact. Unfortunately, the others have an enormous
impact, too.

*Star Wars certainly affected pop culture—in fact, it created a sort of subculture.
My five-year-old and his friends spend half their time being Luke and fighting
the Empire.*
Well, part of it was designed, as I said, to give kids a kind of focus. Again,
it was a conscious attempt at creating new myths. *Star Wars* had a huge
impact. A lot of the other movies I have done didn't have much impact.
You don't go into a movie thinking about that. You make a movie because
you need to say something.

What are you working on now?
Three movies. First, there's *Tucker,* directed by Francis Coppola, the true
story of the innovative car designer Preston Tucker. It's about the life of an
entrepreneur and the fate of creativity in a modern, financially oriented
America. Then, Ron Howard is directing *Willow,* an adventure-fantasy that
takes place a long time ago in a mythical land. It's different than the other
things he's done. It's something I've been working on for about ten years;
I've [finally] managed to get all the pieces put together. The third one is an
animated feature about dinosaurs, with Steven Spielberg.

Are there more Indiana Jones sequels coming?
Steven and I are developing one.

What's going on at Skywalker Ranch these days?
The ranch is an office complex, not, as distorted reports say, a film school
or some Shangri-La. Basically it's an office complex where creative people
can work. Eventually we will have our own special-effects facility here.

*How about the overall direction of Lucasfilm? You have sold Pixar, your com-
puter division; and some recent movies, notably the much-publicized* Howard
the Duck, *didn't make it.*
Over the last five, six years, I learned a lot about business.

Can we expect the much-anticipated sequel or prequel to Star Wars?
I'll do more eventually; I just don't know when. I've done a lot of research,
but my heart is in other areas now. I can make more *Star Wars* and make
zillions of dollars, but I don't need to do that, and I really don't have the
interest right now. There is a story there I would like to tell. It's just that it
isn't beating in my head hard enough to say, "I have to get this out of
here." I'm more interested in other things.

In cowboy movies the good guys won with their bravery and guns. In Star Wars
the good guys had more than phasers; they had the Force. What is the Force?
The Force is what happens in spite of us that we can either use or not use.
We can fight these changes, or we can use them, incorporate them into
our lives, take full advantage of them. One of the most significant
moments in establishing our direction now was when we landed on the
moon. It was the first time we could look back and see us as one planet.
We began to perceive ourselves as a human race, as one world, one little
ball of humanity. We had new information with which to go forward.
Some people got scared, turned inward, became overwhelmed. Others *saw.*

Saw what?
We saw why you cannot blindly set off an atomic bomb, for example. It is
one planet and what you do on one side of the planet will affect the entire
planet. The ecology of the rain forests in Brazil affects everyone. On a cultural level we are seeing it, too. Everything will merge into one culture.
There will be one language everyone will speak. The issues that emerge
then are not which nation is going to beat which other nation in a war but
how to address the problem that there are some people who have and others who have not. We always addressed it on a provincial level, but when
you realize that it is all interconnected, you realize that you have to
address it on a global level.

The opposing view is the nostalgic notion I was talking about—fear of
change: "I don't want to lose myself in the greater ocean of humanity."
Kick and scream all you want, but that is the way things are going. Region-
alism is going to disappear, for better or worse—probably for better *and*
worse. You can preserve little bits of culture here and there, but the new
culture will be global. Multinational corporations are one of the biggest
forces in this. You might as well accept the fact that the McDonald's in

Turkey tastes exactly like the McDonald's in New York City. That's not something to argue with. It is the way it is.

Do you believe that individual cultures will be lost as a result?
Cultures by definition are metamorphosing. Cultures have always grown from other cultures. In each, there were people bemoaning the loss of the way things were. There were also other people celebrating the new challenges. That, to me, is the only way to go. *Star Wars* served to challenge the imagination and say, "For one second take your eyes off your feet and look at the stars."

A Short Time Ago, On A Ranch Not So Far Away...

LISA VINCENZI/1990

AT SKYWALKER RANCH, HIS sanctuary cum corporate complex in Marin County, George Lucas casts an unassuming figure in standard-issue jeans and sneakers. In this setting—the white Main House in a green valley with untrafficked trails, which lead to smaller buildings called the Stable, Carriage House, Gate House, and Brook House—"Hollywood" is a world away. And it seems quite in character when Lucas says that creating hit movies "was not something I expected to do. Never. It was the furthest thing from my mind."

Yet a series of shifts in focus throughout his career have thrust the notoriously low-profile producer-director into a very-high-profile position. After more than a decade of sticking to an established track—resulting in the *Star Wars* trilogy, the Indiana Jones movies, and Lucasfilm, a profitable, multidepartmental corporation that defines the cutting edge of American filmmaking—Lucas is ready to refocus. And when Lucas decides to refocus his energies, it's enough to pique everyone's interest.

"I want to operate more independently," he says. "I'm going back to making movies, and the company is going off to be the company. I've been moving away for the last few years anyway, and the [individual divisions] are more capable of handling their own future. All the divisions are really superior in what they do; they're going into areas I'm not familiar with."

From *Millimeter*, April 1990, pp. 46–56. Reprinted by permission.

George Lucas's feature directorial credits number only three: *THX-1138,*
American Graffiti, and *Star Wars.* His imagination, unthwarted by technological limitations, inspired a segment of the film industry to test boundaries
with new and improved special-effects techniques. Though not all Lucas
projects have had resounding impact (*Willow* performed disappointingly at
the box office and *Howard the Duck* was, simply, an all-around disappointment), his creative influence, as executive producer on *The Empire Strikes*
Back, Raiders of the Lost Ark, Indiana Jones and the Temple of Doom, and
Indiana Jones and the Last Crusade, reached beyond the business of movies
and into the American psyche.

Lucas describes the films he wanted to make as "underground, tone-
poem movies." But he knew that avocation wouldn't pay the bills. After
completing USC's film program, he says, "I figured I would come back to
San Francisco, make movies like James Broughton (the patriarch of San
Francisco's independent scene whose films include *Mother's Day* and *The*
Bed) and the guys who are up here making movies, and then make my living as a documentary cameraman and editor. That's what I really wanted
to do. That was my love."

Perhaps "the Force" was with him long before *Star Wars* was even an
idea. A scholarship connected Lucas with Francis Ford Coppola. "He encouraged me to learn how to write, and he's the kind of director who works
with actors," Lucas says. "So I learned a whole different area, and, in the
process, started writing screenplays, got a chance to direct one of them,
and went off into the world of theatrical filmmaking."

His first venture into the movie mainstream was 1971's *THX-1138,* an
expanded version of his 1965 prize-winning science-fiction short of the
same title. "*THX,* at that time, was about as theatrical a movie as I could
make. And it was sort of between the experimental moviemaking I'd been
doing and what I thought traditional storytelling techniques were. Out of
that came the challenge to do something really normal—to do a regular
movie that was funny and had good characters. It was presented to me as a
challenge, and I said, 'I know I can do it.' So I made *American Graffiti,* and
that became so successful, I realized I could actually make a living that way."

That could be the understatement of the millennium. The tender nostalgia and racy humor of *American Graffiti* painted a detailed portrait of the
late-fifties/early-sixties and scored big at the box office. His next project,
Star Wars, broke the bank. In the film, Lucas created other-worldly creatures

embroiled in a mythic struggle of good versus evil, good fighting the powerful dark enemy on an intergalactic battlefield. In Lucas's universe, aliens drank at a cosmic watering hole, fantastic vehicles roamed the heavens, and light-sabers hummed. To fully realize these concepts, Lucas ventured beyond the contemporary tools of filmmaking.

"George Lucas went around to all the existing remnants, really, of the effects studios and was told, 'No way. The technology's not here. You're dreaming,'" relates Rose Duignan, director of marketing at Industrial Light & Magic, the special-effects division of Lucasfilm. So a group of young, technically creative people, under effects specialist John Dykstra, was assembled to build proprietary equipment that could deliver the necessary computer-controlled camera shots and multiple-elements work. Two years and more than $2 million later, the bugs had been worked out. When *Star Wars* opened in 1977, the megahit revived the dying art of special effects, pioneered the marriage of computer and camera (motion control), and resurrected the VistaVision format.

In 1981, after the *Star Wars* sequel, *The Empire Strikes Back*, and the Lucasfilm-related *Raiders of the Lost Ark*, ILM took on outside projects such as *Dragon Slayer*, *Poltergeist*, *Star Trek II: The Wrath of Khan*, and *E.T. The Extra-Terrestrial*. In 1983, when the third part of the *Star Wars* trilogy, *Return of the Jedi*, was in production, the effects division's work was exclusively devoted to that Lucasfilm project. Over 500 shots were completed for *Jedi*, which required a staff of more that 200 people. Then, in 1984, ILM resumed its work for outside projects, continuing to gain world renown for its effects and amassing 11 Academy Award nominations, nine Oscars, and four Technical Achievement Awards. This year two more ILM projects, *The Abyss* and *Back to the Future II*, vied for Oscars.

Today, ILM is just one division of Lucas's diverse empire. Lucas himself pauses when asked to number them, estimating, in all, 16 subdivisions, including less-publicized segments such as the Games division, Learning Systems, LucasArts Luminaire, LucasArts Attractions, LucasArts Licensing, and the more visible THX Group and Skywalker Group. "Up to a point, I kept a pretty tighthand on the growth of the company. I didn't want it to grow, because it was interfering with my time management," says Lucas, who tries to work only three days a week, between 11 a.m. and 4 p.m., though he admits, "it doesn't always work out that way." Still, Lucas says, "I don't work as hard as I used to."

Yet "the company is growing larger, and in order to really expand," he goes on, "we're splitting it apart. The area I'm mostly focused on, which is actual production of theatrical movies, is coming more under my personal involvement; then, with the other parts of the company, because they need to grow and flourish, I'm now letting them loose, so to speak."

That, however, doesn't mean the other divisions will go the way of Pixar, which was sold to Steve Jobs in 1986. The computer division's original purpose was to develop hardware for ILM's graphics department, as well as several other computer technologies, including the EditDroid, for other divisions. "Once that was developed, then we didn't need a company that manufactured computer hardware. I didn't particularly want to be in hardware manufacturing," Lucas says. "So, we sold that off."

The EditDroid has its own history. The first attempt to launch the optical-disc-based editing system misfired three years ago, and a revamped version made a comeback earlier this year. "We decided that marketing the EditDroid the old way [by selling units] wasn't really going to work," Lucas explains. "So we closed that down and developed a whole new EditDroid [for leasing only]. It's much more advanced than the original. And we're going to try and [lease to facilities]; that makes it easier to maintain and keep quality control, which was a real problem when we tried to sell it."

The inspiration of Lucasfilm's technical developments stem from the company founder's general aim: To expand and improve the filmmaker's creative tools. And, much like the original developments at ILM were the outgrowth of Lucas's own requirements for the *Star Wars* movies, his own roots as a film editor may have set the gears in motion for the EditDroid. "In postproduction, machines like the EditDroid allow you to work faster, to take less time with spliced tape and more time with the actual cut," says Lucas. "It doesn't expand the [filmmaker's] vocabulary, but it's much easier to do your job when you don't have to spend as much energy on the prosaic work."

Yet, just as Lucas's personal interests aren't limited exclusively to motion pictures, not all of Lucasfilms' departments are exclusively related to theatrical motion pictures. His interest in education led him to explore interactive learning systems. "I've always been interested in education and supported educational institutions," says Lucas, who has been developing interactive for several years. "The time has come to build a serious prototype, so people can see the possibilities of this medium," Lucas says of the venture, which he describes as more or less nonprofitable.

The first major product to come out of the Learning Systems division, a joint effort with Apple Computer and National Geographic, is "GTV: A Geographic Perspective of American History," which was released in February by the National Geographic Society. "GTV," published by the NGS, consists of two videodiscs and an accompanying software system that allows manipulation of video images by users to create short shows organized along thematic lines, says Craig Southard, director, Lucasfilm Learning Systems. "The fun part is [a feature] called Showmaker, which is like a junior video editing system."

Showmaker can access 1,600 images and a couple of hundred maps, to create video book reports that can be annotated with word processing. "Most schools have computers but aren't utilizing them 100 percent," Southard notes. Products like GTV, and others in development at Lucasfilm for the Audubon Society and the Smithsonian, are addressing the potential of computers as educational tools. Also on the division's agenda is the development of learning systems for business applications. Southard says Learning Systems is "like a lot of divisions at Lucasfilm, which are branching into other areas."

Another department at Lucasfilm is the extensive book collection housed in a wood-paneled library topped with a stained-glass dome. The volumes number between 15,000 and 20,000; tucked away in 400 drawers are photos collected since 1920 from all over the world. In 1987, with the acquisition of a "major Hollywood studio collection," the library's overall collection more than tripled. The Lucasfilm library, founded in 1978, is one of a handful today designed to specifically support visual research, since most studios no longer house their own libraries. But, says director of research Deborah Fine, "research is not a profitable business. It has expensive overhead, and you can never really cover your operational costs. That's why studios have been reluctant to support them."

Hoping to make the library more profitable and better utilized, Lucasfilm has opened it to outside sources, and will service everything from feature films to commercials in their visual research. Applications include DPs requesting photos of a particular painter's work; art directors looking for visual and written reference material on a period or place, say, New York City's Lower East Side at the turn of the century; location scouts who might want to find out where the greatest concentration of mosques can be found in Morocco; screenwriters looking for inspirational details on a subject; or, simply, ILM model makers who need visual reference to build fantastic creatures.

Though profits may not motivate all activities at Lucasfilm, the company is currently profitable. Revenues from feature work for 1988 were up 75 percent and another 70 percent in 1989. The growth was due to a number of factors: In 1988, for example, *Who Framed Roger Rabbit* required more composite shots than all three *Star Wars* pictures put together, says Scott Ross, ILM vice president and general manager. And in addition to the truly large projects ILM worked on, noneffects films like *Tucker* (for which ILM served as consultant on splitscreen shots) and *The Accidental Tourist* (shots for the opening title sequence) sought ILM's special touch for more reality-based material.

Yet, says Ross, "we find many studios and many producers and directors don't understand what we do and how we do it. To them, [special effects are] a frightening void." He adds, "We tell directors and writers not to write their scripts based on what their understanding of the technology is, to really roam free and take advantage of their creative spirit." And, even though ILM is in the business of creating special effects, Ross says "our job is to cut visual effects out of a movie." ILM also wants to address time-frame expectations. "It's like turning to Vincent Van Gogh and saying, 'Paint Starry Night again, only make it red, and I want it done tomorrow.' This is an art form. You just can't do that."

The most complicated, time-consuming, and vanguard ILM effects, says Lucas, involve the computer-graphics division, which evolved from Pixar, picking up where Pixar left off. Most directors, says Nancy St. John, executive producer and manager of computer graphics imaging (who recently came over from PDI), "don't know how the inside of a camera works, but they have confidence, standing there with their crew and telling the DP what they want. That's all they really need to know to do their shot. Well, unfortunately, they come to computer graphics and think, 'Oh God, I've got to know how to write programs.' Not true. They don't need any of that. All they need to do is tell the animators and technical directors what they want. We'll figure out the mechanics."

In addition to technique, ILM is trying to familiarize the industry with budgeting effects in terms of time and money. Not just the film industry either. ILM is aggressively going after nonfeature business; the company is becoming an integrated studio catering to all sorts of producers—specifically special effects for the commercial realm.

For a long time, ILM was receiving unsolicited boards and inquiries from the advertising industry, and the company finally decided to respond. The initial idea, when Scott Ross joined ILM from One Pass Film & Video two years ago, was to do spots between feature-film projects. At the time, Ross says, "it was feast or famine. We were either doing eight pictures at once, or we weren't really working. We needed to diversify to keep a constant flow."

It was decided, though, that commercial production had its own "mentality," and should stand on its own, apart from features. "We realized," says Andrea Merrim, head of production, San Rafael, Lucasfilm Commercial Productions, "commercials are not something you can just squeeze in between features. It's a different working setup, a different bidding process." The concept was eventually taken beyond special effects. "We wanted to attract a group of high-quality directors who did all kinds of commercials: some special effects, but also live action, comedy, dialogue, and pretty pictures. We'd have the best of all worlds. We'd have A-level directors (including Barry Sonnenfeld, Haskell Wexler, and Vilmos Zsigmond) and the best special-effects company around. We were in the fortunate position to sit back and say, 'Let's start a company.'" And they did. Lucasfilm Commercial Productions, which has offices in New York, Chicago, Los Angeles, and at the San Rafael headquarters, will be one year old next month.

Meanwhile, Lucasfilm is 19 years old and its leader is getting restless again. Whatever paths George Lucas has traveled so far, he says, "I've continued in the independent filmmaking direction—where I started. Now, I'm [taking another turn], allowing the company to expand, grow, and blossom the way it should, which gives me more time to focus on the learning systems I'm developing and the movies I want to write and direct. I just want to get back to what I started doing."

MILLIMETER: *You seem to prefer the producer's chair to the director's . . .*
LUCAS: It's not that I prefer producing, that's just where I find myself these days. It wasn't something I did by choice, I was just more effective in the producing arena, which is where the opportunities have presented themselves over the last few years. Eventually I'll go back and direct.

Ultimately, I'm a director. I've done many other things, but that's really where my heart is.

MILLIMETER: *Many of your films are anchored in your knowledge of mythology. Is that an area that still interests you? Is it something that will continue to factor into your work?*

LUCAS: Yes. In fact, the subjects and themes of all my movies are usually issues I'm emotionally involved with one way or another. I don't just make movies for the sake of making movies. I create mostly everything myself. I don't get six scripts sent to me and say, "I'll take this one and make that movie." I get an idea, then I go out and make the movie, write the screenplay, do the whole process. That's a different way of operating.

MILLIMETER: *Will you go back to making more reality-based films, like* American Graffiti?

LUCAS: Probably. Again it's hard to know where the line between reality and fantasy begins and ends. Because *American Graffiti, Indiana Jones*, and *Star Wars* could all be considered fantasies, though some are more reality-based than others.

MILLIMETER: *You've had a lion's share of blockbusters. Is that important to you?*

LUCAS: No. I've been amused that people equate what I do with making hit movies. All I ever hope for with my movies is that they break even and make everybody whole again. There's always this chance that one will be successful and go beyond that, but I don't create movies just to make them successful. I make movies to make them good—from that has come the success. But it was all unplanned.

MILLIMETER: *You've said the* Star Wars *movies had gotten so expensive that, in the future, you'll need to figure out a way to make them financially feasible. Are you considering filming back to back, like* Back to the Future II *and* III?

LUCAS: Well, yeah. If I do the next *Star Wars* trilogy, I'll do all three at once. That's sort of been the plan from the beginning. And we've been researching various production feasibility studies: How it could be accomplished and where they would get made. Then, of course, we've been advancing the technology at ILM to try to bring costs down. We've been improving postproduction, too. Ultimately, when I get to the point of writing the stories and putting all the technology in place, and if inflation doesn't run over me first, I think we'll do them at a reasonable cost.

MILLIMETER: *What is reasonable today?*
LUCAS: Something under $35 million.

MILLIMETER: *Do you see applications for HDTV in your own work? Are you interested in those developments?*
LUCAS: We're interested. We actually shot a film on HDTV here, which involved ILM. It's a very exciting area that, ultimately, is the future of film and television. That's where it's going to merge, and the electronic medium will eventually take over the celluloid medium. There's no doubt about that. As anybody [who's had to pair] sprocket holes realizes, it's much easier to work with magnetic tape. It's faster and more flexible. And it's not going to be that much longer before the resolution is equal to VistaVision or better. The Japanese are light years ahead of anything that's going on in this country. Celluloid is a 19th-century idea. We're moving into the 21st century.

George Lucas: His First Love Is Editing

DENISE ABBOTT/1991

FIFTEEN YEARS AGO, GEORGE Lucas changed the shape of the movie industry. His *Star Wars* forged new frontiers in sound design and special effects, broke all box office records, won seven Oscars and, with its two sequels, made Lucasfilm over $100 million. Since then, he's had a hand—as a writer, producer, director, or all three—in six of the ten largest grossing films of all time. The list begins with his *Star Wars* trilogy in 1977 and extends to all three *Indiana Jones* movies, for which Lucas wrote the stories that Steven Spielberg directed.

Yet, Lucas has been more out of Hollywood than in it, spending his days at the 2900 acre "ranch" he has built 450 miles north of Los Angeles, just across the Golden Gate Bridge from San Francisco. It's here that he runs Lucasfilm Ltd., one of the most successful independent production companies in the world. Lucasfilm's research and development in special effects and sound quality have earned him a place in cinema history as an unquestioned pioneer of visual and sound technology. This consistent innovation has also earned him ACE's Golden Eddie Award, the first time in two decades the organization has handed out the trophy that honors "notable and conspicuous contributions to the art and craft of film."

For a man who's been receiving top awards ever since he was a film student at USC in the 6os, Lucas seems especially pleased to be honored by ACE. In a sense, it brings things full circle since his first job editing under

From *American Cinemeditor,* Spring 1991, pp. 8–9, 16. Reprinted by permission.

Verna Fields on a USIA (United States Information Agency) documentary covering President Johnson's trip to Asia. "My first love is editing," reveals Lucas. "It's what I came out of, and it's still what I enjoy most."

He enjoys it so much, in fact, that he regularly is asked to re-edit his director's rough cut. "It's a labor of love," he admits with a smile. "Working the Moviola is fun. The director makes a black and white of his cut, and then I do my version. I look at that phase as the last rewrite, a fresh slate. The disadvantage an editor has is that he's trying to bring forth the director's vision. Fortunately, I have the director's permission to throw out his vision and go straight to the heart, what we were aiming for in that very first story conference. But I don't ram anything down the director's throat," he quickly adds. "I simply offer up another possibility. The director always has final say." Similarly, Lucas skips viewing dailies because he doesn't believe in standing over the director's shoulder. "If I've hired someone to direct, I've got to trust him to direct."

His background as an editor has not been lost on Lucas, the writer, director, producer, and post-production czar. "I write as an editor. I understand how scenes go together and how much of the story I need to tell because I've spent so much time fixing and rewriting in the editing room." The gorgeous cutting rooms at Skywalker Ranch are built on the premise that editors are people too. "Creative people need an environment that's conducive to being creative and thinking well. It may be possible to create in small, cramped spaces but, the truth is, it doesn't come out the same," declares Lucas.

He expresses concern that editing, because it comes at the tail end of the filmmaking process, tends to get short shrift. "Film editing is sophisticated and complicated, and there are limits as to how much you can rush it. I've seen so many movies with problems trying to adhere to impossible schedules, throwing away any possible chance of success, just to make an arbitrary release date. The thinking is: put 50 people on it and work them 20 hours a day until they drop; then expect a miracle."

Lucas believes that the sound track is 50% of the filmgoing experience. "Sound is an extremely important part of creating mood and emotional experience. But because sound is the least expensive part of making a film, the track gets little attention. It's a shame how sound has been treated over the years." Lucas brings both his sound editor and picture editor onto a project prior to shooting so they can collaborate. The sound editor works on sound/picture relationships and develops a sound track as the scenes are being shot. "When we see a rough cut, it's got sound and music," he explains. "We may change it all, but everything is not brought up at the last minute with the editor asking the director, 'Do you want this doorknob or that doorknob?' Working sound into the development of the movie makes a huge difference."

After the movie is honed to a point with which he feels comfortable, Lucas invites groups of friends in to screen the picture and offer their opinions. He'll preview once in a movie theater with an invited cross section of an audience. "It's not for marketing purposes but to help me understand editing-wise what's going on. Otherwise, after working on a picture for a while I'm no longer sure what works and what doesn't, but when I sit in a theater I know."

When it comes to hiring an editor, he acknowledges that choosing the right person can be a tough call and that, in fact, he's made some mistakes. "It's very hard to judge editing because a lot of it is very subtle. You don't know who's responsible for the bad cut or the good cut—the director or the editor. I've actually been lucky in finding some extremely talented editors."

One of USC's most illustrious alumni, Lucas made several short films there, including *THX-1138*, which took first prize at the 1967–68 National Student Film Festival. Warner Brothers awarded him a scholarship to observe the filming of *Finian's Rainbow*, directed by Francis Coppola. Lucas recalls, "Francis offered to use me as his assistant. My first assignment was to come up with one good idea a day. Most of the time I ended up hanging out in the editing room with Mel Shapiro. My strength was camera and editing and Francis's was actors and writing . . . so we were a good match."

The following year he got a deal at Warner Brothers to develop *THX* as a screenplay and to work as Francis's assistant on *Rain People*. "We started in New York and traveled across the country. I'd write *THX* from four to six in the morning and then go to work. Simultaneously, I was shooting and cutting a documentary on the making of *Rain People*.

Lucas and Coppola shared a common vision. They dreamed of starting an independent film production company where a community of writers, producers, and directors could share ideas. In 1969, the two filmmakers moved to Northern California, where they founded American Zoetrope. "Francis convinced Warners to invest in our first feature, which was *THX*.

After they saw the film, they pretty much pulled out of American Zoetrope, which forced Francis to go make *The Godfather.*"

Meanwhile, Lucas went off to develop *American Graffiti* and eventually got the green light to make it at Universal with Coppola as producer. "When I first took the project, around town it was considered extremely avant garde to intercut four different stories. Everyone wanted me to tell one story at a time or else have a single character who ran through the entire piece. Now, of course, many TV shows are intercut, but at the time everyone thought I was on Mars. Plus, there was the complicated music situation as well. It was unusual for a story film to have literally wall-to-wall music.

"Editing *American Graffiti* was a nightmare. The first cut was an hour too long. Six months of trimming were required to bring it down to its final form. It was very complicated in terms of intercutting the sequences in order for the movie to make sense. We had to bring the whole thing down line by line."

Three years later, Lucas wrote and directed *Star Wars,* a film that not only brought audiences back to the theater but opened new frontiers for technicians. For that film, Lucas invested his own *American Graffiti* earnings into the establishment of Industrial Light and Magic (ILM) and Skywalker Sound to create the special effects and sound design used in *Star Wars.* "There was no alternative," he contends. "I was making this huge special effects movie, and there was no special effects company around that could handle that kind of project." The ILM team introduced new technology to the film industry and revolutionized special effects, while Skywalker Sound brought new dimensions to sound design as they created voices for aliens, creatures, and droids.

Besides making five more films in the mid 80s, Lucas concentrated on completing the building of Skywalker Ranch and developing individual divisions within Lucasfilm. The facilities were custom-designed by Lucas to accommodate the creative, technical, and administrative needs of the company. The ranch includes a 150,000 square foot post-production and music recording facility, as well as offices used for the research and development of new technologies in editing, audio, and multi-media. Currently, he's working on developing an all-digital post-production system. The first phase is the EditDroid, a compute-based editing station incorporating many different technologies. Lucas reveals, "Now we're trying to get the sound track to be all digital so we can manipulate things by memory without having to lay down a track. Resynching everything is very time-consuming, but if I could get it all on a disc, we could make those cuts instantaneously."

He's gratified that the quality of work at Skywalker Ranch has become the standard to which others in the industry aspire. "Rather than build facilities in keeping with the rest of the world, we said, 'Let's build something better and change the world so it becomes that good too.' It was a bit of a crusade in the beginning, but it's paid off." A little over a year ago, he created LucasArts Entertainment Company to take over all the operations that have grown out of Lucasfilms. "I found myself spending a huge amount of time running a very large corporation," he laments. "I want to get back to what I like to do—editing, writing, and making movies."

Interestingly, Lucas finds writing the toughest part of the creative process. "Writing is hard," he concedes, stroking his slightly greying beard. "I didn't expect I'd ever be a writer. I get a bug, a thought that sits in my brain, and if I can't get rid of it after a few years, I have to write it down. That's how I test an idea."

For someone who's pioneered so many technological advances, it's ironic that he doesn't give it a moment's thought when writing. "Entertainment is good ideas, not technology," he says matter of factly. "Good stories are still the heart of it all. The truth is I'm not that enamored with new technology; I just acknowledge its existence. All that special effects can do is to allow the writer or creator to let his imagination go wild and deal with themes that weren't possible before. It moves the envelope further out as to what the imagination can capture on film. It puts more colors on the palette."

He hasn't directed a film since *Star Wars* but fully intends to return to the director's chair at some point soon. "I've never had much conscious direction in my career," he says with a shrug. "I found myself being a producer because that's what I had to do at the time and the opportunities presented themselves. But I will get back to directing. Being an executive is fun in its own way, but it's like the difference between coaching and playing. Lately," he concludes with a knowing smile, "I've been getting the itch to play."

Lucasvision

IF YOU HAD TO pick just one person who best understands the worlds of entertainment and technology—and who easily traverses both—it would be George Lucas. The creator of the *Star Wars* and Indiana Jones film trilogies has traded in his Hollywood moniker of producer-director to become the ultimate: thinker-doer.

As owner of Lucasfilm Ltd. and several related high-technology companies, he has firmly planted his feet in both worlds and has staked his personal future and professional reputation on a melding of the two. This isn't newfound religion. Years ago, he left behind a Hollywood whose pettiness and lack of vision he abhorred, and moved his company to Northern California, closer to Silicon Valley.

Much the way he created a new standard for special effects with *Star Wars* in 1977, the 49-year-old filmmaker is leading the way in helping to define just how emerging technologies will affect movie-making and entertainment in general.

"Hollywood could be a winner," he says, "if studios cough up vital research and development funds. Technology could help to dramatically reduce the spiraling cost of making films, while offering the promise of making them more exciting."

With his recent TV series *The Young Indiana Jones Chronicles*, Mr. Lucas saved the expense of creating elaborate period sets by using computers to

From the *Wall Street Journal*, 21 March 1994, pp. R20. Reprinted by permission of the *Wall Street Journal*, © 1994 Dow Jones & Company, Inc. All Rights Reserved Worldwide.

"re-create" the backgrounds. He also used them to make a handful of people look like a crowd—winning no friends among extras, perhaps, but gaining the attention of studio bean counters.

An interactive fiber-optic network connects the North Carolina production site of his latest movie, *Radioland Murders,* with the post-production facilities at his Skywalker Ranch here. Mr. Lucas "visits" the set every morning without leaving the ranch, chatting with the crew via a two-way video hookup that allows interaction in real time, using compressed digital video.

The entertainment that comes from Lucasfilm—movies, television shows, computer games and more—will certainly play a role in the much-vaunted multimedia future. Mr. Lucas recently sat down with the *Wall Street Journal,* peered in his crystal ball, and had this to say:

THE WALL STREET JOURNAL: *Where do you think we are headed in the next five, 10, 15 years?*
MR. LUCAS: There's a lot of hype out there, but there's something real happening. It's the upgrading of telecommunications in this country, and that will have a tremendous and powerful impact on the way we live our lives. A lot of the rumbling right now is about home shopping and viewer-on-demand video, and those kinds of things really are going to happen.

If cable operators really want to grow the business, they'll have to compete with the existing home-video market. But a lot of the key issues have to do with pricing. If cable operators get greedy and charge, say, $20 an hour for programming—especially old programming—I don't think much is going to happen. But if they get it down to the level of $1 an hour, there will be an instantaneous revolution that will wipe out the home-video business in a year.

WSJ: *Do you think people really want all these services?*
MR. LUCAS: Definitely. They don't want it at $20 an hour; they don't want it at $10 an hour. But they'll take it at $1 an hour. They'll pay that for movies-on-demand, TV shows-on-demand. I think the only things you'll get on the TV networks will be info-commercials, talk shows and nondramatic programming. I don't think they'll be able to afford to put dramatic programs on the air—it's just too expensive.

"Programming that involves creative talent will end up on pay-on-demand." That's different from "pay-per-view," which will still be used for big events like championship fights. For those, they can charge $20 or $40 an hour. But to sell *Murphy Brown, Roseanne* or any movies, the price will have to be maintained at a very low rate before people will buy into it. And they will buy into it. They would just as soon not go out to the video store if they can get it at home.

WSJ: *What about a generational factor? Will older Americans resist the new technology and leave the 500-channel TV surfing to computer-literate kids?*

MR. LUCAS: I don't see it happening that way. I see it like the cellular phone and the fax machine. People say, "I don't get it; I don't need it." But then they'll see it being used and say, "I have to have one of these things." And it will be hard not to. People will discover that finding information on a computer will be infinitely easier than programming a VCR is today. Plus, audio-command technology is here. That is going to be a major factor. You can tell your TV, "I want to watch *Murphy Brown.*"

Older Americans, I think, will really go for the home-shopping services as they develop. The reality is that many of them would like to order up things at home and not have to go out.

WSJ: *Besides TV shows, movies and home shopping, what else might people order up on these new TV systems?*

MR. LUCAS: Well, I have a game company, and I think view-on-demand games will take off pretty quickly. It's a little bit problematical about how it's going to work, but it seems obvious that home delivery of games is a natural, because it's a digital medium that you're dealing with. Interactive games that involve more than one player—I call them "party-line games"—will be popular. You're playing with two or three other people at the same time at various places over the phone. Visual telecommunications and video conferencing will also add to this. If you're playing a game with two or three other people, you can see them all as you play. It's just like being next to them.

WSJ: *What impact will digital technology have on Hollywood as it relates to movie making?*

MR. LUCAS: The cost of making movies is going to come down. More filmmakers are going to be able to tell bigger stories. Take *The Age of Innocence.* It's hard for most filmmakers to get a movie like that off the ground today. The market isn't big enough, and the cost of doing a period movie like that is too expensive.

But on the *Young Indy* TV series—which was also a period show with horses, carriages, completely different landscapes, costumes—we had exactly the same kinds of production values as *Age of Innocence,* but we did it for 10% of the cost, thanks to digital technology. We used the computer to make crowd scenes, when we only had a handful of actors, and to replicate backgrounds that weren't really there.

That just means that more people will be allowed to make big films like *The Age of Innocence* than just Marty Scorcese, a man who's at the top of the field with a huge amount of clout. More people will be able to do something that's a little bit out of the action or other highly commercial genres. Studios will hopefully be able to make more movies, and they will then be able to take more chances and make more interesting films.

WSJ: *How important is that?*

MR. LUCAS: Listen, a lot of the films that I've made have been offbeat, really high-risk movies. *Star Wars* was a completely high-risk, nobody-out-there-understands-it kind of movie. Once it came out, it was a big hit because it was so fresh and different. Because it was so high-risk.

WSJ: *What kind of savings are we talking about?*

MR. LUCAS: We did a shot in the TV series for $1,500 that would have cost a studio $30,000 if they were doing the same shot for a feature film. *Radioland Murders,* the movie we're working on right now, is an experiment for us in that we're applying the cost-saving technology we learned on the TV series to the big screen. I don't think we can get that same shot done for $1,500, but we may be able to get it to $10,000 or $12,000. But even going to $12,000 from $30,000 is a major leap. And this is just the first step. We're inventing new technology that I feel very confident will allow us to cut that cost in half again. Within the next couple of years, we'll be able to take what was a $30,000 shot and do it on the big screen in full resolution for $6,000 or $7,000.

WSJ: *Tell me about* Radioland Murders.

MR. LUCAS: The budget is under $10 million. The average cost of making a movie today is $30 million. It's the kind of movie I like to make—it's frantic and crazy and fun—but it's difficult to get a movie like this made because it doesn't fit into any of the categories that studios like. This is a really wacko, offbeat comedy, set in 1939—and it doesn't have any movie stars. This isn't a romantic comedy with Tom Hanks and Meg Ryan, so the studio looks at it as this extreme wild card. If it were to cost $30 million, no one would make it. Not even with me attached as producer. But there's this chance it could break out. Universal Pictures will distribute it, maybe in the fall.

WSJ: *Among the studios in Hollywood, how do you rate the various managements and corporate cultures when it comes to melding entertainment and technology?*

MR. LUCAS: They're all struggling to figure out what they're doing, what they should be doing. They come up and we talk about things, but the funny thing is, not many of them listen. They're spending their money in the craziest ways. They won't put it where it has to go, in terms of investing in the technology. They figure somebody else will do it. We're not talking about huge sums of money—$10, $20, $30 million—but it would save them hundreds of millions of dollars if they would just step up to the plate and do it now. You're not going to see giant, overwhelming profits coming from multimedia for a number of years, but the investment has to be made now.

WSJ: *Besides the folks here at Lucasfilm, who are the visionaries in Hollywood?*

MR. LUCAS: There are a lot of people working down there, but there isn't anybody that comes to mind that I would say, "Here's somebody who's really got the picture." The studios are trying to figure out what to do and they're making a lot of interesting decisions.

It's funny. I've been in the game business for 15 years, and now all of a sudden all the studios are jumping in. They don't understand the marketplace or who the players are. Or that the players are bigger than they are.

WSJ: *What will going to the movies be like in the next century?*

MR. LUCAS: Older theaters will be gone. I think today's multiplexes are going to expand and become larger entertainment centers that also have Imax theaters and maybe 3-D theaters. There are going to be bigger, higher-quality images and better sound. There will be a much higher quality of presentation. Things like our THX sound system in theaters will add to that.

W S J : *Some people predict a rise in interactive theaters, where audience members push buttons to determine various changes in a plot to affect the outcome of the movie. What do you think of that concept?*

M R . L U C A S : I think that's "smell-o-vision." People don't want to do that. People do want to have an interactive experience, but I think they want to play interactive games. We've got a CD-ROM game called "Rebel Assault," where players actually get into the "movie." At any given moment, players hit a button or turn left and the action changes. The action shifts according to the way each player responds to certain commands. That is an interactive movie. I call it a game, but somebody else will call it an interactive movie.

If you want to see the future, "Rebel Assault" is the future. These games are going to become more articulate, more sophisticated and have higher-quality resolution. There will be better images, more conversations with the characters, and an appearance of an unlimited ability to move around. But it will be basically the same thing.

W S J : *Isn't the game market kind of a limited business?*

M R . L U C A S : Hardly. "Rebel Assault" just came out at Christmas, and we've already sold about 400,000 units. Before this, the industry saw any CD game that sold over 50,000 as very strong. We can't get it to the stores fast enough, and it's selling through better in Europe than it is here. More importantly, we've obviously hit a brand new population of game players with it. For hard-core gamers, "Rebel Assault" isn't their cup of tea. But there's a whole market of people who want to be able to sit down and have an interactive experience. This is sort of the *Jurassic Park* of CD games.

W S J : *Is there any danger that new technology poses for Hollywood?*

M R . L U C A S : Sure. I think you can make "cookie-cutter" movies with computers, and I'm certain some people will start doing that. Talent is expensive and, at the same time, thinking is hard. But computers or no computers, movies will always be about storytelling. I think you're going to find that the things that are worthwhile will involve the slightly psychotic state of a writer that produces the most interesting things to watch. If you take the "twist" out of movies, you've lost the interest of your audience.

WSJ: *The computer-generated dinosaurs that your company's Industrial Light & Magic division created for* Jurassic Park *left audiences dumbstruck. What was your reaction when you first saw them?*

MR. LUCAS: We did a test for Steven Spielberg; and when we put them up on the screen I had tears in my eyes. It was like one of those moments in history, like the invention of the light bulb or the first telephone call. A major gap had been crossed, and things were never going to be the same. You just cannot see them as anything but real. It's just impossible. Maybe 20 years from now, 50 years from now, they will look clumsy. But I'm not sure even that will happen.

I think we may have reached a level here where we have actually created reality, which of course is what we've been trying to do all along.

WSJ: *Fans of* Star Wars *are eagerly awaiting the next trilogy of movies. Some have been hoping the next movie might be ready for release in 1997, the 20-year anniversary of the first movie.*

MR. LUCAS: That's possible. I plan to start work on the screenplays soon and hope to be in production on the trilogy within the next two years. I think they'll be done in the next four to five years. But it really depends on how fast we can make these technological changes.

There are a lot of interesting aspects to the next stories, but if I were to do them the way I'd done the other *Star Wars* films, they would be astronomically expensive, over $100 million. The first *Star Wars* film cost less than $10 million. Nobody can afford to make a film for $100 million today. So we have to sort of reinvent the wheel. Most of what I'm working for is to be able to do the more fantasy-oriented, high-imagination movies and be able to accomplish them with a reasonable amount of money. It's all sort of dependent on how fast the new technology falls into place, but it's coming along pretty fast now.

Radioland Murders Press Conference

TRANSCRIBED BY SALLY KLINE/1994

Q : *How involved are you in film preservation efforts?*
A : I'm on a foundation with Marty Scorsese and a couple of other directors trying to save old movies and their negatives.

Q : *The announcement you made about the first three in the* Star Wars *trilogy,
the three earlier chapters, have you decided what studio you are going to do those
movies with and when they will go into production?*
A : We haven't made any decisions about the studios yet. I'm just about
ready to get started on writing the screenplays early next year.

Q : *So they'll go into production in 1995, you think?*
A : No. Probably not. We'll probably be doing all three of them at once.
That means it takes three times as long to get through the scripts and all
that sort of thing.

Q : *Will it be 1997 before we see the first one?*
A : I'm not sure. Probably later.

Q : *Could you tell us how* Radioland Murders *came about?*
A : It's an idea that I had that we developed into a screenplay. After *Star
Wars*, I decided that I wasn't that interested in directing at that point, and

---

George Lucas answered questions about producing *Radioland Murders* and other topics
at Pasadena's Ritz-Carlton Hotel on 8 October 1994. Transcribed and amended by Sally
Kline.

I wanted to continue to do the *Star Wars* saga. So I went into producing. And this project I put on the back shelf. I was very interested in it. It was one of my favorite projects, but I just didn't have the time to actually do it. And because I wasn't directing it and because it was sort of designed for me to direct, its very distinct style and the way it was put together, I had to wait until I could find somebody who could understand it and was willing to do it in that style and was not afraid of it.

Q: *How did you come by director Mel Smith?*
A: Well, we obviously interviewed a lot of directors and screened a lot of work. I like *The Tall Guy*. I thought it was very funny and in talking to Mel he seemed to understand the material very well. As these things always are, it's a matter of two minds coming together on an idea and agreeing on what should happen.

Q: *I'm interested in your use of computer-generated sets in putting pieces together, the level of technology used...*
A: What you should remember is that we are using the technology primarily as a cost cutting feature and as an integral part of the production process, just like building sets and using sound stages and that sort of thing. So, um, it's an outgrowth of what we've been doing for the last five years in television and we were very anxious to sort of move the process over the feature film medium, which is a much higher resolution. And I think we've pulled it off very successfully.

Q: *Could you talk about the new technology processes and their impact on film?*
A: Well, I think the techniques that we pioneered in the TV series [*The Young Indiana Jones Chronicles*] that we're now using in features are going to be one of the major differences about the way movies are made. And we are obviously moving that forward considerably to develop complete 3-D sets and build less and less and be able to fill in more extras of people and surroundings and that sort of thing. We'll do that all digitally. And I think that's going to be one of the major impacts, because it does change the whole process of making films.

Q: *To what extent are the digital effects used in this film. And also could you discuss the special video communications you used?*

A : Shot-wise, there are around 100 effects shots in the picture, which doesn't seem like much. But when you consider something like *Jurassic Park*, for which [Lucas's Industrial Light and Magic company] did all of the dinosaur-generated shots, there were less than that. Very few films have more than that. So it's a fairly high rate of special effects for a movie. Not only are we using digital technology, one of the things we've pioneered in the TV series, something that I've used in my productions ever since the beginning of when I started making movies, was a more non-linear way of making films. Which is that normally you write the film, you prep the film, you shoot the film, you do the sound on the film and everything is laid out on an assembly line. And I've never been comfortable with that. Because I'm a writer-director-editor-producer, I'm very much more comfortable working in the medium the way a painter or a sculptor or somebody would. You don't start in one corner and just work down to the bottom of the page. You basically put on a layer, then put on another layer, then you step back and look at it and put on another layer. And that's what we've been doing in the filmmaking process. Now with the digital technology that we've been using, working out of San Francisco, we've pioneered a lot of digital technology in terms of telecommunicating for various directors and producers to use our sound facility, to use I.L.M. And because of making the inroads around the world, we're now using it in the actual production itself. So we can connect the editing machines on the location with what is happening in the editing room and be able to have two-way conversations. And it's just like being there. We've sort of gotten rid of the problem of distance, because film is so immediate and you really need to have answers very quick. Because what ever happens on that set that afternoon is fixed in time, it's great to be able to collaborate long distances daily and talk about what's going on and offer suggestions.

Q : *Why was the* Radioland Murders *story significant to you?*
A : Well, um, I've always been interested in radio. I grew up with radio. We didn't get television until I was 10 years old, so most of my early years were sitting and listening to radio dramas. And I like being able to fill in the blanks with my imagination and hearing a story and I think that's always been very central to what I care about. I've always been very focused on the soundtrack of a movie and how it fits into the whole picture. This project sort of grew out of when I was doing *American Graffiti*, which was another radio listener's fantasy-themed movie. This is sort of an extension

of that idea, of a time I was very fascinated by radio drama. And I wanted to do a real out-and-out comedy, something a little wackier than what I had done with *American Graffiti*. That was the inspiration for doing it. And we developed the screenplay, like I said, but I just didn't have the time or energy to do it or find somebody to do it. So I just put it on the shelf and waited until the time was right.

Q: *What do you get out of producing and what do you like about directing?*

A: Producing, you get to do more different things all the time. For me, I can't direct a movie and produce at the same time. It's very hard. I can only really do one thing and that's direct. When I'm producing, I can produce four or five projects. I've got another TV movie coming out this week with this and with *Young Indiana Jones*. I'm able to go from one to the other. I get more done. I enjoy that. It's the difference between the coach on the sidelines of a football game and being a quarterback and actually doing the plays all the time.

Q: *Going back to technology, what do you think of the idea of scanning the actors into the computer to be used later on?*

A: Well, it's something that is used in games all the time. We use a video interface to capture the actors and then manipulate them around in the environments we need. The idea of taking pictures and then taking that actor for future use, I don't know if people have actually figured out exactly how that's going to work on a lot of different levels. At I.L.M., we've obviously done that. We can create actors that look as real as real actors. The question now is purely a matter of what the cost is. It's a very, very expensive process—to the tune of a few hundred thousand dollars for a few seconds—when you can get an actor to do it for infinitely less. People don't realize that in order to create a computer-generated character and have that character play a scene, there is always an actor involved. The actor may be called an animator, but the animator uses the same craft that an actual actor uses and you have to pay that person accordingly. You don't have to pay them movie star salaries, but you do have to pay them quite a bit of money. And with the technology and paying them quite a bit of money and the number of people involved, it's actually infinitely more expensive than using real actors. That factor's not going to go away for awhile. Instead of recognizing the actor, the actors will be people who are animators who work behind the camera. But the process is still exactly the same. And the human interface, the talent and craft, is still the same.

Q: *How close to your original mental image did you get with* Radioland
Murders? *How satisfied are you with the film now?*

A: I'm very satisfied, actually. I'm very pleased. It came out almost exactly
or even better that I hoped it would come out. There were times when it
was very dubious about whether I was going to be able to make it happen
one way or the other. And the balance—there's a lot of fairly experimental
ideas that are in this movie that aren't obvious. It's stylistically very strong
and there's two completely different levels of humor going on. Combining
this into a thing like this that moves as fast as this does and is paced the
way it is, it was hard to get people to understand how it was going to work.
This is technically a very complicated movie, much more than you'd assume. And it came well, exactly as I was hoping it would do.

Q: *Do you see this next* Star Wars *trilogy as a risk? Or is it a pre-sold thing?
Why did it take you so long before you were ready to tell the next three chapters?*

A: It's just that I've had other stories that I've wanted to do. When I finished the other *Star Wars*, I struggled to get those three finished, because
that was the original script. What I'm working on now is the material that
was developed in order to get to that script. Which is the pre-story. You
sort of have to develop a story, when you're writing a screenplay, about
where everybody comes from and who they are and why they got there
and all that kind of stuff just in order to tell the script that you're going to
do... And then I said, well, I still have this prequel story. It would be nice
to be able to start from the beginning and have it go all the way until the
end. But it wasn't something that I felt I needed to go out and do right
away. I had other things that were more interesting to me at the time and
weren't quite so demanding. Doing something like *Star Wars* is very demanding. Some of the things I wanted to do, I knew the technology wasn't
there... I had to find the right time in my life to fit it in. The biggest difficulty in success is that it brings you an unlimited amount of opportunities.
And at some point, you begin to realize that you have a limited amount of
time. So you have to say you can't do it all.

Q: *Do you see a risk in doing it?*

A: Not really. Part of the reason for doing it is that it's the first question I
get asked. Not "This is who I am" or anything, but "When are you going
to do the next *Star Wars*?" So if I do the next ones hopefully people will
introduce themselves first. Risk-wise, I think the story is good so it's not

esoteric really. I think a lot of people want to see it. And we're using a lot of cost-cutting technology and things we've developed; I don't think it's going to cost very much relative to the top end that I would ever make a movie for. I would never go above the $50 million range. The guys who are making films for $100,000, $120,000, that would be risky. They can never make money at that.

Q: *What are the remaining technological limits with these* Star Wars *movies; are there still things you can't put on the screen?*
A: I'm not sure. Now that we've moved to a digital environment—and that just happened in the last 5 or 6 years—there's a huge shift. So now that we are in that environment, there's almost no limits to what we're able to do. I think from here on, we're just going to perfect everything we've developed and the cost is going to come down. And things are going to be faster. It's basically the same issue as any digital world that you can deal with today. You want more storage and you want it to happen faster.

Q: *Do you see yourself as an artist or a businessman?*
A: I guess I'm both. I've been fortunate that I grew up in a business environment. My father was a businessman and I think he instilled a lot of basic business knowledge in my head so that I was able to survive in this business. At heart, I guess I'm an artist because I've spent my whole life making movies that I like to make. I live to make movies. And I've taken all the money and everything and put it back into making movies. And that's all I really care about. So in that sense I guess, the core of my life is making movies and the art of making movies. I've advanced the art of how you do it as well as the different ways of telling stories and using the medium in different ways. I'm very fascinated with all that as any painter or sculptor or anybody else would be. Painters spend as much time certainly coping with the technology, especially during the Renaissance, figuring out what color, how to invent new colors in order to make their palette more interesting. We're just continuing that. Fortunately, I'm smart enough as a businessman to remain independent. And the reason that I've put the effort in to remain independent, to keep my facility in San Francisco, and not be dictated to by the studios is because I want to tell my own story. I don't want a bunch of people coming in trying to figure out what the market wants. I just like to do what I like to do.

Q : *I was wondering about the role of computers in your life. And what about the role of religion?*

A : I am not focused on computers in my life, interestingly enough. I mean I use computers. But I don't spend my free time on the Internet or anything like that. I don't really have any free time. But it's a tool I use like anything. I have a laptop and a Mac, but I'm not a computer person at all. I have computer scientists who work for me who are the best in the world. I'm not anywhere near that sort of stuff and half the time I'm not sure of what they're talking about. But in terms of religion, I'm an inquisitive, probably fairly spiritual person. But I'm not directly connected with any particular religion.

Lucas the Loner Returns to *Wars*

REX WEINER/1995

GEORGE LUCAS SITS IN his office overlooking the sun-dappled hills of his 2,600-acre Skywalker Ranch and chuckles at the notion of his old friend and colleague Steven Spielberg down in smoggy Hollywood, hammering together his new studio with his partners, Jeffrey Katzenberg and David Geffen.

"Those guys have a lot of work to do," says the 51-year-old filmmaker, at ease in scuffed Nikes, jeans and a blue plaid shirt. "I keep saying, 'Why are you doing this? You own the universe, why do you want to go work in the stables?'"

Lucas is here in his office only because it is Friday, the one day a week when he tackles corporate tasks like opening his mail, attending Lucasfilm board meetings, checking out interactive games at LucasArts and, on rare occasions, talking to the press.

The rest of the time he's nestled in a secret hideaway within walking distance of his San Rafael home, putting on paper the futuristic fantasies that, before the decade is out, will become three more feature film episodes of Lucas's *Star Wars* epic. With some prodding, Lucas admits his intention to direct one of the films—and this is news.

The skinny kid from Modesto, Calif., who burst upon Hollywood in 1973 with *American Graffiti* and practically invented blockbuster motion picture economics with the *Star Wars* trilogy, has not directed a feature film since

From *Weekly Variety*, 5 June 1995, pp. 1, 59. Reprinted by permission.

the first *Star Wars* 18 years ago. Lucas long ago resigned his membership in the Academy of Motion Picture Arts & Sciences, quit both the writers and directors guilds in 1981, pulled up stakes and moved north to Marin County.

Lucas's antipathy toward Hollywood is well known—his feelings based on the experience of having his first two films recut against his will by the studios that owned them, as well his own admittedly conservative and, some say, shy nature. Even now, although the Academy handed Lucas its prestigious Thalberg Award in 1992, he decries what he sees as a lack of filmmaker-friendly types in the ranks of studio execs. Indeed, Lucas left Hollywood to make films his way.

Yet ironically, the filmmaker has spent much of his energy over the last decade servicing other people's films. His special effects division, Industrial Light & Magic, has created groundbreaking digital illusions for such films as Universal's current hit *Casper*—not to mention the dinos in Spielberg's *Jurassic Park.*

But the extremely competitive effects business has become one of shrinking profit margins. And with the exception of the Indiana Jones series, the few films Lucasfilm has produced since *Star Wars* have fared poorly.

Spielberg, on the other hand, chose to work within the Hollywood system, directing many of the most commercial and artistically successful films ever made.

Comparing the two talented peers begs the question of whether the middle years of Lucas's career have not been financially or artistically satisfying—whether or not Lucas is personally happy.

Lucas says he and Spielberg have debated the question many times over the years, often with Lucas grumbling about attending board meetings and Spielberg envying Lucas's autonomy.

"I don't like being chairman of the board," says Lucas.

His goal: "To make the next *Star Wars* with a lot more scope than I was able to do before, at a very reasonable cost, and be able to tell more interesting stories."

In the meantime, Lucas commands a privately owned company that is in many ways what old-line Hollywood studios are still striving to become: a true multimedia company engaged in the production of feature film, TV, commercials, interactive games, theatrical sound and home theater products, visual effects, licensing and post-production services on the cutting edge of the digital era.

But it has been a long and often painful process of trial and error. While Lucasfilm's record in the feature film division includes exec producing the Speilberg-helmed box office bonanzas *Raiders of the Lost Ark* and *Indiana Jones and the Temple of Doom,* the record also includes box office disappointments such as the Francis Coppola-directed *Tucker,* Ron Howard's *Willow* and, most recently, *Radioland Murders.* In 1986, Lucas exec produced Universal's notorious $35 million turkey, *Howard the Duck.*

Lucas's TV series, *The Young Indiana Jones Chronicles,* was canceled in 1993 by ABC, after the web aired 28 of the 32 hours that had been shot. LucasArts, the interactive games division founded in 1982, just after the crash of Atari, was not turning a significant profit until recently. Skywalker Sound sold off its L.A. facilities and retreated northward just last year.

Though isolated geographically from Hollywood infighting and distractions, Skywalker Ranch is beset by local opposition to expansion of its operations, a factor stalling key components of Lucas's long-range plans. Lucas, the father of three adopted daughters, underwent a painful divorce in the mid-80s. And a succession of top-level executive exits over the years hinted at political struggles and dissatisfaction among the rolling hills of Lucas Valley, which was so-named long before George Lucas set eyes upon it.

Given the myriad business uncertainties surrounding Lucas's enterprises, it's not surprising that more *Star Wars* sequels—perhaps the closest things in showbiz history to being sure hits—loom now on the horizon. But Lucas and his execs deny that *Star Wars* is a space race to solvency.

"Each year our business is better than ever," says Lucasfilm Ltd. president Gordon Radley.

Lucas himself shrugs off the executive shuffle and says *Young Indy* and other non-hit efforts were fruitful experiments in new production techniques. He says his company does not stand or fall on the success of its film ventures. Problems with the neighbors, he asserts, are all but settled.

What is important, in Lucas's view, is that he and his empire have at last attained what the entire enterprise has striven for since the very beginning: the technical capability to make the movies Lucas wants to make.

The pivotal moment was *Jurassic Park,* Lucas says. "The fact that you can make a realistic thing, as real as anything on the set, and have it walk around and talk was the big breakthrough."

Lucas's business plan, extending fifteen years into the future, calls for the eventual consolidation of all Lucasfilm operations on the ranch and relies heavily on the idea—technologically a few years off—that all production will flow freely between the various divisions on digital systems.

"I don't know another company like this one," says Radley. His office is on the first floor of the elegantly styled Main House, a handcrafted and antique-appointed manse with a cavernous foyer and winding staircase so magnificent that Robin Williams, on first visit, is said to have cried out, "Tara! I'm home!"

Radley believes Lucasfilm is misunderstood because it is a privately held business that answers to no one but its sole owner and exists far from the center of the entertainment industry. After a decade with the company, Radley, an attorney, speaks of his boss with conviction and a sense of wonder, as if anticipating a listener's disbelief.

"This is not a shareholder that is motivated out of a desire to make money," insists Radley. "This is not an IPO kind of business strategy. This is not about having venture capital or third party investors demanding a return on investment within so many years, or being on a financial timetable."

Although maintaining that ILM, Skywalker Sound and LucasArts are all profitable businesses that could stand on their own, Radley admits that service businesses don't operate on great profit margins. "You don't go into a business like ILM to get rich," says Radley. "I suppose if George had invested in pork bellies he probably would have made a lot more money. Or if he had created an asset that he could then take public."

Of course, there is one part of the company they can, in a broad sense, take public.

Cut to *Star Wars*.

Radley sketches a picture of a company that has wandered near and far, following the central vision of its owner—a vision that is about to reach its goal with Lucas's return to the making of *Star Wars*.

And while Lucas is still in the midst of writing his epic, he appears to know how it all ends: "I know where I've been. I know where I'm going. I just don't know where I am."

Lucasfilm Ltd. and its two subsidiaries, Lucas Digital Ltd. and LucasArts Entertainment Co., employ nearly 1,000 people and together constitute the largest private taxpayer in Marin County. George Lucas is the sole owner.

Lucas Digital includes Industrial Light & Magic and Skywalker Sound. ILM has more Silicon Graphics supercomputers under one roof (close to

200, with new units being plugged in every day) than anybody this side of the Pentagon, according to chief Jim Morris. But the division's bit-stream crested at the high-water mark with *Casper.* The leading digital characters for the Amblin-produced pic required more than 40 minutes of computer animation shots, compared to the less than six minutes of digital dinos in *Jurassic Park.*

The friendly ghosts occupied so much of ILM's man and machine power that the f/x house was forced to turn away other pics, including Universal's *Apollo 13.*

That decision was especially painful, since the film's director is Ron Howard, star of Lucas's first hit, *American Graffiti,* and the director of Lucasfilm's *Willow.*

Morris expects that the upcoming *Star Wars* will occupy as much as a third of ILM's 450 staffers, about the same as *Casper.*

LucasArts Entertainment, the computer games division, has an advantage over all the other CD-ROM titles on the crowded shelves: the *Star Wars* name on its series of combat-simulator games.

But it took the company 10 years to launch a *Star Wars* title. Lucas says earlier efforts were of unacceptable quality.

The company is the only division of Lucasfilm where original content is pitched and developed by staffers. One new title is "Full Throttle," involving a renegade biker battling an evil corporate executive—no doubt a favorite theme of Lucas's. The villain's voice is dubbed by Mark Hamill, who played Luke Skywalker in *Star Wars.*

Another new title is "The Dig," based on an idea from Steven Spielberg as carried out by top game designer Sean Clark.

LucasArts has seen a number of top-level defections over the years, including the recent flight of company president Randy Komisar to rival games company Crystal Dynamics. Jack Sorenson was upped from the ranks to take his place.

But while there are rumors that Lucasfilm may sell all or part of LucasArts, Lucasfilm prexy Gordon Radley denies it for the moment. "There is no need to sell off assets. We are committed to interactivity," he says.

Although Lucasfilm was among the first film companies to venture into the digital interactive realm, the rest of the movie business is catching up. That has brought some pressures to bear on Lucas's empire, particularly in the area of talent.

Responding to rampant talent-poaching from all corners of the industry, Lucas says that Lucasfilm has an informal agreement with DreamWorks that neither will poach employees from the other. Such a pact is highly unusual in the competitive and specialized special effects business. But the friendship between Lucas and Spielberg was the motivating factor.

"We've had discussions about them not raiding us," says Lucas. "I want DreamWorks to succeed. They want me to succeed. And we're going to help each other succeed."

Of the *Star Wars* episodes he is now writing, George Lucas says, "I'd like to see the whole thing finished so I have episodes one through six all done and it's a complete thing, because the first three are mostly background for the other ones. Everything in the three that are done now will make a lot more sense when you know the context in which they happened."

The trilogy will be entirely financed by Lucasfilms and shot back-to-back "like a TV series," says Lucas, using digital production techniques.

The schedule: 1996, preproduction casting, set-building, some second-unit action sequences to be shot. 1997, the bulk of shooting on the three pictures will be completed. 1998: first film release.

Budgets on each of the three films: $50 million to $70 million.

The three existing episodes, *Star Wars, The Empire Strikes Back,* and *Return of the Jedi,* have together grossed more than $500 million domestically, $1.3 billion worldwide total.

No distrib has yet been set for the pics. Twentieth Century Fox, which produced the first three, lost the sequel rights when Marvin Davis sold the studio to Rupert Murdoch.

Letter From Skywalker Ranch: Why Is the Force Still With Us?

JOHN SEABROOK/1997

The Star Wars *trilogy touched audiences around the world in ways that no other movies ever have. It also ushered in the soulless action flick and the kind of merchandising that brings us R2-D2 beverage coolers. George Lucas discusses the making of an American myth.*

THE BIANNUAL STAR WARS Summit Meeting is an opportunity for the licensees who make Darth Vader masks and thirty-six-inch sculpted Yoda collectibles to trade strategy and say "May the Force be with you" to the retailers from F.A.O. Schwarz and Target who sell the stuff, and for everyone in the far-flung Star Wars universe to get a better sense of "how deeply the brand has penetrated into the culture," in the words of one licensee. Almost six hundred people showed up at this year's summit, which took place in early November in the Marin County Civic Center, in San Rafael, California; Star Warsians came from as far away as Australia and Japan. Those arriving by car were ushered to parking places by attendants waving glowing and buzzing Luke Skywalker lightsabres, which were one of the cooler pieces of new product seen at the summit this year; other arrivals, who were staying in the Embassy Suites next door, strolled across the parking lot in the early-morning sunshine of another beautiful day in Northern California.

Originally published in *The New Yorker,* 6 January 1997, pp. 40–53. © 1997 John Seabrook. Reprinted by permission of *The New Yorker* and the author.

It was interesting to stand by the door of the auditorium and reflect that all these people, representing billions of dollars of wealth, depended for their existence on an idea that seemed utterly *un*commercial at the time George Lucas began trying to sell it to studios, in the mid-seventies, when his thirteen-page treatment of "The Star Wars" (as it was then called) was rejected by Universal and by United Artists; only Alan Ladd, who was then at Fox, would gamble on it, over the heated objections of the Fox board. When Lucas would get down on the carpet with his toy airplanes and his talk of the Empire and the dark and light sides of the Force and the anthropology of *Wookiees,* even Lucas's friends thought, "George has lost it," according to the screenwriter Gloria Katz. "He always had this tunnel vision when it came to his projects, but it seemed like this time he was really out there. 'What's this thing called a Wookiee? What's a Jedi, George? You want to make a space opera?' "

The first movie went on to earn three hundred and twenty-three million dollars (more than any previous film had ever earned), and so far the trilogy has brought in about a billion three hundred million dollars in worldwide box-office sales and more than three billion more in licensing fees. Before *Star Wars,* merchandise was used only to promote movies; it had no value apart from the films. But *Star Wars* merchandise became a business unto itself, and it inaugurated modern merchandising as we know it—the Warner Bros. Store, Power Rangers, the seventeen *thousand* different *101 Dalmatians* products that Disney has licensed so far—although *Star Wars* remains "the holy grail of licensing," in the words of one analyst. Last year, *Star Wars* action figures were the best-selling toy for boys and the second over-all best-seller, after Barbie. A large percentage of *Star Wars* action figures are actually bought by adults—*Star Wars* merchandise dealers—who are hoarding them, to speculate on the price. As a result, it has been difficult to find *Star Wars* toys, and some stores have limited the number of action figures that one person can buy. (The "vinyl-caped Jawa" action figures, which sold for around three dollars in 1978, are now worth about fourteen hundred.) In addition, LucasArts, which makes *Star Wars* CD-ROMs, is among the top five producers of video games for computers, while *Star Wars* novels are, book for book, the single most valuable active franchise in publishing. (Most of the twenty-odd novels Bantam has published since 1991 have made the *Times* hardcover- or paperback-best-seller list.) All this in spite of the fact that there has been no new

Star Wars movie in theatres since *The Return of the Jedi,* in 1983—although that is about to change.

What *is* it that makes people crave the *Star Wars* brand in so many different flavors? Somewhere between the idea and the stuff, it seemed to me—between the image of Luke gazing at the two setting suns on the planet Tatooine while he contemplated his destiny as a fighter pilot for the Rebel Alliance, and the twelve-inch Luke collectibles sold by Kenner—an alchemic transformation was taking place: dreams were being spun into desire, and desire forged into product. Here at the summit, you could feel this process drawing energy from the twin rivers of marketing and branding on the one hand, and from people's need to make sense of things on the other. In a world where the stories and images and lessons provided by electronic media seem to be replacing the stories and images and lessons people used to get from religion, literature, and painting, the lessons of *Star Wars*—that good is stronger than evil, that human values can triumph over superior technology, that even the lowliest of us can be redeemed, and that all this is relatively free of moral ambiguity—is a very powerful force indeed.

As an alien at the summit, I wasn't invited inside the auditorium, but several participants debriefed me on the goings on. In the morning, Howard Roffman, the vice-president of Lucasfilm Licensing, talked about the coming "Star Wars Trilogy Special Edition," a digitally enhanced version of the original trilogy. The first movie will appear on nearly two thousand screens starting January 31st, followed three weeks later by *The Empire Strikes Back* and two weeks after that by *The Return of the Jedi.* Then, in 1999, the first of three *new* Star Wars films will début, with the second tentatively scheduled to follow in 2001 and the third in 2003. Yes, it is true, Roffman told the audience, that the first of the new "prequel" movies, which, as everyone present already knew, will begin to tell the back story to the original trilogy—what happened *before* Luke's adventures—will be directed by George Lucas himself, who, as everyone also knew, has not directed a film since the first Star Wars movie.

Roffman warned the licensees not to flood the market with *Star Wars* merchandise this winter—maybe because he was concerned about damaging the prequel's allure. He admitted that no one knew how well the "Special Edition" would do, because nobody has ever given a trilogy of movies already seen on television and video such a wide theatrical rerelease. Still, he believed that a lot of people would go to see *Star Wars* again, because seeing it for the first time had been such an important event. "*Star Wars* has a timeless quality," Roffman had told me earlier. "For a lot of people, it was a defining moment in their lives. There is a whole generation that remembers where they were when they first saw *Star Wars*. Now that original generation has aged, and they'll be looking at the films through different eyes—plus they'll want to take their kids." A movie that was designed to appeal to a feeling like nostalgia in the first place would be revisited by people seeking to feel nostalgic for *that* experience, in the pursuit of an ever-receding vision of a mythic past.

Roffman told the crowd that he still got chills when he saw the opening shot of the rebel Blockade Runner pursued by the Imperial Star Destroyer. Tom Sherak, a Fox executive vice-president, who followed Roffman to the podium, joked that he got chills a little earlier in the film, when he saw the Fox logo come up on the screen. When Lucas approached Fox with the idea of rereleasing the *Star Wars* trilogy, Sherak told me, it was "like Christmas." Fox readily agreed to Lucas's proposal that the studio pay for the use of digital technology to fix some things about the original movies that had always bothered him. Along with every other studio, Fox is hoping to win the rights to distribute the three *Star Wars* prequel movies, and was willing to do almost anything to make George happy. The studio eventually spent fifteen million dollars on the digital enhancements, and will spend perhaps another twenty million marketing the "Special Edition," which is expected to make around a hundred million.

Then John Talbot, the director of marketing for Pepsi-Cola, showed off sketches for its R2-D2 coolers, which will have *Star Wars*-related Pepsi cans inside their heads and will probably be displayed in convenience stores. He talked about all the different ways the company would promote the "Special Edition": not only through the Pepsi label but through Frito-Lay, Pizza Hut, and Taco Bell as well—all part of an unprecedented two-billion-dollar commitment from Pepsi which will help drive the *Star Wars* brand even deeper into the culture, and insure that even if the story were to fade from the surface of the Earth it will remain buried underground in the form of Luke Skywalker pizza boxes and Obi-Wan sixteen-ounce beverage cups.

At five o'clock, a squadron of Imperial Guards, accompanied by white-shelled Imperial Storm Troopers, took the stage, followed by Darth Vader himself, sporting a costume from Lucasfilm Archives. (F. A. O. Schwarz and Neiman Marcus are actually selling limited-edition full-size Vader mannequins for five thousand dollars each—a *Star Wars* product that comes close to having the quasi-religious status of a "prop.") Speaking a recorded version of what sounded like James Earl Jones's voice, the Dark Lord of the Sith sternly upbraided the audience for not inviting him to the summit, but then said that it was actually a good thing he hadn't been invited, because he'd been able to spend the day at "the Ranch" with someone far more important than "you mere merchandisers." With that, George Lucas strode onto the stage.

Wherever Lucas appears, he receives a standing ovation, and he got two today—one on taking the stage and the other on leaving it. It isn't simply Lucas's success as a filmmaker that people are applauding—the fact that, having begun his career right here at the Marin County Civic Center (he had used it as a location for his first film, the dark, dystopian *THX 1138*), Lucas had gone on to create in *Star Wars* and *Indiana Jones* two of the most valuable movie properties ever, and, with John Milius, had also had the idea for *Apocalypse Now,* which Francis Ford Coppola ended up making. Nor is it his success as a businessman: Industrial Light & Magic, which started as essentially Lucas's model shop—a place to do the effects for the original *Star Wars*—has grown into the premier digital-imaging studio in the world, and is responsible for most of the milestones in computer graphics, including the cyborg in *Terminator 2,* the dinosaurs in *Jurassic Park,* and the Kennedy cameo in *Forrest Gump.* No, you applaud for Lucas because he *is* *Star Wars.* It's difficult for brains braised in *Star Wars* from early adulthood to conceive of Lucas in any other terms. The purpose of a myth, after all, is to give people a structure for making sense of the world, and it happens that Lucas's heroic myths are an almost irresistible way of making sense of *him.* "It's like George is Yoda," Tom Sherak told me. "He doesn't say a lot of words, but as you're listening the passion this man feels comes through. He's talking about his own creation. It's this whole thing that just comes over you."

Earlier, during a break, marketing reps from Hasbro had given all the members of the audience their own Luke Skywalker lightsabres, and at Lucas's appearance people turned them on and waved them around. ("It was like being at a Jethro Tull concert in 1978," according to one participant.) After they'd finished, Lucas said a few words about his reasons for

wanting to rerelease the trilogy, which were chiefly that it would allow a
new generation of fans to see the movies in theatres. He later told me he
had made a point of keeping his own son, who is now four, from watching
Star Wars on video, so he could show it to him in a theatre first.

Lucas's aura may be almost palpable, but his *prana*—the Sanskrit word
for life force—is oddly blurry behind the looming shadow of his myth.
(Of course, his lack of presence is also part of the myth: it's what makes
him Yoda-like.) He is slight, and has a small, round belly, a short beard,
black nerd-style glasses, and a vulnerable-sounding voice. According to the
summiteers I talked to, the only really memorable moment in his ten minutes on the stage came when Alan Hassenfeld, the head of Hasbro, gave
him a twelve-inch sculpted Obi-Wan Kenobi body with a George Lucas
head, and the crowd went wild. A George Lucas toy! As one member of the
audience said later, "What a collectible that would make!" George held up
his George toy, and the people all cheered and waved their lightsabres.

Skywalker Ranch, the headquarters of Lucas's enterprises, is that part of
the *Star Wars* universe which juts up above the top layer of the myth, into
the real world. Deep in the hills of West Marin, the Ranch is a three-thousand-acre detailed evocation of a nineteenth-century ranch that never was.
When Lucas was beginning to conceive the place, in the early eighties, he
wrote a short story about an imaginary nineteenth-century railroad tycoon
who retired up here and built the homestead of his dreams. In this story,
the tycoon's Victorian main house dates from 1869; a craftsman-style library
was added in 1910; the stable was built in 1870 and the brook house in 1913.
Lucas gave his story to the architects of the Ranch and told them to build
it accordingly. (He calls this style "remodel" architecture.)

Here, just as in *Star Wars,* Lucas created a new world and then layered it
with successive coats of mythic anthropology to make it feel used. He has
made the future feel like the past, which is what George Lucas does best.
Star Wars takes place in a futuristic, sci-fi world, but Lucas tells you at the
beginning that it existed "a long time ago, in a galaxy far, far away." The
movie has all the really cool parts of the future (interplanetary travel, flashy
effects, excellent machines), but it also has the friendships, the heroism,
and other reassuring conventions of the cinema-processed past (outlaw
saloons, dashing flyboys, sinister nobles, brave knights, and narrow escapes).
It makes you feel a longing for the unnameable thing that is always being

lost (a feeling similar to the one you get from Lucas's second film, *American Graffiti,* which helped make nostalgia big business), but it's a longing sweetened by the promise that in the future we'll figure out some way of getting that unnameable thing back. This was the deliciously sad desire that was being forged into product at the summit down in San Rafael, but up here at Lucas's domain the desire seemed to exist in a purer form.

To get to the Ranch, you head west from San Rafael on Lucas Valley Road, which was named long ago, for a different, unrelated Lucas. It's just a coincidence, but as you wind through the plump, grassy hills of Marin County — America's Tuscany — you feel as though you were entering a sort of Jurassic Park of entrepreneurial dreams, in which there are no coincidences, only destiny. A few yards beyond the automatic wooden gates, you come to a kiosk with a guard whose arm patch says "Skywalker Fire Brigade," and then you drive past Skywalker Inn, where each of the guest rooms — the John Ford room, the Akira Kurosawa room — is decorated in the style of the eponymous director. (Tim Burton was staying in one of them at the time of my visit, mixing sound for *Mars Attacks!*)

As in *Star Wars,* so at the Ranch, you get the sense that some all-controlling intelligence has rubbed itself over every element for a long time. The Technical Building, which is filled with the latest in sound-engineering and editing technology, including a full THX theatre and a soundstage that can seat a hundred-piece orchestra, looks precisely like a nineteenth-century California winery. (According to Lucas's story, it was originally built in 1880, and the interior was remodelled in the Art Deco style in 1934.) Trellises of Pinot Noir, Chardonnay, and Merlot grapes are growing outside, and the grapes are shipped to Francis Coppola's real winery in Napa Valley. Then there are the stables and a baseball field and people on bicycles with Skywalker license plates and an old hayrack and mower that look as if they'd been sitting beside the road for a hundred years. Lucas designed the place so that you can see only one building at a time from any spot on the property, and although two hundred people come to the Ranch each day, you see no cars — only bicycles, except for the occasional Skywalker Fire Brigade vehicle. The Ranch has three underground parking garages, which can accommodate two hundred cars.

Some of Lucas's friends told me that they thought the Ranch was George's attempt to recapture not only America's legendary Western past but his own past, especially his golden days at U.S.C. film school, in the sixties, when he was a protégé of Coppola's (they met when he was a student observer on Coppola's film *Finian's Rainbow*). He soon became friendly with Steven Spielberg, Martin Scorsese, and Brian De Palma. They were all young artists, who just wanted to make artistically worthy films and weren't yet worried about topping one another's blockbusters. (*E.T.* and *Jurassic Park* both surpassed the *Star Wars* box-office record; Lucas is hoping to take the record back from Spielberg with the prequel.) But not many filmmakers come up to the Ranch to conceive and write films; they come to use the technology in postproduction. As Spielberg once wrote, "George Lucas has the best toys of anybody I have ever known, which is why it's so much fun playing over at George's house."

From the outside, the main house looks like the big house on the Ponderosa, but the inside is more like the Huntington Gallery in San Marino, which used to be the home of the nineteenth-century railroad magnate Henry Huntington. Covering the walls is first-growth redwood that was salvaged from old bridges near Newport Beach and has been milled into panelling, and hanging on the redwood are selections from Lucas's collection of paintings by Norman Rockwell, another unironic American image-maker, with whom Lucas feels an affinity. To the Lucas fan, the most exciting things in the house are to be found in the two glass cases in the front hall, where the holiest relics are stored. The "real" lightsabre that Luke uses in *Star Wars* is here, and so are Indy's bullwhip and the diary that leads Indy to the Holy Grail. The Holy Grail itself is stored in the Archives Building.

Two days a week, Lucas comes to the Ranch to conduct business, usually driving himself along Lucas Valley Road. He spends most of the rest of his time at home, writing and looking after his three kids. The oldest, a teen-age girl, he adopted with his ex-wife and collaborator Marcia Lucas (she won an Oscar for editing *Star Wars*); the younger ones—a girl and a boy—he adopted as a single parent, after he and Marcia split up. Because my first visit to the Ranch fell on a Wednesday, which is not one of Lucas's regular days, I had been told there would be no meeting with him. But as we were touring the two-story circular redwood library with the stained-glass roof (there was a cat on the windowsill, a fire burning in the fireplace, and a Maxfield Parrish painting hanging over the mantel), word came that Lucas was here today after all, and would see me now. I was led down the back stairway into the dim recesses of the basement, which was sort of like going backstage at a high-tech theatre, and into a small, windowless room

filled with editing machines, lit chiefly by light coming from two screens—
a television and a glowing PowerBook. There sat the great mythmaker
himself, wearing his usual flannel shirt, jeans, sneakers, and Swatch watch.
He emerged from a dark corner of the couch to shake hands, then retreated
into the dimness again.

Lucas conceived the Ranch as a complete filmmaking operation—his version of the ideal studio, one that would respect human values and
creativity, as opposed to Hollywood studios, which he saw as evil and
greedy and encouraging of mediocrity. Lucas's famous disdain of
Hollywood is partly a result of his father's influence—George Lucas, Sr.,
was a conservative small-town businessman, who viewed all lawyers and
film executives as sharpies and referred to Hollywood as Sin City—and
partly a result of his own bitter experience with his first two films, *THX
1138* and *American Graffiti*. The dark lords at Universal thought *Graffiti* was
so bad that they weren't going to release the film at all, and then they
were going to release it just on TV; finally, when Coppola, who had just
made *The Godfather,* offered to buy the movie, Universal relented and
brought it out in the theatres, although not before Ned Tanen, then the
head of Universal, cut four and a half minutes from it—a move that
caused Lucas terrific anguish. Made for seven hundred and seventy-five
thousand dollars, *Graffiti* went on to earn nearly a hundred and twenty
million.

"I've always had a basic dislike of authority figures, a fear and resent-
ment of grown-ups," Lucas says in *Skywalking,* the 1983 biography by Dale
Pollock (to whom I'm indebted for some of the details of Lucas's early
career). When the success of the first *Star Wars* film allowed Lucas to "control the means of production," as he likes to say, he financed the second
and third films himself, and he built the Ranch. In the beginning, the films
edited at the Ranch were Lucas's own: he was busy working on the *Star
Wars* movies and overseeing the *Indiana Jones* series (which he conceived
the story for and produced; Spielberg directed). But before long people at
the Ranch were spending less time on Lucas's films—*Willow, Radioland
Murders,* and the *Young Indiana Jones Chronicles* television series have been
his main projects in the last few years—and more time doing other people's. Today, Lucas offers a full-service digital studio, where directors can

write, edit, and mix films, and Industrial Light & Magic, down in San Rafael, can do the special effects.

Lucas is the sole owner of his companies; Gordon Radley, the president of Lucasfilm, estimated in *Forbes* that Wall Street would value them at five billion dollars. (*Forbes* estimated that Lucas himself was worth two billion.) He is an old-fashioned, paternalistic chairman of the board, who gives each of his twelve hundred employees a turkey at Thanksgiving, and who sits every month at the head of the locally carpentered redwood boardroom table in the main house and listens to reports from the presidents of the various divisions of his enterprise.

"My father provided me with a lot of business principles—a small-town retail-business ethic, and I guess I learned it," Lucas told me in his frail-sounding voice. "It's sort of ironic, because I swore when I was a kid I'd never do what he did. At eighteen, we had this big break, when he wanted me to go into the business"—George, Sr., owned an office-supply store—"and I refused, and I told him, 'There are two things I know for sure. One is that I will end up doing something with cars, whether I'm a racer, a mechanic, or whatever, and, two, that I will never be president of a company.' I guess I got outwitted."

Lucas's most significant business decision—one that seemed laughable to the Fox executives at the time—was to forgo his option to receive an additional five-hundred-thousand-dollar fee from Fox for directing *Star Wars* and to take the merchandising and sequel rights instead. The sequels did almost as well as the first movie, and the value of the *Star Wars* brand, after going into a hiatus in the late eighties, reemerged around 1991, when Bantam published *Heir to the Empire,* by Timothy Zahn, wherein Princess Leia and Han Solo have children. The book surprised the publishing world by going to No. 1 on the *Times* hardcover-fiction list, and marketers quickly discovered a new generation of kids who had never seen the movies in theatres but were nevertheless obsessed with *Star Wars.*

Lucas's business success as the owner of *Star Wars,* however, has had the ironic result of taking him away from the thing that touched his audience in the first place. He told me he'd stopped directing movies because "when you're directing, you can't see the whole picture." He explained, "You want to take a step back, be the over-all force behind it—like a television executive producer. Once I started doing that, I drifted further and further away.

Then I had a family, and that changed things—it's very hard to direct a movie and be a single parent at the same time." Then his company became a big business. "The company started as a filmmaking operation. I needed a screening room, then a place to do post, then mixing, then special effects—because, remember, I was in San Francisco. You can't just go down the street and find this stuff—you have to build it. Everything in the company has come out of my interests, and for a long time it was a struggle. But six years ago the company started coming into its own. The CD-ROM market, which we had been sitting on for fifteen years, suddenly took off, and digital-filmmaking techniques took off—they are five times larger than six years ago—and suddenly I had a big company, and I had to pay attention to it." He estimated that he now spends thirty-five per cent of his time on his family, thirty-five per cent on movies, and thirty per cent on the company.

Lucas's day-to-day activities in the main house include the management of the *Star Wars* story, which is probably the most carefully tended secular story on Earth. Unlike *Star Trek*, which is a series of episodes connected by no central narrative, *Star Wars* is a single story—"a finite, expanding universe," in the words of Tom Dupree, who edits Bantam's *Star Wars* novels in New York. Everyone in the content-creating galaxy of *Star Wars* has a copy of "The Bible," a burgeoning canonical document (currently a hundred and seventy pages long) that is maintained by "continuity editors" Allan Kausch and Sue Rostoni. It is a chronology of all the events that have ever occurred in the *Star Wars* universe, in all the films, books, CD-ROMs, Nintendo games, comic books, and roleplaying guides, and each medium is seamlessly coordinated with the others. For example, a new Lucas story called "Shadows of the Empire" is being told simultaneously in several media. A recent Bantam novel introduces a smuggling enterprise, led by the evil Prince Xizor, within the time line of the original trilogy. Three weeks before Christmas, he crossed over into the digital realm: he began to appear in the new sixty-four-bit Nintendo playstations. Meanwhile, Dark Horse comics is also featuring the Prince, along with related characters, like the bounty hunter Boba Fett. (Boba had only a few minutes of screen time in the movies, but has become one of the most popular characters among gen-X fans.)

New developments in even the remotest corners of the *Star Wars* universe are always approved by Lucas himself. The continuity editors send him checklists of potential events, and Lucas checks yes or no. "When Bantam wanted to do the back story on Yoda," Dupree said, "George said that was off limits, because he wanted him to remain a mysterious character. But George has made available some time between the start of Episode Four, when Han Solo is a young pilot on the planet Corellia, and the end of the prequel, so we're working with that now." Although Lucas had once imagined *Star Wars* as a nine-part saga, he hasn't yet decided whether he wants to make the final three movies, but he has allowed licensees to build into the narrative space on the future side of *Jedi*; the later years of Han, Luke, Leia, and the rest of the characters have been colonized by other media.

"George creates the stories, we create the places," Jack Sorensen, the president of LucasArts, told me in explaining how the interactive division fits into the Lucas multimedia empire. "Say you're watching the movie, and you see some planet that's just in the background of the movie, and you go, 'Hey, I wonder what that planet is like?' There's a lot going on on a planet, you know. So we'll make that planet the environment for a game. In a film, George would have to keep moving, but the games give you a chance to explore."

I asked Sorensen to explain the extraordinary appeal of *Star Wars,* and he said, "I'm as perplexed by this as anyone, and I'm right in the midst of it. I travel all the time for this job, and I meet people abroad, in Italy, or in France, who are totally obsessed with *Star Wars.* I met this Frenchman recently who told me he watches it every week. I don't really think this is caused by some evil master plan of merchandisers and marketers. The demand is already out there, and we're just meeting it — it would exist without us. I don't know if I want to say this in print, but I feel like *Star Wars* is the mythology of a nonsectarian world. It describes how people want to live. People all view politics as corrupt, much more so in Europe than here, and yet people are not cynical underneath — they want to believe in something pure, noble. That's *Star Wars.*"

Star Wars still seems pure in some ways, but in other ways it doesn't. The qualities that seemed uncommercial about it at the time Lucas was trying to make it — most strikingly, that the literary elements (the characters and the plot) were subordinate to the purely cinematic elements (motion) — are the very qualities that seem commercial about it now. This is one way of measuring how *Star Wars* has changed both movies and the people who go to movies.

"I'm a visual filmmaker," Lucas told me. "I do films that are kinetic, and I tend to focus on character as it is created through editing and light, not stories. I started out as a harsh enemy of story and character, in my film-school days, but then I fell under Francis's mentorship, and his challenge to me after *THX 1138* was to make a more conventional movie. So I did *American Graffiti,* but they said that was just a montage of sounds, and then I did *Star Wars.* I was always coming from pure cinema—I was using the grammar of film to create content. I think graphically, not linearly."

The first *Star Wars* movie is like a two-hour-long image of raw speed. If you saw it when you were young, this tends to be what you remember— the feeling of going really fast. Lucas is a genius of speed. His first ambition was to be a race-car driver, and it was only after he was nearly killed in a terrible accident, when he was eighteen—he lived because his seat belt unaccountably broke and he was hurled free of the car—that his interest shifted to film. (His first moving pictures were of race cars.) Perhaps the most memorable single image in *Star Wars* is the shot of the Millennium Falcon going into hyperspace for the first time, when the stars blur past the cockpit. Like all the effects in the movie, this works not because it is a cool effect (it's actually pretty low tech—merely "motion blur" photography) but because it's a powerful graphic distillation of the feeling the whole movie gives you: an image of pure kinetic energy which has become a permanent part of the world's visual imagination. (The other day, I was out running, and as a couple of rollerbladers went whizzing by I heard a jogger in front of me say to his friend, "It's like that scene in *Star Wars* when they go into hyperspace.") Insofar as a media-induced state of speed has become a condition of modern life, Lucas was anticipating the Zeitgeist in *Star Wars.*

The problems arise when Lucas has to slow down. In *Radioland Murders,* the characters have to carry the narrative, but Lucas couldn't make this work, so he had to speed up the pace and turn the movie into farce. Also, because Lucas has little rapport with actors, his films tend to have only passable acting in them, which forces him to rely unduly on pace and editing. Mark Hamill once said, "I have a sneaking suspicion that if there were a way to make movies without actors, George would do it." Lucas is well known to be impatient with actors' histrionics, and has little interest in becoming involved in their discussions about method. Harrison Ford told

me that Lucas had only two directions for the actors in *Star Wars*; he
replayed them for me over huevos rancheros on the terrace at the Bel Air
Hotel one Saturday morning, using his George-as-director voice—nasal,
high, kind of whiny. The two directions were "O.K., same thing, only better," and "Faster, more intense." Ford said, "That was it: 'O.K., same thing,
only better.' 'Faster, more intense.'"

For serious *Star Wars* fans—the true believers—Lucas's story tends to min-
gle with Luke's, the real one becoming proof that the mythic one
can come true, and the mythic one giving the real one a kind of larger-
than-life significance. Just as Luke is a boy on the backwater planet of
Tatooine—he is obedient to his uncle, who wants him to stay on the farm,
but he dreams that there might be a place for him somewhere out there in
the larger world of adventure—so Lucas was a boy in the backwater town
of Modesto, California. He dreamed of being a great race-car driver, but his
liberal-bashing, moralizing father wanted him to stay at home and take
over the family business. (Pollock's book recounts how his father liked to
humiliate him every summer by chopping off his hair.) Just as a benevolent father figure (Obi-Wan) helps Luke in his struggle against his dark
father, the older Coppola took young George under his wing at film school,
and helped him get his first feature film made. And, just as Luke at the end
of the first *Star Wars* film realizes his destiny and becomes a sort of hero-
knight, so Lucas became the successful filmmaker, fulfilling a prophecy
he'd made to his father in 1962, two years before he left Modesto for U.S.C.,
which was that he would be "a millionaire before I'm thirty."

But both Luke and Lucas have had to reckon with their patrimony.
There's the famous scene on the Cloud City catwalk in *Empire* when Darth
reveals that he is Luke's father. He has cut off Luke's hand and tries to turn
him to the dark side, saying, "Join me, and together we can rule the galaxy
as father and son!": Luke responds by leaping off the catwalk into the abyss.
Just as Luke has to contend with the qualities he may have inherited from
Darth Vader, so Lucas, in his career after *Star Wars*, has stopped directing
films and has become the successful, fiscally conservative businessman
that his father always wanted him to be.

The scripts for the prequel, which Lucas is finishing now, make it clear
that *Star Wars*, taken as a whole story and viewed in chronological order, is
not really the story of Luke at all but the story of Luke's father, Anakin

204 GEORGE LUCAS: INTERVIEWS

Skywalker, and how he, a Jedi Knight, was corrupted by the dark side of the Force and became Darth Vader. When I asked Lucas what *Star Wars* was ultimately about, he said, "Redemption." He added, "The scripts to the three films that I'm finishing now are a lot darker than the second three, because they are about a fall from grace. The first movie is pretty innocent, but it goes downhill from there, because it's more of a tragic story—that's built into it."

I said that the innocence was what many people found so compelling about the first *Star Wars* movie, and I asked whether it was harder for him, now that he is twenty years less innocent, to go back to work on the material.

"Of course your perspective changes when you get older and as you get battered by life," he said.

"Have you been battered by life?"

"Anyone who lives is going to get battered. Nothing comes easy."

I believed him. He was Yoda, after all. He had lived for almost nine hundred years. He had known the sons who triumph over their dark fathers only to find themselves in the murkier situation of being fathers themselves, and that knowledge had made him wise but it had also worn him out. That was the note of loss in his voice—the thing that the *Star Wars* trilogy didn't allow very often onto the screen, but it was there in the background, like the remnants of blue screens you could see in *Empire,* in the thin outlines surrounding the Imperial Walkers on the ice planet Hoth. (These flaws have been digitally erased in the "Special Edition.")

Did Lucas worry about being turned to the dark side himself—did fame, money, or power tempt him? Or maybe it happened more slowly and subtly, with the temptation to stop being a filmmaker and become a kind of master toymaker instead, which is fun until you wake up one day and realize you have become one of your own toys. You could see that starting to occur in *Jedi,* the Ewoks, those lovable furry creatures, seemed destined for the toy store even before they helped Luke defeat the Empire.

"The world is all yours," I said to Lucas. "You could have anything you wanted."

"Like what?" he asked. "What do I want? What do you want? Basically I just like to make movies, and I like raising a family, and whatever money I've made I've plowed back into the company. I've only ever been tempted by making movies—I don't need yachts, I'm not a party animal, and holding and using power over people never interested me. The only dangerous side of having this money is that I will make movies that aren't commercial. But, of course, *Star Wars* was not considered commercial when I did it."

Since *Star Wars* sprang into Lucas's mind first as pictures, not as a narrative, he needed a line on which to hang his images. He studied Joseph Campbell's books on mythology, among other sources, taking structural elements from many different myths and trying to combine them into one epic story. One can go through *Star Wars* and almost pick out chapter headings from Campbell's *The Hero with a Thousand Faces*: the hero's call to adventure, the refusal of the call, the arrival of supernatural aid, the crossing of the first threshold, the belly of the whale, and the series of ordeals culminating in a showdown with the angry father, when, at last, as Campbell writes, "the hero...beholds the face of the father, understands—and the two are atoned"—which is precisely what happens at the end of *Jedi*. Lucas worked this way partly out of a conscious desire to create a story that would touch people—it was a kind of get-'em-by-the-archetypes-and-their-hearts-and-minds-will-follow approach—but it also appears to have been an artistic necessity.

"When I was in college, for two years I studied anthropology—that was basically all I did," Lucas said as we sat in his basement den. The glow of the blank TV screen illuminated his face. "Myths, stories from other cultures. It seemed to me that there was no longer a lot of mythology in our society—the kind of stories we tell ourselves and our children, which is the way our heritage is passed down. Westerns used to provide that, but there weren't Westerns anymore. I wanted to find a new form. So I looked around, and tried to figure out where myth comes from. It comes from the borders of society, from out there, from places of mystery—the wide Sargasso Sea. And I thought, Space. Because back then space was a source of great mystery. So I thought, O.K., let's see what we can do with all those elements. I put them all into a bag, along with a little bit of *Flash Gordon* and a few other things, and out fell *Star Wars*."

He said that his intention in writing *Star Wars* was explicitly didactic: he wanted it to be a good lesson as well as a good movie. "I wanted it to be a traditional moral study, to have some sort of palpable precepts in it that children could understand. There is always a lesson to be learned. Where do these lessons come from? Traditionally, we get them from church, the family, art, and in the modern world we get them from media—from movies." He added, "Everyone teaches in every work of art. In almost everything you do, you teach, whether you are aware of it or not. Some people aren't aware of what they are teaching. They should be wiser. Everybody teaches all the time."

Lucas's first attempt at writing the story lasted from February, 1972, to May, 1973, during which he produced the thirteen-page plot summary that his friend Laddie (Alan Ladd) paid him fifteen thousand dollars to develop into a script. Like *American Graffiti,* which had been a montage of radio sounds, this treatment was like a montage of narrative fragments. It took Lucas another year to write a first draft; he is an agonizingly slow writer. He composed *Star Wars* with No. 2 pencils, in tiny, compulsively neat-looking script, on green-and-blue-lined paper, with atrocious spelling and grammar. Realizing that he had too much stuff for one movie, he cut the original screenplay in half, and the first half was the germ for the three scripts he is finishing now; the second half became the original trilogy. (Lucas's way of making the future into the past is thus part of the structure of *Star Wars.* Many people don't remember this, but the first movie was called, in full, *Star Wars, Episode IV: A New Hope.*)

He showed his first draft to a few people, but neither Laddie nor George's friends could make much sense of it. "It only made sense when George would put it in context with past movies, and he'd say, 'It's like that scene in *Dam Busters,*'" Ladd told me, in his office on the Paramount lot. The only characters that Lucas seemed to have a natural affinity for were the droids, C-3PO and R2-D2. In early drafts, the first thirty pages focused almost entirely on the droids; the feeling was closer to the Orwellian mood of *THX 1138.* Based on his friends' reactions, Lucas realized he would need to put the humans on the screen earlier, in order to get the audience involved. But his dialogue was wooden and labored. "When I left you, I was but the learner," Darth says to Obi-Wan, before dispatching the old gentleman with his sabre. "I am the master now!" Harrison Ford's well-known remark about Lucas's dialogue, which he repeated for me, was "George, you can type this shit, but you sure can't say it."

Lucas also borrowed heavily from the film-school canon. The lightsabres and Jedi Knights were inspired by Kurosawa's *Hidden Fortress,* C-3PO's look by Fritz Lang's *Metropolis,* the ceremony at the end by Leni Riefenstahl's *Triumph of the Will.* Alec Guinness does a sort of optimistic reprise of his

Prince Feisal character from *Lawrence of Arabia,* while Harrison Ford plays
Butch Cassidy. Critics of *Star Wars* point to the film's many borrowings as
evidence of Lucas's failure as a filmmaker. (It is said of Lucas, as it was of
Henry Ford, that he didn't actually invent anything.) But *Star Wars* fans
see this as a brilliant postmodernist commentary on the history of popular
film. Lucas uses these references with a childlike lack of irony that Scorsese, De Palma, or Spielberg would probably be incapable of, because they
grew up with the movies. The critic and screenwriter Jay Cocks, a longtime
friend of Lucas's, told me, "I don't think George went to a lot of movies as
a kid, like Marty and Brian. Before arriving at film school, he hadn't seen
Alexander Nevsky or *Potemkin*; I don't think he even saw *Citizen Kane.*
I remember when I went up to this little cabin he and Marcia had in
Northern California, and I saw he had some *Flash Gordon* comic strips,
drawn by Alex Raymond, on his desk, and a picture of Eisenstein on his
wall, and the combination of those two were really the basis for George's
aesthetic in *Star Wars.*"

But Lucas added many small personal details to the story as well, which
is part of what gives his creation its sensuous feeling of warmth. According
to Pollock, the little robot is called R2-D2 because that was how Walter
Murch, the sound editor on *American Graffiti,* asked for the Reel 2, Dialogue
2 tape when they were in the editing room one day, and for some reason
"R2-D2" stuck in George's mind. The Wookiee was inspired by Marcia's
female Alaskan malamute, Indiana (who also lent her name to Lucas's
other great invention); the image of Chewie came to George in a flash one
day as the dog was sitting next to Marcia in the front seat of the car. Many
of Ben Burtt's sounds for the movie also had personal significance. He told
me that the buzzing sound of the lightsabre was the drone that an old
U.S.C. film-school projector made. The pinging sound of the blasters was
the sound made one day when Burtt was out hiking and caught the top of
his backpack on some guy wires.

Shooting of the interiors began in March, 1976, in Elstree Studios, outside London, and lasted four months. The English crew were awful to
Lucas. "They just thought it was all very unsophisticated," Harrison Ford
told me. "I mean, here's this seven-foot-tall man in a big hairy suit. They
referred to Chewie as 'the dog.' You know, 'Bring the dog in.' And George
isn't the best at dealing with those human situations—to say the least."
Meanwhile, Lucas was struggling with Fox to get more than the nine mil-

lion dollars that Fox wanted to spend (the movie ended up costing about ten million to make), and he was paranoid that the studio was going to take the movie away from him, or, treat it the way that Universal had treated *Graffiti.*

Lawrence Kasdan, who co-wrote the scripts for *Empire* and *Jedi* and also wrote the script for the first *Indiana Jones* movie, thinks Lucas's antagonistic relationship with Hollywood is what *Star Wars* is really about. "The Jedi Knight is the filmmaker, who can come in and use the Force to impose his will on the studio," he told me. "You know that scene when Alec Guinness uses the Force to say to the Storm Trooper outside the Mos Eisley cantina, 'These aren't the droids you're looking for,' and the guy answers, 'These aren't the droids we're looking for'? Well, when the studio executive says, 'You won't make this movie,' you say, 'I *will* make this movie,' and then the exec agrees, 'You will make this movie.' I once asked him, 'George, where did you get the confidence to argue with Ned Tanen?' He said, 'Your power comes from the fact that you are the creator.' And that had an enormous influence on me."

When a rough cut of *Star Wars* had been edited together; George arranged a screening of the film at his house. The party traveling up from Los Angeles included Spielberg, Ladd, De Palma, a few other friends of George's, and some Fox executives. "Marty was supposed to come, too," the screenwriter Willard Huyck told me, referring to Martin Scorsese, "but the weather was bad and the plane was delayed and finally Marty just went home."

"Marty had an anxiety attack is what happened," Gloria Katz, Huyck's wife and writing partner, put in. Huyck and Katz are old friends of Lucas's, who cowrote *Graffiti* with him, and are the beneficiaries of George's generous gift of two points of *Star Wars* for their help on the script.

"Marty's very competitive, and so is George," Huyck went on. "All these guys are. And at that time Marty was working on *New York, New York,* which George's wife, Marcia, was editing, and everybody was saying that it was going to be the big picture of the year—but here we were all talking about *Star Wars.*"

Here, at this first screening of *Star Wars,* a group of writers, directors, and executives, all with ambitions to make more or less artistically accomplished Hollywood films, were confronting the template of the future—the film that would in one way or another determine everyone's career. Not surprisingly, almost every one of them hated it. Polite applause in the screening room, no cheers—a "real sweaty-palm time," Jay Cocks, who was also there, said. It's possible that, just this once, before the tsunami of marketing and megatude closed over *Star Wars* forever, these people were seeing the movie for what it really was—a film with comic-book characters, an unbelievable story, no political or social commentary, lousy acting, preposterous dialogue, and a ridiculously simplistic morality. In other words, a bad movie.

"So we watch the movie," Huyck said, "and the crawl went on forever, there was tons of back story, and then we're in this spaceship, and then here's Darth Vader. Part of the problem was that almost none of the effects were finished, and in their place George had inserted World War Two dogfight footage, so one second you're with the Wookiee in the spaceship and the next you're in *The Bridges at Toko-Ri*. It was like, *George, what-is-going-on?*"

"When the film ended, people were aghast," Katz said. "Marcia was really upset—she was saying, 'Oh my God, it's *At Long Last Love*,' which was the Bogdanovich picture that was such a disaster the year before. We said, 'Marcia, fake it, fake it. *Laddie is watching*.'"

Huyck: "Then we all got into these cars to go someplace for lunch, and in our car everyone is saying, 'My God, what a disaster!' All except Steven, who said, 'No, that movie is going to make a hundred million dollars, and I'll tell you why—it has a marvellous innocence and naïveté in it, which is George, and people will love it.' And that impressed us, that he would think that, but of course no one believed him."

Katz: "We sat down to eat, and Brian started making fun of the movie. He was very acerbic and funny."

"Which is the way Brian *is*," Huyck said. "You know, 'Hey George, what were those Danish rolls doing in the princess's ears?' We all sat there very nervously while Brian let George have it, and George just sort of sank deeper into his chair. Brian was pretty rough. I don't know if Marcia ever forgave Brian for that."

When the movie opened, Huyck and Katz went with George and Marcia to hide out in Hawaii. On their second day there, Huyck told me, "Laddie called on the phone and said, 'Turn on the evening news.' Why? 'Just watch the evening news,' he said. So we turned it on, and Walter Cronkite was on saying, 'There's something extraordinary happening out there, and it's all the result of a new movie called *Star Wars*.' Cut to lines around the block in Manhattan. It was absolutely amazing. We were all stunned. Now,

of course, the studios can tell you what a movie is going to do — they have
it down to a science, and they can literally predict how a movie is going to
open. But in those days they didn't know."

Dean Devlin, one of the creators of *Independence Day,* was fourteen years
old when *Star Wars* came out. He remembers being sixth in line on the day
the movie opened at Mann's Chinese Theatre, in Hollywood, on May 25,
1977. "I don't even know why I wanted to see it," he told me when I went
to talk with him in his office, just off the commissary at Paramount. "I just
knew I had to be there." The movie changed his life. "To me, *Star Wars* was
like the *Sgt. Pepper's Lonely Hearts Club Band* of movies. You know how people like David Bowie say that that was the album that made them see what
was possible in pop music? I think *Star Wars* did the same thing for popcorn movies. It made you see what was possible. He added, "*Star Wars* was
the movie that made me say, I want to do something like that." *Stargate*
and *Independence Day* are what he has done so far, and the day after we
talked he and his partner, Roland Emmerich, were leaving for Mexico, to
hole up and work on their next film, *Godzilla.*

"*Star Wars* was a serious breakthrough, a shift in the culture, which was
possible only because George was this weird character," Lawrence Kasdan
said. "After you saw it, you thought, My God, anything is possible. He
opened up people's minds. I mean, the amazing thing about cinema technology is that it hasn't changed since it started. It's mind-boggling. With
all these changes in technology, and the computer, we're still pulling this
little piece of plastic through a machine and shining light through it. Very
few directors change things. Welles did things differently. But everything
is different after *Star Wars.* All other pictures reflect its influence, some by
ignoring it or rebelling against it." Every time a studio executive tells a
writer that his piercing and true story needs an "action beat" every ten
minutes, the writer has George Lucas to thank. *Ransom,* the recent movie
by Lucas's protégé Ron Howard, is two hours' worth of such action beats
and little else.

Huyck suggested that one of the legacies of the trilogy's success is that a
movie as fresh and unknowing as *Star Wars* wouldn't get made today.
"Truffaut had the idea that filmmaking entered a period of decadence with
the James Bond movies, and I'm not sure you couldn't say the same thing
about *Star Wars,* though you can't blame George for it," he told me. "*Star*

Wars made movies big business, which got the studio executives involved in every step of the development, to the point of being on the set and criticizing what the director is doing. Now they all take these screenwriting courses in film school and they think they know about movies—their notes are always the same. Both *American Graffiti* and *Star Wars* would have a very difficult time getting through the current system. *Star Wars* would get pounded today. Some executive would get to the point where Darth Vader is revealed to be Luke's father and he would say, 'Give me a break.' "

These days, Kasdan said, "the *word* 'character' might come up at a development meeting with the executives, but if you asked them they couldn't tell you what character is." He went on, "Narrative structure doesn't exist—all that matters is what's going to happen in the next ten minutes to keep the audience interested. There's no faith in the audience. They can't have the story happen fast enough."

Twenty years ago, Pauline Kael suggested that in sacrificing character and complexity for non-stop action *Star Wars* threatened to turn movies into comic books, and today, in a week when two of the three top movies are *101 Dalmatians* and *Space Jam,* it is easy to believe she was right. (I know which movies are on top because I read last week's grosses, along with the N.F.L. standings, in Monday's *Times*: another aspect of the blockbuster mentality that *Star Wars* helped to launch.)

When I reminded Lucas of Kael's remark, he sighed and said, "Pauline Kael never liked my movies. It's like comparing novels and sonnets, and saying a sonnet's no good because it doesn't have the heft of a novel. It's not a valid criticism. After I did *Graffiti,* my friends said, 'George, you should make more of an artistic statement,' but I feel *Star Wars* did make a statement—in a more visual, less literary way. People said I should have made *Apocalypse Now* after *Graffiti,* and not *Star Wars.* They said I should be doing movies like *Taxi Driver.* I said, 'Well, *Star Wars* is a kids' movie, but I think it's just as valid an art film as *Taxi Driver.*' Besides, I couldn't ever do *Taxi Driver.* I don't have it in me. I could do *Koyaanisqatsi,* but not *Taxi Driver.* But of course if the movie doesn't fit what they think movies should be, it shouldn't be allowed to exist. I think that's narrow-minded. I've been trying to rethink the art of movies—it's not a play, not a book, not music or dance. People were aware of that in the silent era, but when the talkies started they lost track of it. Film basically became a recording medium."

When you're up at Skywalker Ranch, it's possible to imagine that the future is somehow going to end up saving the past after all, and that we will find on a new frontier what we lost a long time ago in a galaxy far, far away. But in San Rafael, at Industrial Light & Magic, this is harder to believe. Down here, where legions of young geeks work in high-tech, dark satanic mills and stare into computer screens as they build "polys" (the polygonal structures that are the basic elements of computer graphics), the future doesn't seem likely to save the past. The future destroys the past.

Take, for example, the I.L.M. model shop—a high-ceilinged space, full of creatures, ghosts, and crazy vehicles that were used in movies like *Ghostbusters* and *Back to the Future*. It's like a museum of non-virtual reality. There are books on the torque capacity of different kinds of wrenches, cylinders of compressed gas, tools of all descriptions, and a feathery layer of construction dust covering everything. All the monsters, ships, weapons, and other effects in the original *Star Wars* were made in the model shop— by hand, more or less—by the team of carpenter-engineer-tinkerer-inventors assembled by Lucas. They used clay, rubber, foam latex, wire, and seven-foot-two hairy-Wookiee suits to create their illusions. (The only computers used in making the original *Star Wars* were used to control the motion of the cameras.) The modelmakers were so good at what they did that they unleashed a desire for better and better special effects in movies, which ended up putting a number of the people in the model shop out of work. "Either you learn the computer or you might as well work as a carpenter," one former member of the model shop said.

Today, the model shop survives as a somewhat vestigial operation, producing prototypes of the creatures and machines that will then be rendered in computer graphics for the movie screen. (While I was visiting I.L.M., I saw two carpenters working on a C-3PO, whose head, arms, and legs were spread all over the workbenches—he looked the way he did after the Sand People got done with him—and I asked, naïvely, if I would see him in one of the new movies. No, he was just another prototype.) One model-shop old-timer is the artist Paul Huston, who is still around because he has learned how to use the computer. Huston did oil-on-canvas matte paintings for the original *Star Wars*; he did digital matte paintings for the "Special Edition." (No one does any offscreen matte painting at I.L.M. anymore.) He showed me a tape of some of his digital additions to the first film, which occur before and after the famous Mos Eisley cantina scene, where a "C.G."

(computer graphic) Jabba the Hutt will now confront Han Solo in the docking bay where the Millennium Falcon is waiting. (Ford did his half of the scene with a human actor inside a Jabba suit in 1976, but the footage was never used, because it didn't look good enough.) In order to create a crashed spaceship that is part of the background at the Mos Eisley spaceport, Huston actually built a real model, out of various bits scavenged from airplane and helicopter kits—this gave it a kind of ad-hoc, gnarled thingeyness—and he took it outside and photographed it in natural light. Then he scanned that image into the computer and worked on it with Photoshop. A more digitally inclined artist would probably have built the crashed spaceship from scratch right on the computer.

"To me, it comes down to whether you look to the computer for your reality or whether you look out there in the world," Huston said, pointing outside the darkened C.G. room where we were standing to the bright sunlight and the distant Marin hills. "I still think it's not in the computer, it's out there. It's much more interesting out there." He turned back to the spaceport image on the screen. "Look at the way the light bounces off the top of this tower, and how these shadows actually deepen here, when you'd expect them to get lighter—you would never think to do that on a computer."

Huston seemed like kind of a melancholy guy, with sad eyes behind small wire-rimmed glasses. He said he had accepted the fact that creations like the C.G.T. Rex in *Jurassic Park* were the way of the future, and that in many cases C.G. makes effects better. The model shop could never get lava to glow properly, for example, but with C.G. it's easy. Also, C.G. is more efficient—you can get more work done. "The skills that you needed ten years ago to do modelling and matte painting were hard to attain," he said. "Making models was a process of trial and error. There were no books to tell you how to do it. It was catch as catch can. Today, with the computer, you can get modelling software, which has a manual, and follow the instructions."

He gestured around at the monitors, scanners, and other machinery all over the place. "Our company has taken the position that the computer is the future, and we have moved aggressively toward that," he said. "I can see that's what everyone wants. In model-making there aren't many shortcuts. And this is a business of turnover and scheduling and getting as much work through the pipeline as you can. If there is a shortcut to doing something on a computer, and it's going to cost a hundred and fifty thousand dollars, the client will say, 'Oh sure, let's do it.' But if you offer them a model-building project for a third of that there are no takers. Because that's not what clients are interested in. So we're trying to do everything synthetically, with computers, to see how far we can go with that. Part of the interest and excitement is in the surprise—you don't know what is going to happen."

C.G. is supposed to make films cheaper to produce, and its champions continue to promise the nirvana of a movie made by one person on a P.C. for next to nothing. Dean Devlin, a large consumer of C.G., told me about "this British kid who brought my partner Roland and me a full-length film he had shot for ten thousand dollars in a garage." He explained, "It was an excellent film with unbelievably good effects, and the way he shot it you couldn't tell it had mostly been done on a computer, and we looked at each other and said, 'It's coming.' A hundred-per-cent-C.G. live-action film, with no models." But so far C.G. has actually made movies more expensive than ever. When I asked Jim Morris, the president of Lucas Digital, I.L.M.'s parent company, why this was so, he said, "If we did the same shots now that we did in *T2,* those shots would be cheaper today. The fly in the ointment is that very few directors are trying to do what has already been done. The line we hear ninety-nine per cent of the time is 'I want something that no one has ever seen before.' No one comes in and says, 'O.K., I'll take three twisters.'"

A potential milestone in C.G. toward which I.L.M. is racing its competitors—Jim Cameron's Digital Domain and Sony's Image Works—is the creation of the first "synthespian": a C.G. human actor in a live-action movie. *Toy Story,* made by Pixar, a company that grew out of I.L.M. and which Lucas sold to Steve Jobs ten years ago, was an all-C.G. movie, but it starred toys; no one has yet made a believable C.G. human. In *Forrest Gump* audiences saw a little bit of Kennedy: What about a whole movie starring Kennedy? Or a new James Dean movie, in which Dean is a synthespian made up of bits digitally lifted from old images of him?

Recalling Mark Hamill's remark about Lucas—"I have a sneaking suspicion that if there were a way to make movies without actors, George would do it"—I asked Morris if he thought synthetics would ever be the stars of movies. Morris acknowledged that that was "a holy grail for some digital artists" but added that he didn't think a synthetic would be much of an improvement over an actor. "You get a lot for your money out of an actor," he said. "And even if you did replace him with a synthetic you're still likely to need an actor's voice, and you'd have the animator to deal with, so what's the advantage? That said, it does make sense when you're talking about safety. You don't have to have human beings putting themselves at risk doing stunts when you can have synthetics doing them."

One of the lessons *Star Wars* teaches is that friends who stick together and act courageously can overcome superior weapons, machines, and any other kind of technology. At the end of the first movie, Luke, down to his last chance to put a missile in the Death Star's weak spot (a maneuver that will blow up the reactor and save the Rebel Alliance from destruction), hears Obi-Wan telling him to turn off the targeting computer in his X-Wing fighter and rely on the Force instead: "Use the Force, Luke." Clearly, the lesson is that the Force is superior to machines. My visit to I.L.M. made me wonder if that lesson was true. At the very least, the situation seemed to be a lot more complex than *Star Wars* makes it out to be. The gleeful embrace of the latest thing, of the coolest effect, is a force that is at least equal to most other human qualities. The technology to create never-before-seen images also creates the desire to see even more amazing images, which makes the technology more and more powerful, and the people who use it correspondingly less important. And the power of business is not always in the service of human values or of making good films. Lucas has benevolently followed his business instincts into the new world of dazzling, digitally produced effects, and has built in I.L.M. a company that currently earns tens of millions of dollars a year and will probably earn much more in the future—the future! But his success is a sad blow to the fantasy that men are more powerful than machines.

"The possibilities of synthetic characters have grown enormously, and George will rely much more on those in the new *Star Wars* movies," Morris went on. "People in rubber suits worked for back then, and added a certain charm, but there is only so much you can do with that in terms of motion. In C.G., there really aren't physical limitations. There are only believability issues, and George's sensitivity grounds that—he decides what works on the screen. Yoda was a Frank Oz puppet in *Empire,* and that worked for an old, wizened Yoda who could hardly move. But in the prequels we're going to have a sixty-years-younger Yoda, and we'll probably see a synthetic Yoda instead."

Luke Skywalker Goes Home

BERNARD WEINRAUB/1997

JUST BEYOND THE FOG-SHROUDED wooden gates, a guard whose arm patch says SKYWALKER FIRE BRIGADE waves the visitor inside. Within moments, the road opens to Skywalker Ranch — 3000 mostly pristine acres of rolling hills in the appropriately named Lucas Valley. There are mountain lions and bobcats in the hills. Cattle roam the meadows. Down a silent winding road, the visitor sees, in the distance, a grandiose Victorian mansion that was designed by George Lucas to serve not only as his haven but as the nerve center of an empire that has grown immense. It is deep in Marin County, in the town of Nicasio, 425 miles north of Hollywood. But in its psychological distance from the movie capital, the ranch that *Star Wars* built could be, to borrow Lucas' own words, "in a galaxy far, far away."

"I opted for quality of life," the 53-year-old Lucas told a visitor several months ago. "It's a different world. Most of my friends are college professors." He loathes the Hollywood-Beverly Hills-Malibu social whirl. Years ago, he sat with a visitor and pointed south. "Down there" — as he is inclined to say of Hollywood — "for every honest filmmaker trying to get his film off the ground, there are a hundred sleazy used-car dealers trying to con you out of your money."

Following a difficult period in which the normally reclusive filmmaker seemed to retreat even deeper into Skywalker Ranch (he suffered through a

Originally appeared in *Playboy* magazine, July 1997, pp. 118–26. Reprinted by permission of *Playboy* and the author.

divorce, produced a big-budget flop and consumed himself with the lucrative merchandising and special effects businesses that have made him a billionaire), Lucas has abruptly returned once again to Hollywood.

The 20th anniversary rerelease of the newly enhanced *Star Wars* took in $36.2 million on its first weekend, and Lucas has, for the first time in years, turned to writing a trilogy of films that will most certainly outrival, in their technological wizardry, the intergalactic saga that forever changed the movie business. After all, *Star Wars* opened the way for *Alien, Ghostbusters, Batman, Raiders of the Lost Ark* and *Back to the Future,* and dozens of such terrible concept movies as *Last Action Hero* and *Judge Dredd.*

"I'm not saying it's George's fault, but he and Steven Spielberg changed every studio's idea of what a movie should do in terms of investment versus return," says Lawrence Kasdan, who co-wrote *The Empire Strikes Back* and *Return of the Jedi.* "It ruined the modest expectations of the movie business. Now every studio film is designed to be a blockbuster."

Spielberg put a more positive spin on the impact of the film. "*Star Wars* was a seminal moment when the entire industry instantly changed," he said. "For me, it's when the world recognized the value of childhood."

Even before the rerelease earlier this year of *Star Wars, The Empire Strikes Back* and *Return of the Jedi,* Lucas was deeply immersed in writing (he often writes his scripts and ideas longhand in notebooks) and planning the three *Star Wars* prequels. The first will start shooting in the fall, with Lucas himself set to direct for the first time in two decades.

Lucas is as much a businessman as a filmmaker. He's responsible for four of the top 20 highest grossing films in history—he was the hands-on visionary for the *Star Wars* and Indiana Jones trilogies. "George at his heart has a modest vision," said Rick McCallum, producer of the *Star Wars* Trilogy Special Edition and the prequels. "I think he's kind of embarrassed by the huge success of both Indiana Jones and *Star Wars.*"

Embarrassed? *Forbes* has estimated that his personal worth may be as high as $2 billion. And his umbrella of companies, valued at $5 billion, have virtually reinvented the way audiences view and hear movies. All this was possible because Lucas made a daring—and brilliant—decision in 1975.

With the success of his second film, *American Graffiti,* which cost $780,000 and grossed $120 million, Lucas negotiated with Twentieth Century Fox for his next film, *Star Wars.* He gave up a large salary and, instead, asked Fox to give him ownership of the merchandising, music and publishing—

and all sequels. The studio, viewing these as nearly worthless, happily agreed.

Since 1977, Lucas has sold more than $4 billion in *Star Wars* merchandise. There have also been 21 *Star Wars*-related novels published by Bantam Books, all but one making the *New York Times* best-seller list. "The biggest change over the past 20 years is that initially it was only kids buying the products. Not anymore," said Howard Roffman, vice president of licensing at Lucasfilm. "The kids have become adults. They're interested in literary works, and in more sophisticated video games. There's a significant collector market out there." And, of course, it will not end.

Lucas poured his fortune into digital experiments that, he sensed correctly, would transform the movie business. He created the premiere special effects research and development lab, Industrial Light & Magic, which charges studios as much as $25 million a movie and has worked on Hollywood's splashiest special effects films, including *Jurassic Park* and *Twister*. The sound heard in movie theaters worldwide has been enhanced by Lucas' THX Sound System. And many of the entertainment industry's most popular video games were created by Lucas Arts Entertainment, which used the *Star Wars* franchise to create such games as "Rebel Assault," "X-Wing" and "Dark Forces."

Seated atop this empire is a man as complicated as he is private. Lucas gives interviews only in his sprawling office at Skywalker Ranch. His home several miles away, where he lives with his three children, is off-limits to journalists. Although inward and a bit distant, Lucas seems without pretension and enormously self-confident. He invariably wears sneakers, jeans, a plaid shirt and Swatch watch, and his beard and thick black hair are flecked with gray. Lucas seems, in his elaborate office, not unlike any other northern California multi-millionaire whose softspoken style masks his determination. Like his friend Spielberg, Lucas is accustomed to getting his way.

The success of the rereleased trilogy has energized him. *Star Wars*, the highest grossing film of all time, has now taken in overall more than $460 million in box office receipts in the U.S., and at least $200 million overseas. (Pretty good for a movie that was rejected by Universal and, when made by Twentieth Century Fox, cost $10 million.) With the rerelease, the three films have grossed over $1.5 billion around the world.

"*Star Wars* has always struck a chord with people. There are issues of loyalty, of friendship, of good and evil," said Lucas. "The themes came from stories and ideas that have been around for thousands of years."

Actually, the themes of *Star Wars* seem to have come from a variety of sources: mythologist Joseph Campbell, classic films such as *The Wizard of Oz* and Stanley Kubrick's *2001*, the Flash Gordon and Buck Rogers movie serials, plus Lucas's own tortured relations with his father. According to Dale Pollock, author of *Skywalking: The Life and Films of George Lucas,* one of the most significant sources is Carlos Castaneda's *Tales of Power,* an account of a Mexican sorcerer who uses the phrase life force.

"The major theme in *Star Wars,* as in every Lucas film, is the acceptance of personal responsibility," says Pollock. "What Lucas seems to be saying is that we can't run away from our calling or mission in life but have a duty to do what is expected of us. Hard work, self-sacrifice, friendship, loyalty and a commitment to a higher purpose: These are tenets of Lucas's faith."

Lucas himself says, "I mean, there's a reason this film is so popular. It's not that I'm giving out propaganda nobody wants to hear."

By all accounts, the broad details of the prequels have been in Lucas's mind since the trilogy was completed with *Return of the Jedi* in 1983. Lucas says he's aiming for an epic, David Lean look, which will make unprecedented use of digital filmmaking technology.

The prequels, which Lucas will finance with his own money, will explain how young Anakin Skywalker succumbs to the dark side and becomes Darth Vader. "It's bleak, but if you know the other three movies, you know everything turns out all right in the end—that his son comes back and redeems him," Lucas told the *Los Angeles Times.* "That's the real story. It's always about the redemption of Anakin Skywalker. It's just that it's always been told from his son's point of view."

"When the story of the six films is put together," he added, "it has a more interesting arc because you're actually rooting more for Darth Vader than you are for Luke. Until now, you didn't know what the problem really was, because Darth Vader is just this bad guy. You didn't realize he's actually got a problem, too."

People who know Lucas have always insisted that the tortured relationship between Darth and Luke springs, in many ways, from Lucas's relationship with his own father. George Sr. was a domineering, ultrarightwing businessman who owned a stationery shop in Modesto, California. He died in 1991.

"Did you ever meet George's father?" asked Tom Pollock, George Jr.'s attorney in the Seventies and Eighties. "I did not understand him until I met his father and spent some time talking with him about his son. That's when you realize George is his father." Certainly some of Lucas's hostility toward Hollywood, big-city hustlers, bankers and lawyers stems from his father's conservatism. The elder Lucas referred to Hollywood as "Sin City." Lucas also inherited his father's fiscal moderation, "the common sense I use to get me through the business world."

"I'm the son of a small-town businessman," said Lucas. "He was conservative, and I'm very conservative, always have been."

Yet the filmmaker has also recalled being "incredibly angry" at his father. Each summer George Sr. would shave off his son's hair, giving the boy the nickname Butch. They had raging arguments over young George's decision not to take over the family stationery business. Even after his son became extraordinarily wealthy, the elder Lucas, while proud, seemed surprised. He never believed his son would amount to much. "George never listened to me," his father told *Time* in 1983. "He was his mother's pet."

George Walton Lucas Jr. was born on May 14, 1944 in Modesto, a northern California city distinguished mostly by its withering heat in the summer, the Gallo winery on its outskirts and its wide, flat roads perfect for car racing. Lucas was a terrible student ("I was bored silly"), and as he grew older, he immersed himself in music (he kept an autographed picture of Elvis in his bedroom), photography and drag racing.

Weighing only 100 pounds as a teenager, Lucas loved the thrill of drag racing for its freedom. To the horror of his parents, he hung out with a rough crowd: He greased his hair, cruised for girls and listened to rock and roll. "The only way to keep from getting the shit kicked out of you was to hang out with some really tough guys who happened to be your friends," he recalls. (Lucas used his teen experiences for *American Graffiti,* his most personal film.)

Cruising, Lucas told biographer Dale Pollock, is more than a quaint adolescent experience. "It's a significant event in the maturation of American youth," he said. "It's a rite of passage, a mating ritual. It's so American: the cars, the machines, the cruising for girls and the whole society that develops around it."

Cruising also introduced Lucas to sex—a subject that is almost totally avoided in *Star Wars.* (Lucas ordered Carrie Fisher's breasts be taped, leading Fisher to remark, "No breasts bounce in space, there's no jiggling in the Empire.") Painfully shy, Lucas welcomed the anonymity of cars. "Nobody knew who I was," he recalled. "I'd say, 'Hi, I'm George,' but after that night I'd never see the girls again."

Lucas's life changed when he was 18 and a senior at Thomas Downey High School. Speeding home in his Fiat Bianchina, a fast Italian import, Lucas made an illegal left turn onto a dirt road near his home and smashed into a Chevy Impala that was barreling toward him. The Fiat was hurled sideways, flipped over four or five times and wrapped around a walnut tree. Lucas was thrown out the open roof. Had his seat belt not snapped at its base, he would have likely died.

His near-fatal experience—he lingered close to death for several days with serious internal injuries—hanged Lucas. He spent three months in and out of the hospital. "I realized that I'd been living my life so close to the edge for so long," he said years later. "That's when I decided to go straight, to become a better student, to try to do something with myself." The accident, Lucas added, gave him a sense of his own mortality.

"I began to trust my instincts," he told Pollock. "I had the feeling I should go to college, and I did. I had the same feeling later that I should go to film school, even though everyone thought I was nuts. I had the same feeling when I decided to make *Star Wars*, when even my friends told me I was crazy. These are just things that had to be done, and I felt as if I had to do them."

Lucas enrolled at Modesto Junior College, where he became fascinated with cinematography and experimented with an eight-millimeter camera owned by a friend. While racing sports cars—a hobby that continued even after the accident—Lucas also met cinematographer Haskell Wexler, who took a liking to this short, skinny kid who seemed obsessed with camera techniques. Lucas applied to the prestigious film school at the University of Southern California in Los Angeles and—to George's and his father's amazement—got in. "I fought him; I didn't want him to go into that damn movie business," his father recalled years later. Meanwhile, Wexler had phoned friends at the school: "For God's sake, keep an eye on the kid," he'd told them.

USC was a milestone for Lucas. "Suddenly my life was film—every waking hour," he says. He had found his calling. He especially loved editing—partly because, he said later, it offered a way to manipulate the perceptions of audiences. He concentrated on making abstract science fiction films and mock documentaries, which impressed Francis Coppola, who saw one of Lucas's student films and invited him to sit in on the shooting of *Finian's Rainbow*. Later, Lucas directed a short documentary about Coppola's film *The Rain People*.

Coppola persuaded Warner Bros. to sign his protégé to a contract and make a film based on one of Lucas's science fiction student movies. The full-length feature, *THX 1138*, a bleak futuristic tale, was released in 1971 to modest reviews. It was a box office flop. (The film also contains the only erotic sequences in Lucas's oeuvre, including a nude striptease by a buxom black woman.)

But studio executives were impressed with Lucas's obvious talent. He turned his attention to *American Graffiti*, partly because he wanted to dispel the notion that he was a skilled but mechanical filmmaker devoid of humor and feeling.

In the meantime, Lucas had met Marcia Griffin, a film editor. She was the first woman he dated seriously. "My relationships with women were not complex," he said. "Until I met Marcia, it was a very animalistic attraction." (Or, as Pollock put it, "His relationships usually lasted for a few dates and a couple of sessions in bed and then petered out.") Lucas and Griffin wed on February 22, 1969, in a Methodist church near Monterey.

Even before completing *American Graffiti*, Lucas wanted to make a science fiction film, splashed with drama and comedy, that would break the mold of the cheesy futuristic films churned out by the studios. Lucas sensed that audiences yearned for an empowering and bold adventure in the face of all the sexually charged and violent realism produced by studios in the late Sixties and early Seventies.

"I was very interested in creating a modern myth to replace the Western," he said recently. "I realized that it had to be somewhere outside people's realm of awareness. That is where Westerns were. Greek mythology, or mythology from any country, often takes place in an unknown area believable to the audience. The only area we now have that is like that is outer space. So I decided outer space was a good idea."

After researching fairy tales, mythology, movie serials and social psychology, Lucas began writing *Star Wars*, a bizarre saga (no one in Hollywood, including Lucas's agents and lawyers, understood the concept) about intergalactic war, chirping robots, a rebel princess fleeing from an evil sovereign and an intrepid hero named Luke Skywalker who pits himself against a dark, menacing force.

"A lot of stuff in there is very personal," he said years after *Star Wars* was released. "There's more of me in *Star Wars* than I care to admit. Knowing that the film was made for a young audience, I was trying to say, in a simple way, that there is a God and that there is both a good side and a bad side. You have a choice between them, but the world works better if you're on the good side. (It's no coincidence that Lucas chose Mark Hamill, who is about his height, to play the last of the Jedi knights, or that he named the character Luke.)

As for the recent success of *Star Wars*, Lucas says, "If it were just an adrenaline-rush movie, it wouldn't be here 20 years later. There are other things going on that are complicated and psychologically satisfying. It's like sex and love. Sex is a rush for a short period of time, and then it goes away. An adrenaline movie is more like having sex. But if people are still interested in and fond of your movie 20 years later, it was either the best sex they ever had, or it's romantic love, which means there is more to it than just the adrenaline rush."

Lucas's profits from the *Star Wars* trilogy enabled him to purchase the thousands of acres in Marin County. He built a seemingly utopian community (Lucas calls it his "psychological experiment") where everyone speaks in whispers, wears jeans and immerses themselves in some of the world's most advanced film postproduction facilities, where films are edited, special effects added and other enhancements made. "It's my biggest movie. I've always been a frustrated architect," says Lucas, who has lavished at least $75 million on the set of Victorian buildings that makes up the ranch.

Of course, beneath the laid-back style of Skywalker Ranch—and Lucas spent a ton of money, for example, just planting about 2000 mature trees to encourage the foxes and pheasants in the rolling hills of Marin County—there's an aggressive and expanding multibillion-dollar business controlled by the filmmaker: Lucasfilm Ltd., Lucas Digital Ltd. and Lucas Arts Entertainment Co.

"The guiding principle is that the company can sustain itself without having to make movies," confesses Lucas. "I don't want to have to make movies. Your bottom-line assumption has to be that every movie loses money. They don't, of course, but you go on that assumption. It's like baseball. You don't always get into the World Series, but you keep playing."

The Eighties and early Nineties were difficult for Lucas. Marcia, who shared an Academy Award for editing *Star Wars*, left him for an artist who worked on the ranch. The 1983 divorce devastated Lucas (the settlement reportedly cost him $50 million). He had a relationship with Linda Ronstadt, but that broke up. His associates don't know—or aren't saying—anything about his personal life now.

Lucas is raising three adopted children on his own. His older daughter, Amanda, 16, was adopted while George was still married. Lucas also has an eight-year-old daughter, Katie, and a four-year-old son, Jett. In recent years, he has spoken of the children a bit more freely, although Lucas guards his own—and his family's—privacy intensely.

Lucas has produced some disappointing films, including *Howard the Duck*, *Willow*, and, more recently, *Radioland Murders*. His TV show, *The Young Indiana Jones Chronicles*, got marginal ratings.

These days, Lucas drives to his Skywalker Ranch office sporadically. The majority of the time he's home, writing and planning the three films that will consume him past the millennium.

Even Lucas's critics call him a visionary—one of the few filmmakers of the Seventies to grasp the significance of marrying computers to cameras. He now views films (such as the *Star Wars* trilogy) as dynamic creations, forever showcasing the latest technological breakthroughs in sound and image.

"I can take images and manipulate them infinitely, as opposed to taking still photographs and laying them one after the other," he told *Wired* earlier this year. "I move things in all directions. It's such a liberating experience."

The dominant figure in digital moviemaking, Lucas speaks mystically about the untapped potential for computers and film. "Digital technology is the same revolution as adding sound to pictures and the same revolution as adding color to pictures," he said. "Nothing more, nothing less."

Surprisingly, Lucas is hardly consumed with computers on a personal level. He uses e-mail infrequently. "I don't have time to spend on the Web," he told Wired. He added: "For being sort of a state-of-the-art guy, my personal life is very unstate-of-the-art. It's Victorian, actually. I like to sit on a porch and listen to the flies buzz if I have five minutes, because most of my life is interacting with people all the time. I interact with a couple hundred people every day, and it's very intense. I have three kids, so I interact with them during whatever's left of the day. The few brief seconds I have before I fall asleep are usually more meditative in nature."

Since the car accident that nearly killed him at the age of 18, Lucas's credo has been remarkably simple: Work hard, believe in yourself and persevere.

"My films have a tendency to promote a personal self-esteem, a you-can-do-it attitude," he told writer Paul Chutkow in 1993. "Their message is, 'Don't listen to everyone else. Discover your own feelings and follow them. Then you can overcome anything.' It's old-fashioned and very American."

Lucas said he often meets people who are drifting. "All they need is the inspiration to say, 'Don't let all this get you down. You can do it," he said. "It's the one thing I discovered early on. You may have to overcome a lot of fear and get up a lot of courage, sometimes to do even the simplest things, sometimes to just get up in the morning. But you can do it. You can make a difference.

"Dreams are extremely important," he said. "You can't do it unless you imagine it."

Saber Rattler

JACK MATHEWS/1999

WE WERE NEARING THE end of our allotted time with His Eminence, Lord of the Empire, Creator of the Galaxy, Purveyor of the Force, Master of All Jedis George Lucas when, feeling the hot breath of his publicist, we announced the proverbial last question:

"I'm sure that over the last two decades you've heard many times from historians and film critics how you and Steven Spielberg, with *Jaws* and *Star Wars,* changed the course of film history. How you created the blockbuster mentality that ended the golden age of the 60s and 70s. What do you think about that?"

Glad you asked. . . .

"That little myth got started by a critic who didn't know much about the movie business," Lucas said, referring, we would later learn, to David Thomson's "Who Killed the Movies?" essay in a 1996 edition of *Esquire.* "It's amazing how the media has sort of picked it up as a fact."

For the next 20 minutes, Lucas would have plenty to say about his and Spielberg's legacy, maintaining that, far from cramping the styles of serious filmmakers, their successes have helped pave the way for the current popularity of independent and art-house pictures. "There's an ecosystem in the film business," he says. "What happens is when Steven and I make our movies and they make billions of dollars, well, half of that money goes to theater owners. For every billion we make, a half-billion

---

From the *Los Angeles Times,* 17 January 1999, Calendar pp. 4+. Reprinted by permission of the Los Angeles Times Syndicate.

goes to them. What do they do with that money? They make more multiplexes."

More multiplexes means more screens, which means more room for more movies. Thus, room for more non-mainstream films.

"Maybe not in the summer, when there are all these giant films out there, but in the fall and in the spring, you can go to just about any multiplex and two or three theaters playing art films."

If Lucas's theory is correct, look for another multiplex building boom following the May 21 release of the long-awaited *Star Wars: Episode I—The Phantom Menace.* The prequel to the trilogy begun with *Star Wars* (1977), continued with *The Empire Strikes Back* (1980) and completed with *Return of the Jedi* (1983) is as close to a sure thing as a movie gets, even with a $110-million budget.

"Obviously, I'm paying for it, so I don't look at it as quite the sure thing everybody else does," Lucas says. "In order to be a big hit, you have to have repeat business. That's the key to anything getting into the stratosphere of grosses. . . . I know we have a good audience for it, but will they keep coming back? That's the question."

Oh, they will, George. A large number of eager fans have already spun the turnstiles a few times just to see the film's teaser trailer. Eyewitnesses have reported seeing kids cheering through the trailer for *Phantom,* having paid up to $9 to get into the theater, then leaving before the feature started (not a bad idea, anyway, in the case of *Meet Joe Black*).

According to Tom Sherak, head of Fox distribution, business at theaters showing the trailer was up 140% the first night it was shown.

In any case, Lucas doesn't sound very nervous. This is not 1977, when he was a wide-eyed visionary making an epic-sized movie on a parlor-drama budget about a story and characters that had some of his friends turning away in embarrassment. In his book *Easy Riders, Raging Bulls,* which chronicles the films and filmmakers of the '70s, Peter Biskind describes the gloomy scene after the first rough-cut screening of *Star Wars* and quotes Lucas as dismissing his own film as being for kids only.

"I've made a Disney movie," Lucas said, "a cross between *Willy Wonka and the Chocolate Factory* and *The Computer Wore Tennis Shoes.* It's gonna do maybe 8, 10 million dollars."

It made $3 million the first week in just 32 theaters and never looked back. During its first run, *Star Wars* grossed $221.2 in North America. *The*

Empire Strikes Back grossed $181.4, and *Return of the Jedi* $252.5. With subsequent releases, including a back-to-back-to-back reissue of the trilogy in 1997, the saga had reaped $1-billion in ticket sales.

Add in the $4-billion or so spent on *Star Wars* merchandising, videos and other ancillaries, and we're looking at something that Sherak says "belongs to the culture."

"I kid George about this all the time," Sherak says. "*Star Wars* is not his, he's just the caretaker. It belongs to everyone!"

Whatever. Lucas's Industrial Light & Magic gets most of the money. With the exception of *Star Wars* which Lucas directed for Fox, Lucas has controlled everything about the series, except the distribution. Fox famously traded away the merchandising and sequel rights for *Star Wars* to Lucas for lower writing and directing fees, and thus, the empire got its revenge and a whole lot more. So, what's *Phantom* really going to do? How sure a sure thing is it? How much will it rake in on opening weekend?

Sherak says he's making no predictions, and that numbers merely take the fun out of the *Star Wars* experience. Lucas is a little less guarded. "I'm not sure we're going to make it over $100 million [on opening weekend]," he says. "We're not going to be on as many screens as *Jurassic Park,* or whatever the record-holder is [actually, it's *The Lost World: Jurassic Park,* with $90.1 million]."

Lucas says that without repeat business, a movie can't generate $300 million in first-run box office, so he is loath to predict more than that. Of course, few insiders expect *The Phantom Menace* to slow down until it has *Titanic,* with its $600-million record, at least in sight. When it comes to repetitive behavior, love-struck teenage girls may be no match for *Star*-struck kids and their arcade-generation dads—the first generation of turnstile-spinning *Star Wars* fans—who are likely to tag along.

All of which could be striking fear into the hearts of critics like Thomson, who feel *Star Wars* knocked Hollywood off track just when it had got up a head of creative steam, and whose success could only make things worse. It was *Star Wars* and *Jaws,* Thomson maintains in "Who Killed the Movies?," that gave the studios a formula they could nurture, which was a lot more fun and less inscrutable than the egos of filmmakers. Thomson's specific accusations about the damage wrought by Lucas and Spielberg are their films:

*Identified an audience (males, 14–24) whose hunger for sensation was limitless, and easily satisfied.

*Showed how much (the sky's the limit) could be made from a single movie, if it appealed to that audience.

*Created the concept of the mass opening (*Phantom Menace* will be on 3,000 screens, a modest amount compared to *Godzilla's* 7,000; *Jurassic Park* opened on an estimated 3,400 screens) and saturation television advertising (which makes it harder for any other movie to get noticed).

*And wedded film to merchandising, in everything from product placement (the brands the heroes drink) to fast-food tie-ins.

In truth, Thomson's essay is late to this party by more than 10 years. Critics have been blaming Lucas and Spielberg for the dumbing-down of Hollywood since at least the mid-80s, when every other major studio release seemed to be a knockoff of either *Star Wars* or *Raiders of the Lost Ark*. The Lucas-Spielberg popcorn cycle did have those effects, not just in America but in every country where Hollywood movies dominate the cultural landscape.

Lucas, who may rightly claim to be the most successful independent filmmaker in history, disagrees. In fact, the Thomson essay got his dander up enough for him to order a staff analysis of the films of the last 20 years, the results of which he claims put the lie to the whole theory that their blockbusters have killed the art film in America.

"I think the effect Steven and I have had on the business is to help promote the independent art film," Lucas says. "That's the thing the New York critics don't want to acknowledge. They think the films today are worse than they've ever been. Personally, I think they are better than they've ever been."

Lucas's staff report suggests that art films are infinitely healthier in the U.S. market today than in the mid-70s, a period considered by many critics a watershed of mature filmmaking. The report shows a huge increase in the number of successful art films, and anyone flipping through the movie ads on these pages must agree there certainly are a lot of choices among non-mainstream pictures. To a large extent, that is due to the doubling of movie-theater screens, from 16,554 in 1977 to 31,865 at the end of 1997.

But the quantity of foreign and independent films in the market isn't the real issue being raised by Thomson and other critics. Foreign and independent filmmakers have always taken on more challenging subject matter than Hollywood has, with the exception of those years immediately preceding and overlapping the arrival of the Lucas and Spielberg juggernauts.

Beginning with films like *Bonnie and Clyde* and *The Graduate* in the 60s, there was a period when studio heads, a new post-mogul breed better attuned to marketing than story dynamics, trusted good amounts of their production budgets to mature filmmakers who knew how to make movies for a country in turmoil and transition. It was the period in which Sidney Lumet, Francis Ford Coppola, Arthur Penn, Hal Ashby, Alan J. Pakula, Robert Altman, Martin Scorsese and Milos Forman were all doing their best work, under conditions of unparalleled artistic freedom.

That period ended, for those filmmakers and for film lovers who'd gotten used to seeing aesthetically and politically strong movies coming out of Hollywood.

Star Wars and *Jaws,* by example, shifted the balance of power away from the filmmakers—who could, after all, be troublesome—and back to the studio heads, who were encouraged to adopt and follow their formulas, or be damned trying.

Lucas attributes the whining of critics to an artistic elitism unique to this century, and says what's really galling them is the amount of money made by the relatively few blockbusters.

"The rest of the world claims we're cultural imperialists because our films dominate every market," he says. "And the reason we do is that we respond to the audience. Just like Shakespeare, Balzac or Tolstoy—they all related to their audience. Otherwise, they were out of business.

"It's the same today, exactly the same. People complain because their movies don't make money. If nobody wants to go see it, you can't blame filmmakers who are successful for that. That's the nature of being esoteric."

And another thing: Movies in the 70s weren't that great.

"I grew up in that era, and it's a complete myth! There were four or five movies that were really interesting and were about something, and most of the others weren't about anything." In the end, Lucas may be right about the synergy between blockbusters and art films. The trickle-down effect from blockbusters, not to mention the spillover crowds who may try art films if they can't get into *Waterboy 2,* may indeed be seeding the future for diversified film.

In the meantime, there's *Phantom Menace* to look forward to, and we do, we really do.

INDEX